Democracies at the Turning Point

Studies in Modern European History

Frank J. Coppa
General Editor

Vol. 13

PETER LANG
New York • Washington, D.C./Baltimore • San Francisco
Bern • Frankfurt am Main • Berlin • Vienna • Paris

Maarten L. Pereboom

Democracies at the Turning Point

Britain, France and the End of the Postwar Order, 1928–1933

PETER LANG
New York • Washington, D.C./Baltimore • San Francisco
Bern • Frankfurt am Main • Berlin • Vienna • Paris

Library of Congress Cataloging-in-Publication Data

Pereboom, Maarten L.
    Democracies at the turning point: Britain, France and the end of the
postwar order, 1928–1933/Maarten L. Pereboom.
        p.   cm. — (Studies in modern European history; vol. 13)
    Includes bibliographical references and index.
    1. Great Britain—Foreign relations—France. 2. Great Britain—Foreign
relations—1910–1936. 3. France—Foreign relations—Great Britain.
4. France—Foreign relations—1914–1940. 5. World politics—
1919–1932. I. Title. II. Series.
DA47.1.P47   940.5′1—dc20   94-13004
    ISBN 0-8204-2535-4
    ISSN 0893-6897

Die Deutsche Bibliothek-CIP-Einheitsaufnahme

Pereboom, Maarten L.:
Democracies at the turning point: Britain, France and the end of the postwar
order, 1928–1933/Martin L. Pereboom. - New York; Washington, D.C./
Baltimore; San Francisco; Bern; Frankfurt am Main; Berlin; Vienna; Paris:
Lang.
    (Studies in modern European history; Vol. 13)
    ISBN 0-8204-2535-4
NE: GT

Cover design by James F. Brisson.

The paper in this book meets the guidelines for permanence and durability of
the Committee on Production Guidelines for Book Longevity of the
Council on Library Resources.

For Ruth

Acknowledgments

I am grateful to the many people who, in different ways, made this project possible. A generous grant from the Social Sciences and Humanities Research Council of Canada enabled me to spend the academic year 1987-1988 in Britain and France. I received additional funding from these sources: a research grant from the Yale Council on West European Studies, a John F. Enders Fellowship from Yale University, and a grant-in-aid of research from the Mellon-West European Project at Yale.

My research took me to many libraries and archives. In Britain, I would like to thank the staff at the Public Record Office, the British Library, the British Library of Political and Economic Science, the House of Lords Record Office, the Birmingham University Library, the Bodleian Library at Oxford University, the Cambridge University Library and the Churchill Archives Centre at Churchill College Cambridge. In France, I would like to thank the staff at the Bibliothèque Nationale, the Archives Nationales, the Fondation Nationale des Sciences Politiques, the Archives of the Assemblée Nationale, the Archives of the Sénat, and the Archives of the Ministère des Affaires Étrangères. Here in the United States, I would like to thank the staff at Sterling Memorial Library at Yale, the Widener Memorial Library at Harvard, the Hoover Library in West Branch, Iowa, the Lauinger Library at Georgetown University and the Library of Congress.

I am especially grateful to my advisor, Professor Paul Kennedy, for his assistance at all stages of this project. Professors Piotr Wandycz, Brian Sullivan, Peter Gay and Bradford Westerfield also gave many helpful suggestions. Many thanks to Professors Diane Kunz and Aviel Roshwald, who read the whole manuscript in draft form and made many useful and encouraging comments. I thank my parents for their support; their history, no doubt, was a big reason for writing this one. Lastly, many thanks and much love to Ruth, who saw me through.

Table of Contents

Preface xi

Abbreviations xiii

Introduction 1
    Notes 6

1. Europe in 1928 7
    The World Economy 8
    Domestic Political Factors 10
    The Press 12
    Defense 14
    The Mood 15
    The French Outlook 16
    The British Outlook 24
    The Likelihood of War 28
    Britain and French Security 30
    The Kellogg-Briand Pact 32
    Notes 40

2. Liquidation of One War, Fears of Another 45
    The Great War and Public Opinion 47
    The Evacuation of the Rhineland 51
    The Young Plan and the Hague Conferences 54
    The Turning Point and Beyond: Rumors of War 58
    The Decline and the Persistence of Briandism 64
    British Indecision 69
    Notes 76

3. Old Adam: Perceptions of Germany, 1928-1933 81
       Stresemann's Last Years 81
       Revisionism Unleashed 88
       Planning for a Dangerous Future 101
       Notes 111

4. Britain, France and the League of Nations 115
       The Machinery of the League 117
       Britain and the League 118
       France and the League 125
       Disarmament 128
       Manchuria 136
       Notes 140

5. Visions of a New Europe 145
       Growth of the European Idea in France 146
       Germany, Austria and the New Europe 153
       Britain's Response to the Briand Plan 158
       The Demise of the Plan 166
       The End? 170
       Notes 173

6. Life with Nazi Germany 177
       The Economy, Domestic Politics and the Military 177
       Britain: Taking on Public Opinion 181
       France: the Worst Confirmed 184
       Understanding Hitler and National Socialism 191
       And Yet, Talk of Moral Disarmament 203
       Notes 206

Conclusion 211
       Notes 215

Select Bibliography 217

Index 233

Preface

Looking at British and French foreign and defense policies in the 1920s and 1930s from the other side of the Second World War carries certain dangers. Of course history is always a dialogue between past and present, but must the leaders of this period continue to stand in the dark shadow of 1940? One is tempted to look at the interwar period as one of smallminded and shortsighted policies, of blindness to obvious dangers, of decadence and lassitude in the democracies which allowed the evils of dictatorship to proliferate. Especially during the Cold War the apparent lack of vigilance in the face of a clear threat was difficult to understand.

Now that the Cold War is over, however, the interwar years no longer seem so distant and foreign. The absence of a clear "world order," the reluctance of the affluent democracies to make the sacrifices necessary to preserve such order as exists, and uncertainty about long-term economic prospects recall those grim days. Of course, there also are fundamental differences; but the dialogue between that past and our present has become more interesting.

To empathize is not to excuse. Plagued as they were by the memories of the last war, imperial rumblings and economic constraints, British and French leaders exposed their countries to catastrophe by allowing the order they had established at the end of the First World War to unravel. That order was not as "elegant" as the nineteenth-century Concert of Europe or as stark as the U.S.-Soviet confrontation, but it might have worked had Britain and France maintained a cooperative relationship in the 1920s and 1930s to offset Germany's obvious capacity to dominate Europe economically, if not politically. Instead, in their haste to put the Great War behind them, the former allies allowed the order they had established after the war to disintegrate. This book examines the mentality of the British and French foreign policy establishments during the crucial years 1928 to 1933, as the initiative in European politics passed from the victor powers to the revisionists.

Abbreviations

AC	Austen Chamberlain papers
ADAP	*Akten zur deutschen auswärtigen politik, 1918-1945* (*Documents on German Foreign Policy*)
AP	Archives privées
BL	British Library
CAB	Cabinet papers
CSDN	Conseil Supérieur de la Défense Nationale
DBFP	*Documents on British Foreign Policy, 1919-1939*
DDF	*Documents diplomatiques français, 1932-1939*
FO	Foreign Office
HNKY	Maurice Hankey papers
HR	Horace Rumbold Papers
JO	*Journal Officiel des débats parlementaires* (French parliamentary debates)
JS	John Simon papers
KNAT	Hughe Knatchbull-Hugessen papers
LKEN	Leo Aubrey Kennedy Papers
MAE	Ministère des Affaires Étrangères
n.a.fr.	Archives of the Bibliothèque Nationale
PA	Papiers d'Agents
PHPP	Eric Phipps papers
PRO	Public Record Office
SDN	Société des Nations (League of Nations)
VNST	Robert Vansittart Papers
WO	War Office

Introduction

'What war?' said the Prime Minister sharply. 'No one has said anything to me about a war. I really think I should have been told. I'll be damned,' he said defiantly, 'if they shall have a war without consulting me. What's a cabinet for if there's not more mutual confidence than that? What do they want a war for, anyway?'
— Evelyn Waugh, *Vile Bodies*

Vile Bodies appeared in 1930, the same year that European leaders proclaimed the "liquidation" of the war of 1914-1918. The former allies evacuated the Rhineland and put reparations on a more manageable schedule for Germany, only to cancel them altogether two years later. But public opinion seemed nervous: rumors of war began to circulate to such an extent that some leaders sought to reassure the public of their pacific intentions. Waugh did not foretell the kind of war that came in 1939, but the war he described at the end of *Vile Bodies* reflected the fear that many people felt already at the beginning of the decade. He also recognized the basic instability of the postwar international system: one of the characters, Father Rothschild, replied to the prime minister's tirade by saying that "wars don't start nowadays because people want them. We long for peace, and fill our newspapers with conferences about disarmament and arbitration, but there is a radical instability in our whole world-order, and soon we shall all be walking into the jaws of destruction again, protesting our pacific intentions..."[1]

For many years, conventional wisdom held that the severity of the 1919 peace treaties nourished a German spirit of revenge and made another war inevitable. The opinion dated back to Keynes' scathing critique at the time of the peace conference. Scholars subsequently focused a great deal of attention on the treaties themselves, as well as on the rise of Nazism and the response of the democracies to the Nazi revolution. Of course they did not ignore the 1920s and early 1930s, but the events of that period — squabbling over treaty terms, dreary conferences and occasional public-relations successes — essentially marked time against the coming German backlash. Though no one could accept the Nazis' brutality, their resentment was justified, for the allies had blamed Germany for the war and forced it to pay huge reparations. Somehow, in this case, the losers wrote the history.

Many scholars have worked to revise our understanding of this period. In some ways, the Fischer controversy of the 1960s, which established that Germany had pressed for war in the summer of 1914, began the process. Beginning in the 1970s scholars challenged the "myths" of reparations, demonstrating that Germany was by no means the long-suffering victim of allied, particularly French, treachery.[2] Exploration of newly available archival material produced the conclusion that the Treaty of Versailles, though flawed, was a reasonable settlement in the circumstances. In the meantime, the older views had done their damage, and even continue to do so.

This book rests on the belief that maintenance of the Versailles order, whatever its problems, provided Europe's best chance for peace in the 1920s and 1930s. Had Britain and France cooperated as allies to enforce the terms of the treaty, or even to revise them, Germany eventually might have taken its place among the peaceful nations of Europe. But between 1928 to 1933, in "liquidating" the war, Britain and France left a void in European politics, which German revisionism filled. In retrospect, the turning point came in June 1930: as the last allied occupation forces evacuated the Rhineland, surrendering the former allies' most important source of leverage against an unrepentant Germany, paramilitary demonstrations and demands for further concessions revealed the defeated nation's contempt. Three months later the National Socialists won 6.4 million votes in the Reichstag elections, capturing 107 seats and becoming the second-largest party in the government. In liquidating the war, the former allies liquidated the peace.

Of course, nothing was inevitable; Germany's contempt for the postwar order did not make a war of revenge certain. But the conduct of the former allies, especially Britain, created circumstances in which that contempt flourished. German voters put Hitler in power, and the Nazis and their supporters bore responsibility for the atrocities that followed. But the unwillingness of the former allies to enforce the treaties cooperatively and their failure to create structures to accommodate and contain German strength — to "organize the peace," as Aristide Briand put it — allowed Germany to exploit the weaknesses of the European order to its advantage.

Britain and France had emerged from the war victorious, though much of northeastern France lay in ruins and both allies had suffered huge losses.[3] Some scholars even describe an illusion of victory, since Germany's enormous economic and military potential remained intact, and very little of the war had been fought on German soil. Others note the imbalance of power that resulted from the collapse of the Austrian and Russian empires, destroying the old concert of Europe and opening the region up to ethnic conflict over new national boundaries. But the fact remains that, even abandoned by the United States, the British and French people together outnumbered and outproduced the Germans. Together the democracies possessed the means to shape a stable European order; instead, the failure of Anglo-French cooperation allowed Germany to assume the initiative.

In 1925, the Locarno agreements established the inviolability of the border between Germany on one side and Belgium and France on the other; Germany's Rhineland was to remain demilitarized. Britain and Italy guaranteed the pact, which many hailed as ushering in a new era of peace. Though the "Locarno era" provided some relief from the acrimony of the immediate postwar years, Franco-German reconciliation remained an elusive goal, hampered on one side by hostility toward the peace treaty and on the other by continued fear and suspicion. Britain's position of neutral guarantor, meanwhile, further undermined cooperation with France.

This study begins with a look at the Locarno era at its height in 1928, when its realities were beginning to set in: namely, that British leaders would make no additional security commitments in Europe and that they were ready to eliminate the elements of the peace treaty which had caused so much bitterness. Reliant upon the treaty for key elements of its security, France called for "organization of the peace," a concept which had no real counterpart in Britain. The Kellogg-Briand Pact, still hailed today as the epitome of naïve liberal internationalism, was, for France in any case, the unintended consequence of an attempt to secure relations with the United States. For many British leaders the pact, coming as it did after several years of tense relations with the United States, expressed a hypocritical idealism typical of their American cousins.

The prosperity of the later 1920s, which individuals experienced directly through increased purchasing power and an improving standard of living, did not correspond to a sense of unbounded optimism with regard to European politics. Few people, for example, could claim to be optimistic about the future of Polish-German relations; wartime allies France and Italy grew increasingly antagonistic; and Soviet Russia's place in Europe remained mysterious but vaguely menacing. British leaders, coping with domestic economic problems and increasingly burdensome imperial commitments, sought simplicity in their European commitments. While France remained committed politically to its East European allies, its military leaders were making no plans to defend them. The former allies essentially retreated before the problems that faced them.

They did not do so out of ignorance of developments in Germany, though subsequent errors of judgment allowed the state of torpor in the conduct of British and French foreign policy to persist. Observers tended to underestimate the Nazis, remaining more fearful of earlier demons; few could imagine the Nazis gaining control of Germany's industrial and potential military might. British politicians and diplomats would describe the brutality of the Nazis, then lapse into the usual talk of the distress of the German people, the harshness of the treaty, and the responsibility of the French for the miserable state of affairs. Some of their French counterparts shared these views, attacking the policies of the early 1920s and calling for conciliation before it was too late. But it already was too late, and these recriminations and *mea culpa*s, which assumed that Germany's grievances were legitimate, further undermined the Versailles order.

The League of Nations, that experiment in liberal internationalism, did not help matters. Rather it underscored the differences in British and French approaches to the postwar world. British supporters of the League saw it as a moral force, a forum in which the nations of the world would see their actions subjected to the scrutiny of world public opinion, and conduct themselves accordingly. In practice, however, British leaders did not invest it with much confidence. French supporters wanted to give the League teeth to enforce its resolutions, but Britain refused to commit its military forces. Ultimately, the League complicated European politics during this period, introducing a pious vision of how international relations ought to be conducted, while tainting traditional diplomatic practices. It also engaged the nations in a futile disarmament conference just as a new menace to European peace emerged in Germany.

Into the early 1930s, Aristide Briand continued his efforts to organize the peace, launching a proposal for a European union in Geneva in September 1929. But his vision of a new Europe clashed with present realities. Striking as the proposal may look today in light of subsequent developments, it did not have much substance at the time. The vision in itself was commendable, but the Briand Plan was not really a plan. It merely put forth an idea, which Britain, Germany and Italy, among others, rejected contemptuously as a French effort to secure the status quo and dominate Europe.

In 1933, Germany rejected democracy and hailed Hitler as its new leader. The Nazi revolution produced no policy changes in Britain and

France; rather, it accelerated the abandonment of the Versailles order. Ramsay MacDonald, in charge of British foreign policy, worked with Mussolini to establish a four-power directory to address Germany's demands and contain France. The French displayed a keener sensitivity to the brutality of the new regime, but did nothing. There was little sense of solidarity between the two remaining great-power democracies in Europe as the Nazi menace grew.

Though Nazi Germany would destroy much of Europe in its bid for dominance, it did not destroy the order established by the Treaty of Versailles. The former allies, Britain and France, already had abandoned it, most significantly with their evacuation of the Rhineland in 1930. Unleashed, German revisionism, aided to a degree by the economic depression, produced the Nazi revolution. Fears of another war date, not from 1933, but from the beginning of the decade. Arnold Toynbee wrote in his essay "Annus Terribilis 1931":

> the general state of the World — in the Far East, in India, in Latin America, in Europe — bore eloquent witness to the truth of the dictum that 'the one thing you cannot do with bayonets is sit on them. 'Were the blades going to be beaten into harmless sewing-machines and safety-razors or were they going to be buried once again in human breasts? That was the question which men and women all over the world were asking themselves — even amid the preoccupations of a world-wide economic depression — during the early months of 1932, while one Disarmament Conference in Geneva was waiting upon the outcome of the Sino-Japanese conflict in the Far East.[4]

Toynbee and others expressed surprise that people could worry about war in the middle of a severe depression, suggesting that the grim outlook that emerged in the early 1930s was not economic in origin; at least it was not perceived to be at the time. Fear of war arose, not from falling prices and unemployment, but from the sense that, after all the conferences and meetings, the ancient disputes remained unresolved, and all Britain and France's leaders seemed to be able to do about them was to arrange more conferences and meetings. The following chapters examine more closely the perceptions and policies of these leaders as the world unravelled around them and as their fears of another war hastened its arrival.

Notes

1. Quoted in S. Hynes, *The Auden Generation: Literature and Politics in England in the 1930s* (Princeton, 1972), p. 61.
2.   William R. Keylor, "The Versailles Settlement after Seventy-Five Years: A Retrospective Assessment," paper given at the 1994 meeting of the Society for Historians of American Foreign Relations, Waltham, Massachusetts.
3. France lost 10 percent of its active male population; Britain lost 9 percent of its men under 45. B.E. Schmitt and H.C. Vedeler, *The World in Crucible, 1914-1919* (New York, 1984), p. 458n.
4. *Survey of International Affairs 1931* (London, 1932), p. 161.

1

Europe in 1928

What dominates this whole debate — let us say it frankly — is what I will call the spirit of peace; it already has allowed us many things, and it will allow us other things tomorrow, because I remain optimistic in spite of everything.

— Aristide Briand[1]

Diplomatic histories of the interwar period usually list the Kellogg-Briand Pact to "outlaw war" as the main event of 1928 and the crowning achievement in an era of illusions and hopeless idealism.[2] But Europe's leaders knew that idealistic declarations would not sweep away the problems that continued to bedevil relations among them. The negotiations among the major powers which led to the pact reflected all the calculation and self-interest of traditional diplomacy. Briand no doubt hoped that a new spirit of peace would emerge in Europe, but in the meantime he wanted to reestablish good relations with the United States, against the day that Germany would seek its revenge against France. The Herculean task of "organizing" the peace was a race against time. Though Briand continued to pursue better relations with Germany, privately he doubted that a firm basis for Franco-German understanding existed.[3]

Europe in 1928 was still recovering from the profound shock of the war of 1914-1918. Serving as guardians of the peace was but one challenge Britain and France faced in the tumultuous postwar world. The following assessment of the two powers' economic, political and military situations in 1928 will establish a global context for their European diplomacy. While European security problems remained unresolved, Britain and France also faced stiff economic competition from the burgeoning United States, and the colonies showed signs of restlessness under foreign rule. France's continuing preoccupation with Germany alienated British leaders who hoped to put the struggles of the previous decade behind them. Even Briand's attempts to build a constructive relationship with the former enemy met with suspicion from France's former ally. Though the atmosphere was relatively calm compared to what had come before — and what would follow — the governments of Britain and France viewed the future with concern.

The World Economy

In general, the world economy boomed in 1928, though not all regions shared in the prosperity. In Asia, Japan's economy grew sluggishly by comparison with previous decades, despite the stimulus of the war; the massive earthquake of 1923 had had far-reaching effects, and a tight credit policy hindered reconstruction and further expansion; but Japan's economy was not yet tightly bound to the world's. A prolonged civil war in China concerned the larger imperial powers, whose economic interests in this "Sick Man of Asia" were still strong. The rest of Asia remained under the control of Britain, France, the Netherlands, and the United States. The fledgling Soviet Union, which had held on to the old regime's vast Asian empire, remained a mystery to Western observers, its economy isolated and its politics inscrutable; but the specter of revolution haunted them.

The economic boom of the later 1920s manifested itself in the lives of ordinary citizens in America and Europe. Particularly in the United States, the automobile and related industries burgeoned. By 1928 radios, refrigerators and vacuum cleaners, rarities in 1920, became common in American homes.[4] The average American family was about ten times more likely to own a car than was its British or French counterpart, with one in five Americans owning a car.[5] In 1928 there were 758,000 private cars in use in France, 885,000 in Britain, but only 343,000 in Germany.[6]

In Latin America, the United States replaced Britain as the chief trader in the region during World War One, eventually dominating most of the countries in the region. Only Argentina, with its large middle class, could compete with the United States, particularly in meat and grain production. Close cultural ties to Europe were matched by close commercial ties: about three-quarters of exports crossed the Atlantic, while regionally Argentina sought to foster "Pan-Hispanic" solidarity among its neighbors to counter American domination. Nevertheless, during the war the United States had replaced Great Britain as the top exporter of goods (especially manufactured) to the country. The British, however resentful of this U.S. intrusion, continued to import a great deal of Argentine meat and wheat; total imports averaged about £80 billion annually, while exports averaged only about £30 billion.[7]

In Europe, meanwhile, living standards varied widely, in general increasing as one moved north and west. In Italy the Fascists' cult of virility failed to manifest itself economically; throughout the decade, poor finance of industry thwarted growth.[8] Having survived defeat, coup attempts and hyperinflation, Germany prospered in the late 1920s, but recessions interrupted this growth in 1926 and 1928; the major stimulant — short-term American loans — illustrated a basic financial weakness, complicated by political instability. Despite these problems, however, Weimar Germany led Europe in steel production, placing second (behind Britain) only in the disastrous year 1923; in coal production the lead had shifted back and forth in the early 1920s, but Germany surged ahead in the year of Britain's coal strike (1926) and afterward. Though businessmen complained about the perils of socialism, they had never had it so good.[9]

Britain, however, did not prosper in the 1920s. After a brief postwar boom, Britain's economy had gone into recession in 1920; throughout the decade unemployment remained above one million (about 12%), due to depressions in the "older industries": coal, steel, shipbuilding, textiles and housing. Conditions were worse in the north than in London and the southeast, where the newer industries created relatively good conditions. The domestic automobile industry, for example, flourished after a 33⅓% tariff on American-made Fords put a large dent in the market for imported cars. Even after Ford beat the tariff by building a plant east of London at Dagenham in 1928, Morrises and Austins would outsell Fords by a vast margin.[10] By and large, however, the automobile remained a luxury.

For France the late 1920s provided welcome relief from the financial crises of the first half of the decade. Prices, which in 1926 reached seven times their 1913 level, levelled off after the Poincaré government stabilized the franc.[11] After 1926 the French government's budget ran surpluses which enabled it to pay off its debts to the Bank of France. With the franc stabilized but undervalued, French goods, always desirable, were now affordable to foreigners, and orders would keep French industry busy for many months after the slump hit Germany and the United States.

France, which as an industrial power had fallen far behind Britain and Germany before the war, now gained on its rivals. In 1928 the French automobile industry, in the early days second only to the American, regained the lead over Britain it had lost in 1926, producing 223,000 private cars and commercial vehicles to Britain's 212,000.[12] André Citroën's mass-produced four-cylinder car competed strongly with Ford's new Model A.[13] In August 1928 the *Economist* reported the general industrial index (1913 = 100) for June at 128, up from 125 in May and 123 in March.[14] Official French figures showed only 16,000 unemployed, compared to Britain's 1,217,000.[15] Inflation figures also compared favorably, and restrictions on rent increases and tax breaks translated into comparatively good conditions for the average citizen: using prices in gold as an index, the *Economist* reported that "the Paris workman's living expenses are now rather less than 4 per cent more than in 1914, whereas his British counterpart has to spend well over 50 per cent more."[16]

The volume of world trade, meanwhile, grew at a rate of about five percent per year between 1924 and 1928, though it had taken until 1924 to regain its 1913 level. But the trend toward protectionism, which had begun before the war already, also increased.[17] The League of Nations' Economic Conference at Geneva in May 1927, though short on concrete results, fostered hopes for greater liberalism, especially in European trade.[18] The war had upset Europe's monetary systems, but by the later 1920s order had returned, though Britain's return to the gold standard in 1925 had resulted in an overvalued pound and overpriced British exports.   Real national income exceeded the 1913 level in all of the major economies; with 1913 as an index of 100, Britain stood at 113 in 1928-1929, Germany at 109, France at 124, the United States at 166. In manufacturing output, Britain stood at 106, Germany at 118, France at 139, the United States at 172.[19] Despite its recent ordeal and its present concerns, Europe in 1928 was richer than ever.

Domestic Political Factors

Mainstream politicians in Britain and France could not compete with the theatrics of their reactionary and revolutionary counterparts elsewhere. Stanley Baldwin's Conservative government had been in power with a large majority since November 1924. The Conservatives' handling of the General Strike in 1926 won the approval of the middle classes, even though the government had contributed to the deterioration of the situation leading up to the strike. The prime minister handled the coal strike, which continued after the General Strike ended, less adeptly, and many concluded that the Conservatives lacked direction; the Cabinet, a group of tired men without ideas, opted for traditional solutions to remedy unemployment and to protect Britain from the threat of war.[20] For all his political acumen, Baldwin lacked charisma. Foreign Secretary Austen Chamberlain, basking in the glory of Locarno and his Nobel Peace Prize but unable to build on his success, contributed to the public's sense of governmental inertia.

The Liberal and Labour parties, meanwhile, longed for the election which had to come by 1929. The Liberals, though still affected by the wartime split between Asquith and Lloyd George, enjoyed a brief renaissance, with success in by-elections and some fresh ideas about handling unemployment from Lloyd George himself, ideas which Labour would appropriate in the following year's campaign.[21]

For all of the war's disruptive political, social and economic effects, Britain had emerged from the conflict with an enlarged empire.[22] But the 1926 Imperial Conference had established greater independence for the dominions, like Canada and Australia, which had sent millions to fight for the mother country. In India and Egypt, however, the British resisted demands for equal treatment.[23] Canada and Australia, their economies increasingly linked to that of the United States, enjoyed pronounced growth in the second half of the 1920s.[24]

The French government watched European developments with greater concern than did the British, but it was no better equipped to deal with crises, domestic or foreign, in the postwar world. The constitution of the Third Republic had given little power to the executive branch, making the legislature the seat of power; but cabinets survived only as long as shaky coalitions of self-interested, undisciplined political groups lasted. As a result, France experienced far more frequent changes of government than did Britain, though the personnel in chief Cabinet posts remained fairly constant, and Aristide Briand's long tenure at the Quai d'Orsay brought continuity in foreign policy. The elections of 1928 marked a shift to the right, for example, creating a power base more suited to Raymond Poincaré than to the independent socialist Briand, but the latter remained foreign minister until he retired, four months before the 1932 elections.

France's political parties, such as they were, lacked structure and discipline. The Radicals typified the politics of the Third Republic. Between 1924 and 1936 they formed the single largest group in the Chamber of Deputies, and remained a fixture of the Senate. Also known as Radical Socialists, they were neither radical nor socialist; despite a sentimental attachment to a common-man philosophy and such revolutionary figures as Robespierre and Danton, twentieth-century Radicals were not keen on reform. They distinguished themselves from the mainstream conservative groups mainly by their anticlericalism. The Constitution of 1875 had been a compromise between republicans and pro-restoration conservatives; the result was a government of which the people could expect little, especially in the area of social legislation.[25] Gradually the radicals became entrenched in the new republican system, and the working class found its champions among the real socialists.

A government that did little suited a political culture in which people distrusted a powerful state, but the government also had become estranged from the life of the country. The Radicals could easily defeat attempts at reform simply by allying themselves with the reformer's opponents on either end of the political spectrum. If, by chance, some bold new initiative passed the Chamber of Deputies, it was sure to fail in the Senate, where conservative rural and small-town interests held sway.

The French Empire also had expanded as a result of the war. Except for the new League of Nations mandates, Syria and Lebanon, Paris did not have to devote much energy to the suppression of colonial nationalism.[26] Though investment in and trade with the colonies was increasing, the French public seemed indifferent. To remedy this apathy, the national school curriculum included instruction in colonial history and geography after 1925, and propaganda portrayed France as the heir to Rome.[27]

The Press

The diversity of opinion in Britain found expression in the press, which in 1928 was engaged in fierce competition for readers. Newspapers could be divided between "serious" and popular, with the competition concentrated in the latter category. Of the former, the *Times* of London enjoyed the closest relationship with the ruling Conservatives. The paper had become increasingly conservative under the editorship of Geoffrey Dawson, an alumnus of Alfred Milner's "kindergarten." London papers dominated the country, with the exception of the traditionally Liberal *Manchester Guardian*, edited by C.P. Scott.

The popular press catered to public opinion, and in turn helped to shape it. Lord Rothermere owned the *Daily Mail* and *Daily Mirror*, while the Canadian Lord Beaverbrook owned the *Daily Express* and the *Evening Standard*. The *Daily Telegraph*, which imitated the *Times*, was the "business-man's paper."[28] The politics of these papers tended to be conservative, pro-imperial, and chauvinistic.[29] The disposition of editors towards the public tended to be paternalistic: "As always," writes Stephen Koss, "editors knew far more than they saw fit to communicate, perhaps even more than they themselves wished to know."[30]

Judgment of the French press of the same period also has been severe: "the French press could not explain to the French people the difficult realities of the time. It indulged the passions of its readers and its backers. It was not the reasonable guide which public opinion needed in these times of instability and disorder."[31] Many papers blended news and opinion in the old style, but the newer mass-market, illustrated dailies reached far more readers.

The most influential paper, and the most balanced, was *Le Temps*, which was closely linked to the Quai d'Orsay. Its editors, Chastenet and Mireaux, were backed by two of the most powerful cartels in France, the Coal Mines Committee and the Comité des Forges. This combination created an interesting dynamic: the Comité was strongly nationalistic in outlook, and its president, François de Wendel, was "strongly pro-English and a firm believer in renewed German aggressiveness in the future."[32] Meanwhile, Henri de Peyerimhoff of the Coal Mines Committee worked to reconcile Germany and France through the integration of their coal industries.[33] Wendel, whose family dominated the iron industry of Lorraine, owned controlling shares in no less than twenty French newspapers, including the oldest, the conservative *Journal des débats politiques et littéraires*.[34] Among the *Journal*'s frequent contributors was André Géraud, better known as Pertinax, who was an open enemy of Briand and therefore *persona non grata* at the Quai d'Orsay. Pertinax's name was even more closely associated with the *Écho de Paris*, an equally conservative paper aimed at a less high-brow mass market. William Tyrrell, who became Britain's ambassador to France in 1928, wrote that Pertinax, who often criticized British policy, was "generally considered the strongest writer in the French press."[35] However, the first secretary at the embassy, R.F. Wigram, later suggested that Pertinax was taken more seriously in Britain than he was in France.[36]

Though important, *Le Temps* (circulation about 70,000) and the *Journal des débats* (circulation about 35,000) were not the papers that most people in France read.[37] The Paris press, with some notable exceptions, tended to be conservative in outlook. Of the four mainstream newspapers, *Le Petit Parisien* had the largest circulation (about 1.5 million); though traditionally favorable to England, in 1928 it was less so, but it supported Briand's policy toward Germany. *Le Matin* also favored Franco-German reconciliation. Its best-known reporter, Jules Sauerwein, attended all major diplomatic conferences, and was close to Briand. For obscure reasons, *Le Matin* had broken with its Anglophile tradition after the war, taking a pro-American line instead. *Le Journal* (circulation about 700,000) was more critical of Briand and strongly anti-communist, while *Le Petit Journal* (300,000) watched Germany vigilantly.[38]

Many of the major Radical papers came from the provinces, such as Albert and Maurice Sarraut's *Dépêche de Toulouse*, "the Manchester

Guardian of French journalism," according to Tyrrell. *Le Populaire*, with Léon Blum as editor, was the Socialist party's main newspaper; *Humanité* was the Communist party mouthpiece. The overall assessment of the press of the interwar years is not positive; Bernard and Dubief write that, "[on] the whole, the French press was corrupt, biased, anti-parliamentarian and xenophobic, and much of what it printed was noxious."[39]

Defense

In the 1920s Britain's political leaders cut military budgets, arguing that the services would not be required for some time to come. The Cabinet in August 1919 had approved the "Ten Year Rule," requiring that the services draw up their budgets assuming no major conflict in the next ten years. In 1925 a Treasury committee had been formed to propose drastic cutbacks. In addition, advocates of disarmament and collective security nurtured the idea that armaments themselves caused wars, and that their elimination would make the world a more congenial place.[40]

David Lloyd George, still a strong political presence, could quickly rattle off a rationale for these spending cuts. Maurice Hankey, Secretary of the Committee of Imperial Defence, wrote that Lloyd George believed

> that we are in for a long era of peace. Nowhere in the world does he see any risk. America does not want to fight us. Neither does Japan — she could not afford it if she did. France, our greatest danger, owing to the air menace, is so friendly that we have nothing to fear. Russia cannot get at us to grapple. Germany in a military sense, is down and out. A dangerous situation takes long to develop.[41]

Hankey struggled to maintain what he considered to be levels essential to the Empire's defense, but the government agreed with Lloyd George.[42] The Treasury, bolstered by widespread rosy assumptions about the prospects for peace in the Far East, blocked improvements at the naval base at Singapore.

In 1928 the French Army struggled to meet both the political and strategic demands of the postwar era. Philip Bankwitz writes that the three major laws passed in 1927 and 1928 produced an army that represented "a curious alliance (or, as it eventuated, misalliance) between the hoary ideas of the citizen army held by the political left and the general theory of the importance of matériel in total war," in an attempt to prevent a recurrence of "the bloody tactical and strategical defeats of 1914-1917."[43] The new laws eliminated the traditional large professional army, which left-wing legislators viewed as the domain of a privileged military elite. The army was to become a school: each year 240,000 conscripts would receive one year of training by a professional officer corps and spend the following three years in the reserves. The reduction of military service to one year (from three) was politically very popular, but legislators realized at the same time that they could not afford to alienate career officers in face of the danger, actual and potential, from Germany. They therefore expanded the corps and increased salaries.

Three themes defined the French military establishment of the interwar years: the nation in arms (a "total war" strategy for economic and industrial mobilization), defense of the frontiers and maintenance of the peace treaties.[44] But the vigor and vigilance which these doctrines called for was not forthcoming; what was popular politically and what France needed to defend itself were at odds with one another, and the best that could be achieved was compromise. Yet civilian and military leaders alike scarcely could countenance another war on the scale of the last one; the result was an exclusively defensive strategy.[45] Militarily, therefore, France ceased to function as a great power.

The Mood

The Dawes Plan and the Locarno agreements had helped to diminish the acrimony of postwar European politics. But the warm acclaim that greeted these events did not diminish the difficulty of "liquidating" the war: ending the Allied occupation of the Rhineland, establishing definite terms for reparations, making Europe's new states secure and reducing armaments. *Le Temps'* Wladimir d'Ormesson greeted the new year with hope and caution:

> [1928] has begun under auspicious circumstances, in an atmosphere of international cordiality essentially favorable to the work of peace. Traditionally the chiefs of state and the men entrusted with power make promises in response to popular hopes for a renewed sense of security, on which the moral and material prosperity of the nations depends; but the optimist must consider the actual circumstances, which, taken alone, might create a real danger if they gave rise to facile illusions among the people.[46]

Locarno had fed a growing public appetite for reassuring diplomatic agreements. Diplomacy had become no less difficult, but politicians were beginning to discover the weight of public opinion in the process. Briand, who understood these dynamics well, was eager to maintain the momentum of Locarno in 1928: "I am confident that the year we are entering will mark a new step in the development of the international spirit, the application of methods of arbitration, and the organization of the peace."[47]

In London, the *Times* began the new year with a somber review of the past year. The naval conference had failed, leading to the resignation of Lord Cecil, a founding father of the League of Nations, and a strong advocate of disarmament. The account of the League's work in the past year indicated that delegates to the League from smaller nations felt that Britain had not pursued peace — i.e., disarmament — with the alacrity they expected. Austen Chamberlain had stated bluntly that Britain's primary obligation was to its own empire.[48]

The French Outlook

The French national curriculum required schoolteachers to disseminate propaganda about France's mission to civilize faraway peoples, but most leaders in Paris did not preoccupy themselves with imperial matters. After all, the ongoing German problem affected the future of the *métropole* itself. Another war on the scale of the last one, which had claimed one tenth of the active male population, was unthinkable, but the old adversary was still there, 70 million strong and much better equipped industrially to wage modern war. The situation called for creative solutions and inspired leadership, and Aristide Briand provided that leadership.

More than any other leader at this time, Briand was chiefly responsible for the "new internationalism" of the 1920s, attempts made to foster cooperation among Europeans.[49] Though these efforts failed in the 1930s as extreme forms of nationalism gripped Italy, Germany and other countries, the great strides toward European unity made since the Second World War have given Briand the aura of a pioneer and an "apostle of peace." Briand himself was a reflective and intuitive person, not given to poring over despatches and memoranda, as the journalist Louise Weiss wrote: "To observe his catlike movements, to know that he hardly consulted his files, his nonchalance had become legendary. Never has a myth appeared to me to be more false. The moment he opened his eyes, Aristide Briand thought. The moment he closed them, he dreamt. With him, meditations and thoughts intertwined ceaselessly. Intuition was the main weapon of his oratory arsenal."[50] Unfortunately, his personal style also meant that little record remains of Briand's private thoughts and opinions. His ideas developed over lengthy multi-course dinners rather than in consultations with other Quai d'Orsay officials, which perhaps helps to explain the originality of his ideas, if not also their impracticality.

Briand's sponsorship of a pact to outlaw war did not mean that his perceptions of the state of Europe were naïve. In pursuing what became the Kellogg-Briand Pact, he had intended to improve relations with the United States, to which France still owed 21 billion gold francs.[51] Moreover, his support in the National Assembly came from members who recognized the dangers lurking in European affairs. Before the elections of 1928, that support came primarily from the Cartel des Gauches. Speaking in the Chamber of Deputies for the Radicals and Radical-Socialists, Jean Montigny presented an assessment of the European situation in November 1927 which harbored no illusions; it was an affirmation of Briand's policies, calling for increased collective security through the League of Nations. In the meantime, economic and financial weakness seemed to be the chief factors restraining the forces of war:

> The picture which Europe presents us does not inspire us with complete confidence. If we turn our attention to the Albanian frontier, to the borders of Bessarabia or Lithuania, we see only nervous tension and even military rumblings. I will not enumerate all the trouble spots of Europe, all the feverish tremblings with which she is gripped. Some even say that the Europe of today harbors more possibilities for conflict, more pretexts for war, than the Europe of 1914. At least today economic and financial crises are of a nature to constrain the governments and people to some wisdom and moderation. The more the nations recover their strength, however, the more those constraints will be relaxed.[52]

By this logic, Europe's increasing prosperity actually would encourage revisionism.

Moreover, Montigny argued that France could not rely on a long-term economic and financial advantage over such potential adversaries as Germany. The effect of the Great War on France's birth rate meant that the "curve of the forces" — that is, the number of men reaching military age — would be at its lowest in 1935. This, he said, called for a "vigorous solution," because France could not meet these dangers alone. "We stress again that it would be extremely dangerous to put off problems and defer solutions, allowing them to accumulate until a time of crisis. What we want is that, when the hour of danger sounds, the troublemakers will be confronted with an organized, pacified and resolutely peaceful Europe."[53] The Radicals' plan for peace called for confidence in the League of Nations as well as a "loyal" assessment of France's relations with Italy and Germany.

The Radical party applauded France's strong support of the League: the National Assembly had voted in favor of compulsory arbitration; it supported delegates to the League who were pursuing the question of disarmament. The organization was still young, its authority resting only on the assent of its members, but it would have to be allowed to grow. "How," asked Montigny, "will the League of Nations develop its authority sufficiently to impose its solutions in the serious disputes that threaten to pit the larger powers against each other, if it persists in ignoring the everyday conflicts that divide its members?"[54] Traditional diplomacy would continue to play a role, but it would not be allowed to weaken the League Council, which gradually would develop the ability to deal with major disputes.

Such disputes were bound to arise eventually from the dissatisfied powers of Europe. With respect to Italy, the Radicals believed that France ought to be concerned primarily with Mussolini's foreign policy, even though domestically he restricted individual rights. Most worrisome was Mussolini's call for a military buildup; the *duce* had spoken in very bellicose terms:

> [Italy] must be able to mobilize and arm five million men at a moment's notice. We have to strengthen our navy. Our air force, in which I believe more and more, has to be so large and so powerful that the drone of its engines obliterate all other noise on the peninsula and its wings obliterate the sun above our heads. On that day, sometime between 1935 and 1940, we will be at a critical point in European history, when we will be able to make our voice heard and finally see our rights recognized.[55]

Montigny drew attention to Mussolini's choice of the year 1935 as the year in which Italy would begin to flex its military muscle, the very year in which France would be at its greatest disadvantage demographically. Montigny's opinion of Mussolini had strong support from the center and the left of the Chamber, but interruptions from the right of the Chamber caricatured Montigny's concerns as typical of a person from the Midi, the southern region of France where an influx of Italian immigrants was creating tensions; others took exception to Montigny's criticism of right-wing newspapers that portrayed Mussolini favorably.

In the face of such dangers, France could count on the support of Great Britain, Poland and the Little Entente, as well as on the "moral force" of the League, but unless France resolved its differences with Germany it might be faced with a "union of malcontents" after 1935: "I envision, not without concern, that at that time a kind of syndicate of malcontents will be formed, of which Russia, Italy and Germany will make up the board of directors."[56]   The right remained opposed to such a conciliatory policy toward Germany, but Montigny argued that it was the logical consequence of the Locarno agreements and of Germany's entry into the League.   He assured the government that he was not issuing an ultimatum, but he did not want to see these matters ignored; the present situation would not last indefinitely: "No doubt Germany has to choose as soon as possible between the spirit of Tannenberg and the spirit of Locarno.   But it will be necessary as well for France to choose between the spirit of Versailles and the spirit of Geneva."[57]   From the right came the rejoinder, from Prime Minister Poincaré, that there was no contradiction between the spirit of Versailles and the spirit of Geneva, that the League always pledged to respect the Treaty.

To charges that his position on the treaties was weak, making collaboration impossible, Montigny replied that his critics were pessimistic and cynical: "Would you tell us that the lots have been cast, that it is already too late, that the German nationalists will be more and more the masters of power, that the only chance of peace for France is in preparation for war? I would say that such pessimism is a form of laziness, that the cause of peace asks that one struggle for it to the end."[58]   At this point Briand joined the debate, saying that he was disposed not only to struggle but also to organize the cause of peace, and that in so doing he was in full accord with his government.   Such moments were awkward; Briand and Poincaré no doubt still had private differences of opinion on foreign policy, but the two managed a cohabitation within the government.   On foreign policy, Briand held sway; Poincaré had been called back for his domestic political skills.   Poincaré could sound like an internationalist and a patriot at the same time, when the need arose.[59]

Briand's diplomacy met with little threatening opposition in France. True, he had some very outspoken critics in the parliament and in the press, and much of the political right remained highly suspicious of Germany. Conservatives believed that evacuation of the Rhineland, for example, would lead not to German cooperation, but to the annexation of Austria. Despite the powerful rhetoric, however, strong support for Briand from the center and the left made it impossible for critics in the Chamber, such as Charles Desjardins, Henri Franklin-Bouillon and Louis Marin, to pose a threat to his control of foreign policy.

Even Poincaré seemed to express a new spirit of internationalism in his ministerial declaration before the National Assembly on June 7, 1928.[60] But rather than focusing on French relations with Germany or Italy, he turned to a problem on which most could agree: the greatest threat to

France and its colonies now was the "systematic campaign of hatred" being executed by the international Bolshevik movement. In light of this, France needed to cooperate with other European countries to promote stability:

> Away with these sad visions! We want to work: for the good of the *patrie*, for the good of Europe, for the good of humanity. The war is over. We came out of it victorious, but bruised. After every bloody conflict, it is up to the victor to extend a hand to the vanquished, if the latter is prepared to observe honestly the treaties and if the former does not wish to perpetuate the painful memory of the hostilities. However, it is up to all the peoples affected — victors, vanquished, even neutrals — to realize that none of them can recover fully unless they all cooperate in the gradual establishment of economic, intellectual and moral understanding.[61]

He added that France preferred arbitration to force and would be prepared for all forms of rapprochement, provided that no questions of treaty revision were raised.

Needless to say, Poincaré, in his appeal for European cooperation, had not ceased to believe in the nation-state, as others seemed to have:

> Far from seeking to isolate France, we have a firm desire to associate her more closely with European life and the life of the world. We are not among those who believe or pretend to believe that the nations have had their day and that one day, aged and impotent, they will absorb themselves into an inorganic humanity, deprived of its principal sources of warmth and light. We believe, on the contrary, that the nations retain and will continue to retain their nobility, their strength and their necessity. But we are convinced that, in a world in which science every day upsets our notions of time and space, no nation has the right to turn in on itself or the right to try to dominate others. The prosperity of each depends on the prosperity of all; among nations, as among individuals, there will be no progress for anyone if there is no progress for all.[62]

Here, then, were some lofty motives for French international cooperation, to which Poincaré could appeal while at the same time asserting the inviolability of the status quo.

Reports from French diplomats in Europe's more troubled regions concurred with the politicians' assessments. Jean Herbette, the French ambassador in Moscow, wrote in a long telegram, entitled "How to Avoid War in Europe" (January 1928), that the Soviet Union and Italy were the two countries most likely to start another war on the continent. The Soviet Union was engaged in intensive military preparations, which he saw as motivated both by internal social crisis and by Anglo-Russian rivalry. Herbette took the view that "men were not of a calibre sufficient to alter the course of events."[63] Italy's attitude, he continued, was clear from its alliances with Hungary and Bulgaria, both defeated powers. Whether or not war was Italy's intention, its diplomacy was aimed at repairing the injustices of the peace treaties, which had failed to provide Italy with its desired share of the spoils. Domestic problems as well might push Italy into foreign adventures.

To the dangers from Russia and Italy, Herbette added a possible third: a recovering Germany could push Europe towards war, even though at the moment it had no dictatorial government or powerful military demanding change. Herbette's perspective from Moscow was that the dynamics of Russo-German relations were a destabilizing factor. Germans today had peaceful intentions towards France; but even if they were indifferent to the word "Alsace," they trembled at the word "corridor," and certain basic traditions remained driving forces in German foreign policy:

> One tradition pushes the Germans towards Danzig, towards Posen, towards Katowice. Another reminds Germany that one can make use of Russia against Poland. Right now, while we occupy the left bank of the Rhine, the will of Germans preparing a war of revenge in the east is stronger than the will of Germans who want peace. One feels it only too strongly in Moscow: it is not the Stresemann of Locarno who directs Germany's eastern policy; it is another Stresemann, or other men.[64]

These considerations led Herbette to consider the possible consequences of France's commitments to Poland and the Little Entente, should the status quo be disturbed. Of course, as the French ambassador in Warsaw, Jules Laroche, had written, relations among the powers sandwiched between Germany and the Soviet Union were hardly stable themselves. As a general rule, countries that shared borders had bad relations. France therefore had to preach patience and mutual confidence among the nations of the Little Entente and Poland, lest their disputes should tempt their stronger neighbors to take advantage of their weakness.

To prevent a major conflict in the East, which Herbette considered to be a very likely possibility, France had to try to influence the policies of the greater powers as well. The Locarno agreements with Germany had been a very important step in this direction, but more had to be done to secure peace along Germany's eastern frontier. Regarding Italy, Herbette believed that there were no insurmountable obstacles to an entente with France, but he also felt that the goal of Mussolini's policy was not so much to consolidate peace as to make his policy of expansion as efficient as possible: to secure what he could through peaceful means, saving the military for the more difficult cases.

As for the Soviet Union, Herbette believed that Dogvalevsky, the new ambassador in Paris, was sincere when he said that he wanted to negotiate a non-aggression pact with France. The Soviet government could use a few years to remedy the deficiencies in its military forces for the war that communist doctrine deemed inevitable. However, French influence on Soviet policy was only slight compared to that of Great Britain, and profound internal financial and social crises might tempt Soviet leaders to adopt Bismarck's doctrine, that the great questions of the day would be resolved, not by discussions and the will of the people, but by "blood and iron."

Herbette recognized the limits of French foreign policy with respect to all three of these potential troublemakers, and he stressed the importance of alliance with Britain. The United States played an increasingly important role in the world, and France did well to try to encourage U.S. participation in the pacification of Europe, but in the event of a crisis Britain could act more effectively:

> It is not American policy that can act most effectively in a moment of crisis in Germany's relations with her eastern neighbors. It is not the United States Navy that can open or close the eastern Mediterranean to Italian ambitions. It is not the United States that has to defend India against Moscow....England, more than any other power, can reinforce or paralyze France's efforts for peace in all domains.[65]

The only hope, then, lay in intimate Anglo-French cooperation: "If England wants peace in Europe, it cannot achieve it without us any more than we can achieve it without her. The situation right now is too serious to be handled by only one of these two governments. This need to act together can be beneficial. Provided that both parties are clearly aware of this need, it cannot fail to bring them together."[66]

Among the socialists, Pierre Comert, who later became director of the press and information service at the Quai d'Orsay, already had given up on rapprochement with Germany. At the meeting of the Socialist International at Brussels in August 1928, he spoke with Hugh Dalton, who a year later would become parliamentary undersecretary at the Foreign Office in Ramsay MacDonald's second Labour government.[67] Dalton had said "a few mild pro-Polish things" and was amazed at the Comert's indiscreet response:

> [H]e, an international official, begins an anti-German tirade. He had hoped for an Anglo-French-German understanding, on which the peace of Europe might rest securely. But it is clear now that the Germans won't play the game. They have a most peculiar psychology. Whenever they get one thing they ask for more. One piece of

cake after another. Now they concentrate on the evacuation of the Rhineland. Next it will be the Anschluss and then the Polish Corridor.

The Polish Corridor question would bring "the gravest European political crisis since the war in a few years. The French would be quite willing that Poland should cede the corridor to Germany, on terms, but the Poles will never agree.... An Anglo-French understanding on all these matters is, therefore, the only hope for peace," Comert had concluded.[68]

Less constrained by contemporary politics than either the politicians or the diplomats was Marshal Ferdinand Foch, the great war hero. Leo Kennedy, foreign correspondent for the *Times*, interviewed him in Paris at the end of May. Foch, who had encouraged Clémenceau to seek harsh terms for Germany at the Paris Peace Conference, was not active in post-war French politics, but nevertheless remained "Briand's most vociferous and prestigious critic."[69] Popular in all the allied nations (he was the only French commander to be created an honorary field-marshal in the British Army), Foch struck Kennedy as "essentially French and soldierly. He is keenly and nationally French and full of brain; and now, as...is of course natural at 76, looking backward rather than forward."[70]

"Looking backward" meant that Foch had little use for the League of Nations or for disarmament: against the latter he argued that there always remained the potential for war, and Kennedy had to agree. Germany was the focus of his thoughts:

His mind was absolutely fixed on Germany — and on the Rhine — throughout our conversation; and he instanced the recent escape of phosgene gas from a tank at Hamburg. I actually mentioned it first, I remember, but he thought it a very good example of the uselessness of limitation. The Germans were only supposed to produce so much gas; and here was a 'usine illicite', where there was a lot undeclared. And they could at once in war time make ever so much more, the same with aeroplanes.[71]

When Kennedy raised the matter of the Kellogg-Briand proposals to renounce war, Foch said that he did not think that Germany agreed with them, in spite of Stresemann's acceptance:

The German Empire had been built up by war since the days of Frederick the Great, and on the whole it was a success, and the work remained substantially intact in spite of the great failure of 1914-1918. The USA might think it was a good moment to get us all to renounce war as a method of policy; but 'le désarmement des esprits' was absolutely first. It had not yet come in Germany, said Foch, but he had some hope that it might under the Republic. He seemed to think the republican form of government important.[72]

Foch had retired from public life and therefore did not play a direct role in the formation of French foreign policy. Yet he enjoyed tremendous prestige in his own country and abroad, and his views found echoes in many quarters in France, particularly among the military and the older generation.

These various perceptions of a continuing danger from Germany and Europe suggest that the "spirit of Locarno" was not so much illusory as necessary. Unwilling to countenance another war on the scale of the last one, the French public embraced Briand's foreign policy, with its combination of cautious conciliation towards Germany and continued appeals to Britain for solidarity. Briand combined an internationalist idealism with a realistic concern for French security in his attempt to address the unavoidable reality, that in one way or another Germany eventually would dominate Europe.

The British Outlook

Members of Stanley Baldwin's Cabinet strongly opposed further British commitments in Europe. Locarno was a minimal commitment as far as Britain was concerned; as Paul Kennedy has written, Locarno "was more significant for what was *not* guaranteed."[73] Britain had refused to join France in defensive alliances with, among others, Germany's eastern neighbors, Poland and Czechoslovakia. The Rhineland Pact itself put Britain and Italy in a neutral position between France and Germany, creating a situation in which Anglo-French military cooperation actually would violate Britain's position as an impartial guarantor. In other words, Locarno secured Belgium and France against Germany, but it did so by undermining the Anglo-French cooperation on which the peace of the whole continent rested.

Cooperation with France was not popular in Britain. Foreign Secretary Austen Chamberlain, considered too pro-French by his colleagues, had encountered strong opposition from them in the spring of 1925, when he had sought some form of assurance for France in the wake of Britain's rejection of the Geneva Protocol.[74] After this confrontation, Chamberlain encountered little opposition to his conduct of foreign policy, but largely because he pushed for no further commitments, even though he remained strongly suspicious of Germany. He did not have to endure the interference and second-guessing that his successors would under Ramsay MacDonald, for Stanley Baldwin had little to say in the realm of foreign affairs. Until 1927 he had to contend with Robert Cecil, but Cecil's zeal for the League and the "new diplomacy" received an even less enthusiastic reception in the Cabinet than Chamberlain's "pro-French" policy.

Chamberlain basked in the accolades that followed Locarno, sharing the 1926 Nobel Peace Prize with Stresemann and Briand. Knowing that Locarno was the extent of Britain's commitment to Europe, he tended to exaggerate its significance and to stress its "moral" effect. Chamberlain placed a great deal of emphasis on the "spirit" of Locarno which transcended the written pacts, "as if the ethereal *bonhomie* created in 1925 between Briand, Stresemann and himself could somehow permeate the conduct of diplomacy generally and create the sort of international society for which men of good will had sought in vain since the end of the Great War."[75]

The word 'moral' also came to be attached to words like 'disarmament,' on the assumption that consensus would emerge on all major issues once leaders overcame their postwar grumpiness and saw the wisdom of seeking their goals in a peaceful, orderly spirit of compromise. Correlli Barnett has analyzed this mentality extensively; the scrappier English ruling class of previous generations (whose passing Barnett seems to regret) had been replaced by sensitive Oxonians and Cantabrigians reared on a nineteenth-century evangelical moral code.[76] To a degree, Austen Chamberlain fit this description, though his personal opinion of German behavior was not sentimental. In later years, while out of office, his private letters would demonstrate a keen understanding of the dangerous developments in Germany and Europe. Yet the fear — or rather the assurance — of failure prevented Chamberlain from seeking further British guarantees of the status quo; between December 1926 and September 1928 German affairs appeared only once on the House of Commons agenda.[77]

Chamberlain's diplomacy was of the old style, and his attitude towards the League of Nations was markedly cool; he had the unfortunate habit of addressing it as "your council" and "your assembly." The Conservative government had resisted efforts to give "teeth" to the League by committing Britain militarily to the defense of its interests. Chamberlain saw the League as young and unproven, but potentially a great forum for arbitration. After one League failure he noted that "if it teaches people that the League is not yet a gathering of angels wholly freed from human feelings and passions but a very human instrument, the best yet devised, but still singularly imperfect, it will have done good and perhaps have saved the League from undertaking, or having thrust upon it, tasks which it is not yet strong enough to perform."[78]

The statement of the government's foreign policy in April 1928 revealed no great anxiety over the general state of the world, though one can infer an undercurrent of concern about the integrity of the British Empire. Independence movements within the colonies (especially India and Egypt) demanded a great deal of attention, of course, but this statement focused on external threats. The European powers presented no serious dangers to Britain or the Empire. Relations with Germany were "good, even cordial"; the only slightly rancorous note was dissatisfaction with Britain's Safeguarding of Industries Act, which protected British manufacturers from German competition. The question of Austrian-German union was mentioned only in the context of relations with Italy; the Italians appeared to have softened their stand on the issue (*Anschluss* would give Italy a border with Germany), and now seemed inclined to use the issue as a bargaining tool with France and Germany. Italy's relations with France continued to be strained: "Unpleasant incidents have been frequent along the Franco-Italian border, whilst the large Italian emigration into the South of France is a cause of serious misgiving."[79]

The statement confirmed British opposition to further commitments in Europe. A year earlier, the government had expressed its hope that the Locarno treaty system could be extended to central and southeastern Europe, but that hope could no longer be maintained. Instead, the government expressed its desire that the principles laid down at Locarno and the efforts of the League of Nations would guide the nations in this region. The stated aim of British policy in eastern Europe was peace and stability, but to that end the government put its trust in the League "experiment."

In 1926 Austen Chamberlain had identified Russia as the "greatest danger at the present time," and relations did not improve in subsequent years.[80] Britain severed diplomatic ties in May 1927 after officials had concluded that the Soviets had been carrying out "military espionage and subversive activities throughout the British Empire" through the offices of Arcos Limited and the Russian Trade Delegation. Though the USSR would "not be in a position for many years to wage war on a considerable scale outside [its] boundaries... the action which is to be feared from her (apart from its persistent anti-British propaganda) is that of gradual extension of her influence in directions which affect British interests."[81] Though Russia and Britain had long been imperial rivals, British concern now focused on Soviet Russia's ideological weapons. The ultimate stakes remained territorial, but communist subversion posed a greater danger to the British Empire — especially to India — than had Imperial Russia's military might.

After the failure of the 1927 naval conference, Britain's chief foreign policy concern was the peril of unrestrained naval competition with the United States and Japan. With Japan relations were "polite rather than cordial." Misgivings about Russia and China kept Britain and Japan united, as did a less tangible "admiration on the part of the Japanese ruling classes for the kind of democratic monarchy which now presides over the British Empire," a perception presumably shaped largely by the happy visit of the crown prince (who had become Emperor Hirohito in 1926) to Great Britain in the early 1920s.[82]

Though British leaders were horrified at the thought of war with the United States, relations with that country had deteriorated alarmingly in recent years. The 1922 Washington naval convention had established parity on capital ships, but the two largest naval powers failed to reach agreement in Geneva in 1927 on cruisers and submarines. Now the danger of unrestrained naval competition reminded British leaders of another recent adversary:

> [It] must be frankly admitted that, as long as the element of veiled naval competition exists, relations are unlikely to improve and may, indeed, gradually deteriorate. Commercial and financial competition is a necessary and permanent evil, but its effects are only likely to become serious if an acute and determined naval competition is superimposed. The situation has certain analogies with that existing as between Great Britain and Germany before the war, and for this reason needs careful watching. But there are also fundamental differences, chief of which is the fact that the American people is, as a whole, pacific in its outlook.[83]

The potential for trouble existed wherever Britain had commercial or imperial interests — in other words, almost everywhere. In March 1928 Stanley Baldwin told Ramsay MacDonald: "The American money power is trying to get hold of the natural resources of the Empire. They are working like beavers."[84] Relations deteriorated further in 1928 when someone at the Quai d'Orsay in Paris leaked news of a naval compromise between Britain and France (struck in the wake of the 1927 failure) to an American journalist.[85] With the Empire facing both internal and external difficulties, how would policy makers respond to signals from "danger areas" in Europe where they would rather not make further commitments?

The Likelihood of War

Europe in 1928 was still full of potential conflicts, despite the pacific sentiments being expressed. French military planners took no chances with respect to Germany. The British government, however, attempted to evade European questions altogether. Earlier in the decade, the Cabinet had advised military planners to carry on their work with the assumption that Britain would face no major war in the next ten years. Now nearly everyone in the Cabinet affirmed that assumption.

Military leaders were less comfortable with this assumption. On May 23, 1928, Field Marshal Sir George Milne, Chief of the Imperial General Staff, addressed the Central Council of the Territorial Army Association. He observed that, historically, the horrors of war and the exhaustion that followed produced a tendency among statesmen to economize on armaments, assuming (or hoping) that another war was a long way off.[86] Today, however, the world situation would not allow such a rest:

> It is impossible to say that we shall be free from a war in Europe for 40 years after the Great War, but it is clear that we are in no immediate danger of having again to fight for our existence in Europe. In one way, however, the world situation is very different from what existed 100 years ago. Now experiments in systems of Governments are being made in various countries. Spain, Italy and Russia have all made far-reaching changes in their form of Government, and China is undergoing the pains of finding some new form of government that will bring her peace and opportunities for development. There is little danger, therefore, that we shall be tempted to allow our military organizations to become atrophied, but with so many countries of the world still working under new forms of government, the conditions of the problem we have to face are continually changing, and this brings great difficulties in their solution.[87]

The actual choices as to what form preparedness ought to take were rendered extremely difficult by rapidly advancing technology. The internal combustion engine, radio, and the airplane had already revolutionized warfare and would continue to do so. Tanks would play a key role in any future conflict; Milne hoped never again "to see as in 1915 naked divisions going into war — men armed with rifles and field guns only," but the use of tank strategy required more training than simply handing out weapons to raw recruits. This in turn required greater expenditure, which, given the fact that "we can put out of our mind the immediate danger of a national war in Europe," might be very difficult indeed to wrest from the government.[88] Investment now, as Milne realized, meant investment in the current technology, whereas delay could allow for the use of more advanced technology. This was the dilemma, or the gamble, that the government faced.

The Cabinet chose to wait. On June 15, 1928, Chancellor of the Exchequer Winston Churchill asked his colleagues for firm decisions on the "general assumptions which now govern our preparations for war."[89] He believed that the Ten Year Rule, which he himself first advocated in 1919, should be confirmed and put on a rolling basis, subject to annual review by the Committee of Imperial Defence (CID).[90] He made a proposal to this effect at a special meeting of the CID on July 5, at which he said he believed there was "no likelihood of a great war" in the next ten years. First Lord of the Admiralty Bridgeman supported him, provided that the Royal Navy would not be allowed to drop to second place behind the United States Navy. Sir Samuel Hoare, the Air Minister, also concurred, though he worried — with good reason — that the Treasury would use the rule to block necessary modernization. Churchill replied that this would be a way to check mass production and prevent the stockpiling of weaponry soon to be rendered obsolete.

Only Arthur Balfour dissented; he believed that "nobody could say that from any one moment war was an impossibility for the next ten years, and that we could not rest in a state of unpreparedness on such an assumption by anybody." Examining the logic of the rule, he added that "to suggest that we could be nine and a half years away from preparedness would be a most dangerous suggestion. We had but a small Army and a Navy that we could hardly reduce. These must be maintained in the highest pitch of perfection. It would be wholly impracticable to suggest a scheme which allowed our arms a period of ten years in which to prepare."[91]

Austen Chamberlain supported Churchill's position.[92] Asked by Baldwin to assess the world situation, he affirmed that major war was indeed unlikely in the next ten years. He could not conceive of war with France in its economically weak state. Germany and Italy also were economically unfit to wage war, whereas war with the USA would be madness. He could not say whether Japan would never be a menace to Europe, but it "did not constitute such a menace now."[93] The "greatest danger spot" was Russia, but, despite uncertainty as to its aims, Britain knew that the Russian army was at this time incapable of offensive operations on a large scale. Given these assurances, the CID put the Ten Year Rule on a sliding track.[94]

Economics played a key role in Chamberlain's opinions of the war potentials of the other great powers, and particularly of the western European powers. Of course a country in financial and economic distress would be in no condition for war, but how safe was it to assume that this situation would last? Was it safe to assume also that a power would not go to war unless its "war potential" had reached some kind of acceptable level? British leaders, sensing their own economic limitations and the consequences of these limitations for overseas commitments, projected the same feelings and conclusions onto the French, the Germans, and the Italians. They resented what they perceived to be the attempts of French leaders to wield their relative prosperity as a diplomatic club. Yet, unlike the British and the French, the Italians and Germans had ambitions that conflicted with the status quo, and therefore might be inclined to view war in a rather different light. Financial and economic distress might hamper their chances for success, but would sound financial sense restrain revisionist leaders?

Britain and French Security

Tensions between "old" and "new" diplomacy and the traditional rivalry between Britain and France combined to skewer relations between the two countries after the war, and the relatively peaceful conditions of 1928 allowed frictions to continue. Those, like Robert Cecil, who favored the "new" diplomacy, calling for peacemaking through disarmament and arbitration of disputes through the League of Nations, regarded France's large standing army as an emblem of the "old" diplomacy, with its dangerous reliance upon alliances and military preparedness. Briand's efforts to build relations with Germany attracted less attention than France's neurotic insistence on the precise terms of the Treaty of Versailles. French supporters of the League, meanwhile, could cite Britain's refusal to give the League teeth with which it could enforce its resolutions. British leaders seemed cavalier about France's security, indulging Germany while strictly curtailing its commitments to France.

But those directly responsible for Britain's foreign and defense policy recognized that France played a key role in the maintenance of peace in Europe. Members of the Committee of Imperial Defence (CID) resisted calls from their countrymen to pressure the French to disarm. As Churchill wrote to Sir Warren Fisher,

> We are frequently told that Germany would disarm on the understanding that other nations would disarm too, and that further France in particular is bound morally to disarm. However I do not admit that any moral obligation exists....The only securities for the defense of France are the French Army and the Locarno Treaties. But the Locarno Treaties depend for their efficiency upon the French Army. As long as that

army is strong enough to overpower a German invasion no German invasion will be attempted.[95]

France had given up the Rhine frontier on the assurance that the United States and Britain would guarantee its security; now it had no American guarantee, and British (and Italian) assurance only in the form of the Rhineland Pact.

The size of the French Army not only compensated for the lack of a guarantee; it served British interests as well:

> [T]he British undertaking to protect Germany from the misuse of the French Army affords Germany full security, and it is unthinkable that France would attack Germany in defiance of England and Germany together. Thus the strength of the French Army protects us against the most probable danger of our being forced to intervene in Europe, and it is not in our interest at all to press for the whittling down of this force below the point of security. Moreover France will never consent to such a whittling down and all expectations that she will are futile.

Churchill reasoned that an increased sense of security eventually would convince French leaders to make their own reductions, because of the great "expense and burden of maintaining so large an army."[96]

For League enthusiasts, however, reliance on large armies revealed an unwillingness to embrace the new faith. In 1927 Robert Cecil had written to Churchill:

> we do completely disagree on the main issue. You believe that future war is practically certain, that the best way of avoiding it is the old prescription of preparedness, and that in any case the first duty of Government is to collect such armaments as may be necessary to prevent defeat. I regard a future war on a big scale as certainly fatal to the British Empire whether we win it or lose it, and probably also to European civilisation. I think therefore that the first duty of the Government is to throw their whole strength into the effort to substitute some other method for settling international disputes for war, and that therefore the main purpose of maintaining armaments is not to reduce our fighting strength at present to such a low ebb as to invite attack. In other words, perhaps our differences may be put in this way, — you hold the old maxim 'si vis pacem para bellum'. I would rather say: 'si vis pacem para pacem'.[97]

For Cecil the establishment of the League of Nations had been a tremendous achievement:

> until we get a definite abandonment of the idea of war as a legitimate means of dealing with international differences, I do not feel that we shall be on firm ground. I hoped that we should be able to do it by a direct attack on armaments, but as long as this

Government is in office there will be no determined lead in that direction from here or I think any country which is really ready to take the matter up whole-heartedly. As [Joseph Paul-] Boncour used to say to me repeatedly at Geneva, it was only he and I who were in earnest about disarmament. On the other hand, I do think we might do something with arbitration; and to establish arbitration is a step toward dis-establishing war. Anyhow, it seems to me that these views, if not certainly true, are possibly true, and in view of the enormous stakes we are playing for we ought to try and take the safest course, even if there is another which may also be safe.[98]

But was this the safest course? Cecil's views did not take account of realities with which the Foreign Office and the CID dealt much more directly. Nevertheless the League of Nations Union became a pressure group with a good deal of public support; it was by far the largest such organization in any country.[99] By taking the moral high ground on matters of disarmament and arbitration, the Union could make the government appear to be operating in bad faith. Many of Cecil's former colleagues regarded him as an eccentric nuisance.

The Kellogg-Briand Pact

The Kellogg-Briand Pact, signed in Paris on August 27, 1928, was an agreement to "condemn recourse to war for the solution of international controversies and renounce it as an instrument of national policy..."[100] The gathering at the Quai d'Orsay of foreign leaders, including Gustav Stresemann, generated a good deal of public enthusiasm. Such events helped to foster an atmosphere of international goodwill — French crowds cheering Germany's foreign minister could not hurt — but the pact alone could not resolve Europe's outstanding disputes, and leaders harbored no illusions that it could. Briand said "Peace proclaimed, that is good, that is a lot. But it will be necessary to organize it."[101] The pact bore an unmistakably American mark, and the United States took responsibility for distributing it to its signatories. Maurice Hankey described the pact to Arthur Balfour as a "great fraud and an American electioneering move."[102] Nor was it what French leaders had had in mind at the outset, but they had no desire to offend the great creditor across the Atlantic.

Though Briand believed that a renunciation of war by the nations of the world could have a positive effect, he had set out to improve relations with the United States through the renewal and expansion of a bilateral arbitration convention signed in 1908. In April 1927, ten years after U.S. entry into the war, he proposed that the two powers ban war between them with a "solemn declaration...more of mystical and moral value than a treaty of friendship and arbitration."[103] President Coolidge's Secretary of State, Frank B. Kellogg, replied eight months later (December 27) with a proposal to extend the pact to all the world's great powers. Public opinion, he thought, would not accept a pact that appeared to make the USA a passive observer of any adventures the French might undertake in Europe or elsewhere. Briand accepted this, but reminded Kellogg that League members had pledged in the Covenant to take action against any member that violated its articles, and war remained one such possible action. France might have to fight to defend itself, an ally or a League member.[104]

The correspondence among British leaders during the negotiations leading up to the signing ceremony revealed considerable animosity towards the United States. In February 1928, the British ambassador in Washington, Sir Esmé Howard wrote to Austen Chamberlain to discuss "all this business." Howard had met with Salmon O. Levinson, a Chicago lawyer, and concluded from their conversation that the isolationist Republican Senator William Borah was behind the whole scheme, and Levinson was his agent, having gone to Paris the previous spring to suggest to Briand that he take the initiative.[105] "In any case" wrote Howard, "it all fits in so well with Borah's well-known penchant for resolutions outlawing war without incurring any risks or responsibilities, that we can well believe it has his fullest support."[106] For his part, Kellogg had taken his time to act on the idea.[107]

Yet, no matter how shallow-minded the thinking behind the proposal, the pact might be of some value to Britain. Howard continued: "Would it or would it not be a benefit for the peace of the world if [the United States] which is now the most powerful in the world can be brought to subscribe to some general Treaty renouncing war, and would it or would it not be in the interest of Great Britain if this could be brought about without sacrificing any of the pledges His Majesty's Government have given in the interests of peace and security in Europe?"[108] Howard thought so. A pact renouncing war, while it would have to brought into line with the League Covenant, the Rhineland Pact and other defensive treaties, would also render war between the U.S. and the British Empire less likely; at least it would "make the United States pause before attacking us."

At the same time, Howard recognized that "a declaration renouncing *all war* in the future on the part of any government is really nothing but sheer hypocrisy and humbug because no Government can obviously consent to renounce the right to defend itself if attacked." He wondered, therefore, "how M. Briand could have proposed such a treaty in the first instance, even with the United States which France certainly has no reason to fear."[109] Yet if events developed as Howard thought they had, Briand's proposal made sense. Neither the French nor the British wished to offend the United States; they hoped, on the contrary, to attract the Americans into the peace-keeping system organized after the war, and it could not hurt to assure the U.S. of their pacific intentions. Regardless of the proposal's naïveté, one could hardly disapprove of the sentiment.

Privately, however, Chamberlain expressed annoyance at what he also considered to be an American electioneering ploy. He wrote to Howard that he saw the long delay on Kellogg's part as indicative of a concern not so much for international peace as for "the victory of the Republican party."[110] The Americans had drafted the proposal carelessly, failing to distinguish between defensive and aggressive war. Kellogg himself immediately repudiated the idea that nations would abandon the right to defend themselves if attacked, but did not deem it necessary to alter the wording.

Chamberlain wondered whether in fact there was any benefit to be gained from such a pact. Sir Edward Grey, foreign secretary in the years before the outbreak of the war, had drawn a lesson from Britain's experience with the Hague and London Conventions on the conduct of war, that in the future Britain ought not to sign any similar document that did not bind all signatory powers to take action in case of violation. Chamberlain, therefore, saw little to be gained from a "platonic" declaration, with mental reservations, from the United States:

> [It] would be a very fair question to put to Mr. Kellogg. If you invite us to sign such a treaty not merely with the United States but...with Germany or Russia, what action will the United States take if either of them break this provision while we remain loyal to our engagement? It may be one thing to sign such a treaty with a Government and people in whose loyalty you have total faith, but it is quite a different thing to involve us in signature of a multilateral treaty with powers who have not our standard and whose past does not encourage us to put unlimited faith in their loyalty to 'a scrap of paper'. I can see many disadvantages in doing anything which Mr. Kellogg may regard as a rebuff, but I confess that I don't think the world will gain anything by merely helping Mr. Kellogg over his electoral fence.[111]

Responding to Chamberlain, Howard suggested that he was perhaps too critical of Kellogg's motives. Kellogg had told Howard more than once that he believed the proposals would have a moral and educative value, and the ambassador was "equally sure he would never have cared enough about them to propose them if there had not been a serious demand in great sections of the country that the Government should do something towards helping to promote the cause of world peace."[112]   Rejection would satisfy only "the isolationists, big Navyites and jingoes" who believed that "Europe will never take any real peace measure. She believes only in force, so we must arm as much as we can to protect ourselves."[113]

Chamberlain did not intend to oppose the Kellogg plan, but he remained suspicious of, or at least baffled by, American motives. He felt he could more or less predict how the Italians, the Germans or the French might behave in a given situation, but he saw American foreign policy as a ship drifting "at the mercy of every gust of American public opinion." The Kellogg proposal was an example:

> Who could guess when they left Briand's suggestion unnoticed for months that it would suddenly become the cardinal feature in their attitude to the rest of the world? And what do they mean it to be even now on the eve of signature — a 'moral' gesture, vox et pretera nihil, or a new Monroe doctrine? It will be one or the other according as the trend of American public opinion makes the rest of the world think that they are in earnest or the reverse? I end as befits the whole correspondence with an enormous mark of interrogation.[114]

Rumors of Chamberlain's hostility to the Kellogg proposal circulated in Geneva and alarmed Eric Drummond, Secretary-General of the League of Nations. The League's purpose in part was to help eradicate such cynicism, and his despatch to the foreign secretary, mentioning the rumors in a postscript, had a reproachful tone:

> Some of us who have been working for the League for a long time past believe that the reply made and the treatment given to the recent note from Kellogg on the possibility of the abolition of war must be of the very greatest importance to the whole future of the League.   That note raises some... fundamental problems with regard to the relationship of the League to war, and it seems probable that American opinion toward the League and its decisions will in the future be very largely influenced by what now happens. This being the case, is it really wise that any Power, however important [i.e. France], should speak on behalf of the League as a whole? So much depends on the answer, that I cannot think that the other Members of the League should disinterest themselves in the matter.   It may be that the American proposals come at an inopportune and inconvenient time, but I hope that they will be considered very seriously.[115]

Chamberlain's prompt reply employed a favorite stalling tactic, invocation of the principle of Imperial unity: "I know of no such hot-bed of gossip as Geneva and no place where more baseless rumours are current. I have not expressed any opinion on Kellogg's proposals at present and shall not give expression to any opinion until I have been able to consult the Dominions and reached a conclusion with my own Government."[116] Chamberlain did not bother to provide Drummond with any of the explanations he had given to Howard a month earlier.

Leo Kennedy, the *Times'* chief diplomatic correspondent, followed the debate over the proposal in Geneva.[117] Frustrated with Austen Chamberlain's leisurely conduct of foreign policy, he described in his diary a conversation he had with the foreign secretary in June. They discussed the recent revelation that the Germans were producing phosgene gas at a plant in Hamburg. Chamberlain, eager to end the Allied occupation of the Rhineland, did not wish to raise the matter in Geneva: "AC said nobody had brought it up before the council, and he did not feel inclined to. This strikes me as very typical of AC's *laissez-faire* foreign policy. He is not a man to shape events."[118]

In the weeks that followed Kennedy discussed the Kellogg proposal with various representatives at the League of Nations. Friedrich Gaus, the German delegation's jurist, agreed with Fromageot, his French counterpart, that "they will make no difference whatever. Once you allow the validity of all pre-existing engagements, some of which imply war, the Kellogg proposals become an empty declaration." But Lord Cecil, whose view Kennedy personally preferred, believed that "up till now every nation had kept the right to make war whenever it liked; now for the first time we proposed to renounce that right."[119]

The League experiment had raised philosophical questions about war and its place in international relations. The acceptance of war as a national prerogative had begun to give way. A conversation with Sir George Grahame about the future of Germany's relations with its neighbors and the Kellogg Pact surprised Kennedy, for he considered Grahame "essentially a Continental diplomatist," and therefore inclined to be cynical : "He took the view (which I hold rather strongly) that [Chamberlain] has in the Kellogg negotiations shown himself rather continentalized and legalistic, and has not responded enough to the big idea behind the actual Treaty."[120]

Austen Chamberlain was too ill to attend the signing ceremony at the Quai d'Orsay on August 27, but Walford Selby described the atmosphere as similar to the one at the Foreign Office when the Locarno Treaties were signed there in December 1925. The solemnity of the occasion was marred only by shouts of "*assis*" ("down in front") from the numerous reporters and photographers in the back of the room whenever someone in front tried to get a better look.[121] Fifteen nations signed the pact at this time, including Britain and the Dominions individually, but before long nearly all nations, including the Soviet Union, also signed.[122]

The Kellogg-Briand Pact met with a good deal of public enthusiasm in 1928, but it did not change the European diplomatic situation substantively. Perhaps it kept alive the "spirit of Locarno," but it did not change the way European nations' leaders perceived each other's intentions. Many thorny problems remained. Of course, the pact addressed only the matter of using war as an instrument of national policy; it made no provision for enforcement of the new law. Nevertheless, at least among the major powers, a war of aggression was either undesirable or inviable at this time.

The renunciation of war as an instrument of policy in 1928 was not a difficult step for British and French leaders to take, at least with respect to war in Europe. One potential trouble source was fascist Italy, but it seemed to have settled down after the Corfu incident in August 1923, and Mussolini had a number of prominent admirers in Britain. Franco-Italian relations were bad, but, in this case, the status quo power was the stronger power. The popular press helped to create a favorable image of Mussolini in British public opinion. Lord Rothermere "scooped" all other newspapers with his revelation in the *Daily Mail* that Mussolini had saved Western Europe from a Bolshevist victory in Italy, which "seemed inevitable" in 1922: "Our escape from so great a danger we owe to Mussolini alone, who... not only carried through a bloodless revolution, but has since given his country the most efficient Government in Europe. There can be no doubt as to the verdict of future generations on his achievement. He is the greatest figure of our age. Mussolini will probably dominate the history of the twentieth century as Napoleon dominated that of the early nineteenth."[123] Cabinet members Chamberlain and Churchill also admired Mussolini. Baldwin dismissed concerns about this friendliness: "Isn't it a great blessing that Austen has some hold on a wild man like Mussolini — that someone can restrain him!"[124]

In Germany, meanwhile, the extremists seemed to lose ground. In the May 20 elections the National Socialists got 100,000 votes fewer than they had in 1924 (when they had received 908,000 votes). Sir Ronald Lindsay, Britain's ambassador in Berlin, described the "Hitlerites" as

at the point where extreme left and extreme right touch. These crazy people are actuated by a combination of anti-Semitism and acrid nationalism carried to its extreme logical conclusions. They become anti-Dawes plan, anti-Locarno, anti-capitalist, nearly Communist. Dr. Stresemann calls them 'Communists who sing the "Wacht am Rhein" instead of the "International".' Their communism separates them from the Conservatives, and their militant nationalism is a gulf dividing them from the Communists. The only pleasant thing about them is that they have lost three out of fifteen seats in the Reichstag.[125]

Paris also received the news gladly. *Le Temps* interpreted the result as a "direct disavowal of the German people of the political elements in Germany which have preached resistance to the policy of Locarno."[126]

Chamberlain hoped that this "disavowal" would enable Britain and France to continue a successful policy of moderation towards Germany, which would solidify the republic:

> We have made it possible for the republic to live and for the German people to give a striking proof of their desire for peace....Doubtless the French Government are fully alive to these considerations, but I feel that you should take an early opportunity of impressing them upon M. Briand. I trust that, far from disputing their cogency, he will be prepared to recognise that in the circumstances which have now arisen high policy requires that we should respond to the demonstration accorded by the German elections by showing that to a peaceful Germany we accord willingly and promptly what a Germany pledged to a policy of revenge would never have wrung from us, and that we should therefore do all we can to make it possible for republican Germany to achieve without further delay that state of complete normality in her international relations which has always been her aim and which the Nationalists have hitherto always declared to be impossible of attainment by means of the policy of Locarno.[127]

Chamberlain had just read a report from Lindsay on Germany's economic outlook. The financial adviser at the British Embassy in Berlin, Ernest Rowe-Dutton, believed that German industry was in a "normal, though not in a stable, position." A steady rise in wages required either increased production or increased prices; the latter appeared to be the preferred choice, because of "the traditional belief of German industry in high prices, but also...the uncertainty of the future course of events in Germany, which will prevail until a final settlement of Germany's reparation liability is effected." The effects of price increases would be complicated, but Rowe-Dutton believed they might derail the progress made on the issue of reparations during the past few years:

> it is by no means improbable that, without in any way impairing the real economic strength of Germany, a period of severe economic depression may set in during the next winter, at a moment when the Dawes annuities reach their maximum. The political importance of such a conjunction may be very great, and may lead to an instant clamour in this country for a revision of the reparations burden.[128]

Though uncertain about Germany's future, both British and French leaders felt sure that, at least as long as Gustav Stresemann remained foreign minister, Germany would not start a war in the East. Chamberlain had been convinced already at the time of Locarno that Stresemann, energetically restraining the nationalists, sincerely wanted rapprochement with the western European powers and would continue to pursue it, though not at the expense of a revisionist agenda:

> As for western Europe, there was nothing to fear. As far as the east was concerned the situation was obviously less certain, but, nevertheless, one could most sincerely desire that Germany would not attempt anything by force. Mr. Stresemann said to Sir Austen: 'you understand that I cannot commit myself to never using war to resolve the problems in the east. But my desire is to resolve them, not by force, but through conciliation and through peaceful arrangements.[129]

Of course this was only reassurance from Stresemann, not from the German people, and much depended on his continued success at the Wilhelmstrasse and his rapport with both Chamberlain and Briand. Considering the age and state of health of all of these men, this unique equation might not last much longer, but for the moment it put tensions on hold.

To French leaders, Stresemann did not truly represent Germany when he signed the Kellogg-Briand Pact; while they hoped that his conciliatory policy would continue to enjoy support, the Germany of the Great War had not faded from memory. The fact that Italy and other dissatisfied powers also signed offered some comfort, but the fact of these countries' fundamental dissatisfaction with the status quo remained. Despite the sentiment expressed in the pact, therefore, the French government remained committed to the status quo in Europe, and had to be prepared and willing to defend it. Briand believed that the best way to forestall such a test was to organize the peace and organize Europe, rather than pessimistically and passively wait for events to develop.

Britain, however, was not prepared to play a greater role in Europe; it had done its part to maintain the balance of power there and could not afford to do more without further jeopardizing its imperial interests. Yet the Foreign Office and the Committee of Imperial Defence recognized that France was the only power on the continent whose interests they could know with some certainty to be the same as their own. But the British were in no mood for experiments; experiments in peacekeeping were laudable, but economical, limited arrangements were more desirable. The prevailing mentality among members of the Baldwin government was in line with

British tradition, that European entanglements meant trouble. The result of this was a passive pessimism, the very attitude which Briand's supporters believed would have leaders allow events to take their course, without attempting to have an impact on them. Yet difficult as efforts to consolidate the peace appeared to be in 1928, circumstances did not improve. In the years that followed, leaders would look back upon this relatively peaceful time as one of lost opportunities.

Notes

1. From a speech on disarmament at the 10th plenary session of the League of Nations, Geneva, September 10, 1928. A. Elisha, ed., *Aristide Briand: Discours et écrits de politique étrangère* (Paris, 1965), p. 209.

2. Most recently Henry Kissinger has described the treaty as a retreat from the order established by the Treaty of Versailles, for the way in which it pressured a France pledged to peace to disarm, leaving no material deterrent to a resurgent Germany. See *Diplomacy* (New York, 1994), pp. 280-282.

3. Geneviève Tabouis, *They Called Me Cassandra* (New York, 1942), p. 73.

4. C. Kindleberger, *The World in Depression, 1929-1939* (Harmondsworth, Middlesex, 1987), p. 44.

5. D. Dimbleby and D. Reynolds , *An Ocean Apart: The Relationship between Britain and America in the Twentieth Century* (New York, 1987), p. 108.

6. B.R. Mitchell, *European Historical Statistics, 1789-1975* (London, 1975), pp. 668, 670.

7. "Argentine Exhibition Number," the *Times*, March 10, 1931. See also William R. Keylor, *The Twentieth-Century World: An International History* (New York, 1984), pp. 213-214; P. Snow and G. Wynia, "Argentina" in H. Wiarda and H. Kline, *Latin American Politics and Development* (Boulder, 1990), pp. 132-136.

8. Kindleberger, p. 43.

9. Henry A. Turner, German Big Business and the Rise of Hitler (New York, 1985), pp. 3-37.

10. Dimbleby and Reynolds, pp. 111; 121-122.

11. David Landes, *The Unbound Prometheus* (Cambridge, 1969), p. 361.

12. Mitchell, pp. 488-489. In 1931 Britain resumed the lead, which lasted for the rest of the 1930s, with Germany emerging as the chief competition.

13. W. Klingaman, *1929: The Year of the Great Crash* (New York, 1989), p. 121.

14. The *Economist*, August 18, 1928, p. 314.

15. Mitchell, pp. 174-176. France's economy was still largely agricultural, compared to Britain's; four times as many active males were involved in that sector, and unemployment in the countryside was easier to hide (the same was true of Italy). France's population in 1928 was about 40.5 million; the population of Great Britain and Northern Ireland was about 45 million.

16. The *Economist*, August 18, 1928, p. 315.

17. Landes, pp. 359-361.

18. A. Orde, *British Policy and European Reconstruction after the First World War* (Cambridge, 1990), pp. 316-321.

19. Landes, p. 368.

20. C. Mowat *Britain Between the Wars, 1918-1940* (Chicago, 1955), pp. 299-302, 324-7, 331-5.

21. Mowat, pp. 346-352.

22. A.J.P. Taylor, *English History, 1914-1945* (London, 1965), p. 163-193.

23. B. Porter, *The Lion's Share: A Short History of British Imperialism, 1850-1983* (London, 1984), pp. 295-300; J. Darwin, "Imperialism in Decline? Tendencies in British Imperial Policies Between the Wars," *Historical Journal* 23:3 (September 1980), pp. 657-679.

24. Mowat, pp. 44, 46.

25. Education was the exception which proved the rule; the enormous struggle between clerical and anticlerical forces in the early decades of the Third Republic illustrated the difficulties the state faced in imposing its will on society. Stanley Hoffmann has described the Third Republic as the "stalemate society" in his article "The Paradoxes of the French Political Community" in *In Search of France* (New York, 1963), pp. 3-26. On the Constitution of 1875, see J.-M. Mayeur and M. Rebérioux, *The Third Republic from its Origins to the Great War* (Cambridge, 1987), pp. 18-36.

26. C. Andrew and S. Kanya-Forstner, *France Overseas: the Great War and the Climax of French Imperial Expansion, 1918-1925* (London, 1981), p. 245.

27. Ibid., pp. 247-249; Bernard and Dubief, pp. 196-200.

28. R. Graves and A. Hodge, *The Long Week-End: A Social History of Great Britain, 1919-1939* (New York, 1963), p. 57.

29. Mowat, pp. 244-245.

30. S. Koss, *The Rise and Fall of the Political Press in Britain*, volume 2, *The Twentieth Century* (London, 1984), p. 542.

31. C. Bellanger, *Histoire générale de la presse française*, volume 3, *De 1871 à 1940* (Paris, 1972), p. 482.

32. FO 425/409/22, Tyrrell to Henderson, April 14, 1930.

33. Ibid. Stephen Schuker explains that the French steel industry depended on foreign sources for coking coal. Germany had an abundant supply, but many members of the Comité favored force over reconciliation as a means of gaining access. *The End of French Predominance in Europe* (Chapel Hill, 1976), pp. 222-229.

34. W.R. Sharp, *The Government of France* (New York, 1938), pp. 282-283.

35. FO/425/405/20, Tyrrell to Henderson, April 14, 1930.

36. FO 800/292/34-35, lecture by Wigram, May 1933.

37. P. Bernard and H. Dubief, *The Decline of the Third Republic, 1914-1938* (Cambridge, 1985), p. 263.

38. Bellanger, pp. 513-522; Bernard and Dubief, p. 263.

39. *Decline of the Third Republic*, p. 264.

40. The covenant of the League of Nations expressed this sentiment in article 8, which spoke of the "evil effects" attendant upon the private manufacture of arms. See text in S. Fischer-Galati, *Twentieth-Century Europe: A Documentary History* (Philadelphia, 1967), p. 39.

41. CAB 63/40/86-90, March 26, 1928.

42. S. Roskill, *Hankey: Man of Secrets*, vol. 2, *1919-1931* (Annapolis, 1972), p. 417.

43. Bankwitz, *Maxime Weygand and Civil-Military Relations in Modern France* (Cambridge, Mass., 1967), p. 41.

44. Bankwitz, p. 43.

45. J. Doise and M. Vaïsse, *Diplomatie et outil militaire, 1871-1969* (Paris, 1987), pp. 275-292.

46. *Le Temps*, January 2, 1928, p. 1. Several other articles on the front pages of Le Temps during the first days of 1928 demonstrate a French preoccupation with peace, including a regular column entitled "The Regulation of the Peace."

47. Ibid.

48. "The *Times* Review of the Year 1927," December 31, 1927, pp. iii-iv.

49. See Jon Jacobson's article, "Is There a New International History of the 1920s?" *American Historical Review* 88:3 (June 1983), pp. 617-645.

50. Quoted in B. Oudin, *Aristide Briand: La paix: une idée neuve en Europe* (Paris, 1987), p. 518.

51. The French parliament thus far had not ratified the 1926 Mellon-Bérenger agreement, which had established a payment schedule. J.B. Duroselle, *France and the United States* (Chicago, 1978), pp. 122-128. To get an idea of the size of the debt: the French government's annual budget for 1913 had been five billion gold francs. The U.S. refused to recognize a connection between reparations and war debts, and furthermore had established tariffs averaging 38% (by the Fordney-McCumber Act of 1922), making it difficult to increase income through trade.

52. *Journal Officiel de la République Française*, *Débats parlementaires* (hereafter JO), Chambre des Députés, sessions extraordinaires, November 30, 1927, first session, p. 553.

53. Ibid., p. 554.

54. Ibid.

55. Ibid., p. 555.

56. Ibid., p. 556.

57. Ibid., p. 557.

58. Ibid.

59. Nevertheless, Stresemann believed that Poincaré obstructed the progress of Franco-German relations. R. Poidevin and J. Bariéty, *Les relations franco-allemandes 1815-1975* (Paris, 1977), p. 273. Briand and Poincaré retained their positions after the elections of 1928, which marked a shift to the right.

60. Poincaré had been premier during the military occupation of the Ruhr in January 1924, when France had attempted to force Germany to pay reparations. The *déclaration ministérielle* was the statement of a new government's policy presented to the Chamber for approval.

61. Poincaré Papers LV, n.a.fr. 16046/235-252.

62. Ibid.

63. MAE, series Z (1918-1929), Italy 85/129-140, Herbette to Briand, Moscow, January 10, 1928.

64. Ibid.

65. Ibid.

66. Ibid.

67. M. Vaïsse, *Sécurité d'abord: La politique française en matière de désarmement* (Paris, 1981), p. 355.

68. Dalton Papers, Diary (summer 1928), I/12/12-14.

69. V. Pitts, *France and the German Problem* (New York, 1987), p. 339.

70. Leo Aubrey Kennedy Papers (LKEN) 6 (Diary), Paris, June 1, 1928.

71. Ibid.

72. Ibid.

73. *The Realities behind Diplomacy* (Glasgow, 1981), p. 268.

74. A. Orde, *Great Britain and International Security, 1920-1926* (London, 1978), pp. 94-97; S. Marks, *The Illusion of Peace* (New York, 1976), pp. 59-60. The Geneva Protocol for the Pacific Settlement of International Disputes would have provided the League with a procedure for settling disputes; it was the work of Ramsay MacDonald, devised following the previous (Conservative) government's rejection of the Draft Treaty of Mutual Assistance, which France and much of Europe had supported. Baldwin's government in turn rejected the Geneva protocol. In both cases pressure from the dominions played a role; Canada in particular did not wish to be locked into a protocol-ordained course of action in a dispute involving Britain and the United States.

75. D. Dutton, *Austen Chamberlain: Gentleman in Politics* (Bolton, 1985), p. 259.

76. *The Collapse of British Power* (London, 1972), pp. 19-68.

77. Dutton, p. 259.

78. Dutton, p. 270.

79. FO 425/401/51, Memorandum: The Foreign Policy of His Majesty's Government, April 5, 1928.

80. M. Howard, *The Continental Commitment* (London, 1972), p. 90.

81. FO 425/401/51; see also C. Andrew, "British Intelligence and the Breach with Russia in 1927," *Historical Journal* 25:4 (December 1982), pp. 956-964.

82. FO 425/401/51 (Memorandum cited above).

83. Ibid.

84. Quoted from T. Jones' *Whitehall Diary* by D.C. Watt in *Succeeding John Bull: America in Britain's Place, 1900-1975* (Cambridge, 1984), p. 60.

85. Essentially, Britain supported France's policy of conscription and her desire for submarines; in return France supported the British position on cruisers. S. Roskill, *Naval Policy Between the Wars*, volume 1, *The Period of Anglo-American Antagonism* (New York, 1968), pp. 545-547.

86. WO 32/2672, Address of the CIGS, May 23, 1928.

87. Ibid.

88. Ibid.

89. M. Gilbert, *Winston S. Churchill*, volume 5, *1922-1939* (London, 1976), p. 289.

90. For a contentious view of the origins of the rule, see J. Ferris, "Treasury Control, the Ten Year Rule and British Service Policies, 1919-1924," *Historical Journal* 30:4 (December 1987), pp. 859-883.

91. Gilbert, p. 290.

92. N. Gibbs, *Grand Strategy*, volume 1, *Rearmament* (London, 1976), p. 58.

93. Gilbert, p. 290.

94. Gibbs, p. 70. The rule was reaffirmed in 1929 and 1930. At the spring 1930 meetings of the Three Party Committee on Disarmament, Austen Chamberlain (no longer Foreign Secretary) expressed doubts about the Ten Year Rule.

95. M. Gilbert (ed.), *Winston S. Churchill*, part 1 of companion to volume 5, *Documents: The Exchequer Years, 1922-1929* (Boston, 1981), letter from Churchill to Fisher, September 14, 1928, p. 1337.

96. Ibid., pp. 1337-8.

97. Cecil Papers, British Library (hereafter BL) MS 51073/132, Cecil to Churchill, July 26, 1927.

98. BL MS 51166/25-6, Cecil to Lady Gwendolen Cecil, February 24, 1928.

99. D. Birn, *The League of Nations Union 1918-1945* (Oxford, 1981), p. 79. The French League Society had more than 120,000 members in 600 branches at the end of 1927, about a quarter of the British organization's membership.

100. See text in S. Fischer-Galati, pp. 118-120.

101. G. Suarez, *Briand*, volume 6, *L'Artisan de la paix* (Paris, 1952), p. 273.

102. S. Roskill, *Hankey*, volume 2, p. 469.

103. Papiers 1940/Léger 2/29-31, Briand to Paul Claudel, French Ambassador to Washington, Paris, December 26, 1927.

104. MAE, series SDN (Société des Nations), IH 738/51-55, Briand to Claudel, January 2, 1928; IH 738/120-128, Briand to Fleuriau, Paris, January 10, 1928.

105. Actually, Briand had discussed the pact proposal beforehand with James T. Shotwell of the Carnegie Endowment for International Peace. Levinson arrived in France after the announcement, but he was very enthusiastic about it. Duroselle, *France and the United States*, pp. 130-133.

106. FO 800/262/93-97 (Private Collections: Austen Chamberlain), Howard to Chamberlain, Washington, D.C., February 2, 1928.

107. Indeed, New York *World* columnist Walter Lippmann wondered how the State Department could be wasting its time on "a project so obviously absurd." R. Steel, *Walter Lippmann and the American Century* (Boston, 1980), p. 254.

108. FO 800/262/93-97. Despatch cited above.

109. Ibid.

110. FO 800/262/158-166, Chamberlain to Howard, London, February 13, 1928.

111. Ibid.

112. FO 800/262/256-59, Howard to Chamberlain, Washington, D.C., March 9, 1928.

113. Ibid.

114. FO 800/263/29, Chamberlain to Sir Malcolm Robertson (personal), London, July 27, 1928.

115. FO 800/262/250, Drummond to Chamberlain, Geneva, March 7, 1928.

116. FO 800/262/251, Chamberlain to Drummond, London, March 7, 1928.

117. He later wrote the first draft of the now infamous leading article of September 7, 1938 suggesting that Czechoslovakia cede the Sudetenland in the interest of peace.

118. LKEN 6 (Diary), Geneva, June 4, 1928.

119. Ibid., Geneva, June 9, 1928.

120. LKEN 7 (Diary), Geneva, July 20, 1928.

121. FO 800/263/38-40, Selby to Chamberlain, Paris, August 27, 1928.

122. R. Albrecht-Carrié, *A Diplomatic History of Europe Since the Congress of Vienna* (revised edition: New York, 1973), p. 442. The only nations not to sign were Arabia, Argentina, Bolivia, Brazil, and Yemen.

123. *Daily Mail*, March 29, 1928, reported in French diplomatic correspondence: Series Z (1918-1929), Italy 85/156.

124. Thomas Jones, *Whitehall Diary*, volume 2, *1926-1930* (London, 1969), p. 129-131.

125. FO 408/51/42, Lindsay to Chamberlain, Berlin, May 24, 1928.

126. FO 408/51/44, Chamberlain to the Marquess of Crewe, London, May 30, 1928.

127. Ibid.

128. FO 408/51/43 Lindsay to Chamberlain, Berlin, May 26, 1928.

129. Series Z (Europe 1918-1929), Poland 113/292, M. de Gaiffier d'Hestroy, Belgian Ambassador in Paris, to Philippe Berthelot, Secretary General, French foreign ministry, Paris, May 11, 1928.

2

Liquidation of One War,
Fears of Another

I am going to see this confounded thing through. It is the end of a great historical episode — the end of the Paris Peace Conference in a sense, or at least a great part of it, and as I am one of the two people who can sign the final Act, I am going to sign, I am and I won't have any blooming foreigner signing for me, I won't.
— Maurice Hankey[1]

The Hague Conference of 1929 was subtitled "The Conference for the Final Liquidation of the Great War."[2] What did this mean? Specifically, it meant that in Geneva the previous October, Germany, Britain, France, Italy, Belgium and the United States had agreed on a protocol for resolving the problems which had most directly affected their relations in the postwar period: reparations and the Allied occupation of the Rhineland. Beyond this narrow definition of "liquidation," however, lay the more general hope that, after all the upheaval and acrimony of the past fifteen years, Europe would live in prosperity and security.

Between 1928 and 1933, a series of agreements "liquidated" the war: in 1929 the Young Plan created a specific schedule for German reparations payments; in 1930 the former allies completed their evacuation of the Rhineland five years ahead of schedule; in 1932 the Lausanne Conference in effect cancelled reparations. These events brought no catharsis, however; the German people, encouraged to blame their growing economic distress on the Treaty of Versailles, cast their votes for parties sworn to revenge. German leaders demanded equality of rights in armaments. The "liquidation" of the war ended discussion of issues which could be resolved peacefully, leaving exposed those issues which could not, such as Germany's eastern frontiers. The liquidation of the Great War cast in sharp relief both persistent dangers to European peace and the unwillingness of Britain and France to face those dangers resolutely.

This chapter discusses the perceptions surrounding the process of "liquidation," the emergence of renewed fears of war, and the inability of both the British and French governments to address the new realities effectively. For the peace to last, the rapprochement between France and

Germany had to continue on terms acceptable to both nations. It did not. In retrospect, the summer of 1930 — the period between the evacuation of the Rhineland and the German Reichstag elections — was the turning point between the two world wars. The occupation of the Rhineland had been valuable insurance for France and its allies: with French troops on German soil, Germany had to abide by the terms of the Treaty. Evacuation was, therefore, a leap of faith. Noisy paramilitary demonstrations in the Rhineland immediately following the final evacuation in June 1930, followed by the National Socialist victories in the September elections, demonstrated German contempt for the Versailles order and a willingness to use force to revise it.

Hindsight might suggest a fuller definition of "liquidation": the reestablishment of a balance of power, in which each of Europe's larger powers could accept the consequences of the war, including the appearance of new states carved from the collapsed or reduced Russian, German, Ottoman and Austrian Empires. However, models of harmonious states systems possess a simple beauty rarely found in reality. In any case, war originates not simply from faulty balances, but also from leaders who exploit them. Issues such as reparations and postwar occupation seem ephemeral by comparison, but these were issues on which British and French leaders could agree, though the negotiating process was often complicated, contentious and exhausting. Pacifying Germany was a far more formidable task.

Again from hindsight, one could argue that Britain's leaders suffered from a form of cognitive dissonance, failing to consider adequately Britain's security interests in a new era, one in which the English Channel, as a barrier to attack, was not what it had once been. As a matter of policy, the Rhine had become Britain's line of defense, but the conduct of diplomacy suggested that the English Channel continued to play the psychological role it had for centuries. Leaders fell back on a more traditional definition of security: isolation, as much as possible, from European entanglements. Ultimately, liquidation meant withdrawal.

Of course, the French also desired security above all, but they did not even have an English Channel to protect them, physically or psychologically. Demographics militated against seeking safety in a large army: Germany's could always be larger. Technologically, France might be able to keep up with Germany but could not hope to secure an advantage. As an industrial power, Germany was still far ahead of France, despite considerable French progress in the 1920s.[3] Regardless of current figures, Germany's *capacity* to wage total war, her potential, was far greater than

France's. French leaders had been aware of these realities for some time; before the war, the answer had been alliances. But allies had not prevented the deaths of over one million Frenchmen or the destruction of northeastern France, and after the war they had proven to be unreliable. Now the League of Nations theoretically offered collective security, but the best hope for peace lay in cooperation with Britain and reconciliation with Germany.

The Great War and Public Opinion

During a visit to Cambridge in December 1929, Hugh Dalton spoke with Professor "Goldie" Dickinson, and later noted in his diary: "He is impressed by the effect of the ten-year period of stunned consciousness after the war, and the signs of its passing, with the flood of war books and the spreading interest in international relations, and by the immense power of wireless to reach those who read little."[4] The "liquidation" of the war coincided with an outpouring of books, plays and films dealing with the wartime experience. In 1928, twenty-one books about the war appeared in Britain, up from six in 1926 and fifteen in 1927; in 1929 twenty-nine books appeared on the subject.[5] These works influenced public opinion about war and international politics at a critical time. Their direct influence on leaders is difficult to assess, but in Britain the revulsion against war and the general sentiment of "never again" bolstered the arguments of those who sought greater economy in defense budgets and narrow circumscription of military commitments. In France, a similar weariness was evident, but leaders could not avoid the German problem so easily.

Public opinion during this period is difficult to quantify; though A.L. Bowley had hit upon the idea of random sampling as far back as 1915, the first polls in both Britain and France were conducted only in the second half of the 1930s.[6] Of course, election results suggested broad currents in public opinion, at least among those who could vote.[7] The critical and popular reception of films, books and plays is a limited indicator of general public opinion, but it does suggest the mood among society's more affluent and educated members, a group which includes political leaders.

For many Britons who wrote about the war, the visceral experience of life and death in the trenches tended to obscure any intellectual convictions of the war's purposes.[8] For example, Edmund Blunden's *Undertones of War* (1928) made no attempt to place the individual experience of war within a broader context. Richard Aldington's *Death of a Hero* (1929) shrilly attacked the "older generation" of Victorian leaders for sending their sons to their deaths.[9] These authors, writes Noreen Branson, "expressed a growing uncertainty about motives on both sides. People were now not sure that Germany had been solely to blame. And many of those who thought the war had been unavoidable also believed that it had been unnecessarily and brutally prolonged by the Allied governments for ignoble purposes."[10]

Erich Maria Remarque's *Im Westen nichts Neues* (*All Quiet on the Western Front*), appeared in both German and English in 1929, and became an international best seller, selling 250,000 copies in Britain alone within the first year.[11] It was less successful in Germany, where works glorifying war outsold anti-war books; for example, Ernst Jünger, who was heavily influenced by Oswald Spengler, was a more popular writer.[12] The film version of *All Quiet* was both a critical and financial success in the English-speaking world. In Germany and Austria, however, the film met with violent demonstrations, and the Austrian Minister of the Interior subsequently banned it.[13]

Much of the new literature focused on the horrors of war generally rather than specifically German atrocities. Indeed, these descriptions were so graphic that one irritated critic wrote in the *Times* that these authors were "determined, like the old fresco painters when they pictured Hell, so to scare, horrify and revolt the reader that he shall never think of the war again without trembling and nausea"; but this was their intention.[14] The play *Journey's End*, by R.C. Sherriff, after being rejected by many London theaters, finally opened at the Savoy in January 1929, and became a great commercial success.[15] It portrayed life in the trenches for a group of ex-public school boys (whose fate the title suggested). Though it did not address overtly the question of the war's purpose, Germans were at one point referred to as "quite decent...outside the newspapers."[16] Later on in 1929 a radio version of the play broadcast on Armistice Day topped a *Radio Times* survey of the year's most "enjoyable" programs.[17] A year later it became a successful film, the first Anglo-American co-production.

In this atmosphere *Dawn*, a film which portrayed the German army's arrest and execution of the British nurse Edith Cavell, provoked controversy. Produced and directed by Herbert Wilcox, the film depicted the story of Nurse Edith Cavell, who helped 210 English soldiers to escape from occupied Brussels before her capture.[18] In September 1927 the German Embassy had tried without success to get the Foreign Office and the producer to stop the film's release. The following January, Austen Chamberlain declined an invitation to the premiere, saying that he disapproved personally of this evocation of an episode "sorrowful to English hearts" and likely to provoke discussions "around the grave of a heroine respected the world over."[19] He also had made a "personal call" on the chairman of the Board of British Film Censors, which in turn called for the withdrawal of the film.[20]

Though many approved of Chamberlain's stand, the film's distributors protested that the film was meant to inspire a more general horror of war.[21] Anxious to dispel the notion that the government would engage in political censorship, Chamberlain emphasized his "personal call" as a gesture of loyalty to the memory of an English heroine. His objections to the film, which he had not seen, arose from the director's description of the execution scene: "One of the firing party definitely refuses to level his rifle at Nurse Cavell, and he is shot on the spot. The rest are lined up, and, on the order to fire, each one raises his rifle so that he fires above Miss Cavell's head. Nurse Cavell, however, falls down in a faint, and the officer then steps forward and despatches her."[22] Chamberlain believed this account to be wholly apocryphal and shamelessly manipulative of the facts for "the purposes of commercial gain." Opposition critics in the Commons, however, pointed out that British representatives in Germany failed to protest films like *The World War through German Spectacles*, which portrayed incidents tending "to perpetuate German hatred of Great Britain and her Allies."[23]

The government could hardly declare that the war had been a mistake and that thousands of British families suffered losses as a result of diplomatic, bureaucratic and military incompetence, but this did not mean that Britain could not adopt a more conciliatory attitude towards Germany. The role that the "will of the people" played in the minds of foreign policy makers in the interwar years is an evasive problem. In Britain, the government cited "public opinion" as justification for its policies, yet used various means to control public opinion.[24] Newspapers like the *Times* maintained a cozy relationship with members of the government and a paternalistic disposition towards the public; as the diaries of Leo Kennedy illustrate, confidences were not passed on to readers if public opinion might be alarmed by them. In return, of course, correspondents could expect greater candor from their sources.

In France, too, the arts scene demonstrated a mellowing of attitudes. There was a similar outpouring of memoirs; already in 1929 Jean Norton Cru published a survey and analysis of existing works in the genre. Marcel Bucard, whose *Paroles d'un combattant* appeared in 1930, hoped that war veterans would play a role in postwar society equal in importance to that which they had played during the war. Veterans' movements failed to transform the political system, however, in part because a slightly younger generation of writers, too young to have fought in the war but nonetheless brilliantly disillusioned by the experience (or lack thereof), attracted attention away from the former combatants, at least in the literary world.[25]

In Paris, the success of Jean Giraudoux's play *Siegfried* suggested that Briand's conciliatory policy enjoyed wide support, at least among affluent Parisians. Already successful as a diplomat and writer, Giraudoux had adapted the piece from one of his novels; it received great critical acclaim and ran for 283 performances at the Théatre des Champs Elysées in the Avenue Montaigne.[26] *Siegfried* dealt frankly with relations between France and Germany. Set in postwar Germany, the title character is the republic's new chancellor, a leader of mythical proportions (as the name suggests) cultivated from an unidentifiable amnesiac soldier who had ended up in a German army hospital during the war. An advisor who wants to seize power for himself hatches a plot to reveal the Chancellor's true identity: Siegfried is actually Jacques, a Parisian artist. Siegfried/Jacques reacts to this revelation with irony: "I am no longer German. How simple! It's enough to change everything. My glory days are no longer Sedan and Sadowa. My flag no longer has horizontal stripes. East and West will switch places around me. What I believed to be examples of supreme loyalty and honor may come to seem treasonous and brutal."[27]

Giraudoux did not argue that the French and the Germans were essentially the same; Germans were deeply romantic in spirit, great lovers of nature, whereas the French prized the intellect and rationality. Though Siegfried/Jacques feels an impulse to escape both cultures, a sense of duty to these troubled nations prevails:

> I'll tell you that the day before yesterday I thought about disappearing, about seeking asylum in some third country, one that I would have chosen because it had no neighbors, no enemies, no dedication ceremonies for war memorials, no dead. A country with no war in its past and no war in its future. But the more I looked at the map, the more attached I felt to the countries that suffer, the more clearly I felt my mission....My mission is to serve.[28]

While acknowledging the cultural differences between France and Germany, Giraudoux clearly saw the enmity between the two as senseless. A great sense of weariness, engendered by the seemingly endless conflict, pervades the play. Yet the tone is conciliatory and hopeful.[29]

Siegfried was one of several manifestations of a changing attitude toward Germany in Paris. According to the British ambassador, the Marquess of Crewe, "all the important elements of Paris society" were present at a sold-out performance of the Berlin Philharmonic under the direction of Wilhelm Furtwängler at the Faubourg Saint-Honoré on May 11, at the end of which the German ambassador, mounting the stage, was "greeted with loud applause." At the Opéra between 5 and 17 May the Vienna State Opera Company gave a series of performances of German operas by Wagner, Strauss and Mozart, which also were sold out. "I consider that these three events should be carefully noted," concluded Crewe. "I question whether the German Ambassador could have appeared at all on a Paris stage, much less have been loudly cheered on his appearance, at any time between 1871 and 1914."[30] *Le tout-Paris*, at least, was willing to readmit the best of German culture.

The Evacuation of the Rhineland

Early in 1928 Philippe Berthelot, secretary general at the Quai d'Orsay, envisioned a scenario whereby the questions of reparations, interallied debts and the evacuation of the Rhineland could be resolved by the end of the year, after elections in France, Germany and the United States. He believed that the Americans then would agree to cancel the French debt to them in return for a large reduction of the reparations bill. Once the Germans issued railway and industrial bonds to generate the revenue needed to pay the rest of the reparations, the Rhineland could be evacuated.[31] The linkage of the reparations question to the occupation of the Rhineland had antecedents, he believed; after the Franco-Prussian War, German troops had evacuated occupied French territory, department by department, as the French paid off their indemnity.[32] The scheme was simple from Berthelot's point of view, but unfortunately neither the United States nor Germany would accept it; U.S. officials refused to recognize a connection between reparations and debt, and the Germans rejected any link between reparations and evacuation.

For France, evacuation of the Rhineland represented a major concession; in return Germany would have to provide assurance that her rehabilitation was genuine. Not all in France were prepared to make this leap without safety nets; leaders considered schemes whereby surveillance of the region would continue by other means. Briand took up in the Senate a scheme developed by the Socialist deputy Joseph Paul-Boncour calling for the establishment of a Geneva-based permanent body of investigation for the demilitarized zone. At the British embassy in Paris, Eric Phipps found Paul-Boncour's proposal to be rather reactionary for a Socialist; he wrote to William Tyrrell at the Foreign Office of Paul-Boncour's vanity and jealousy of Léon Blum, whose leadership he did not recognize. The Germans would reject the scheme in any case, since it exceeded anything called for in the Treaty of Versailles. In conversation, Paul-Boncour had vigorously rejected Phipps' rather perverse suggestion that the commission be empowered to investigate on *both* sides of the frontier.[33]

At stake for the French was their "last card," as right-wing journalist André Chaumeix, a frequent contributor to the *Écho de Paris* and the *Journal des Débats*, put it. When Phipps suggested to him that French delays might ruin whatever chances France had to use this issue to obtain something in return from Germany, such as a more friendly disposition, Chaumeix invoked the "usual arguments as to the persistence of the German militarist spirit, the teaching of that spirit to the young, etc."[34] Phipps would have been mistaken to take this attitude as typical, but, unfortunately, the right wing in France, with its sharp opinions, made an impression in Britain out of proportion to its influence in France.

In any case, the French government did not intend to evacuate the Rhineland without a quid pro quo: "it is important to maintain very firmly the principle of our right by the Treaty to not proceed with evacuation without compensation."[35] French troops on German soil were the best means of assuring German payment of reparations; in addition, they also made it difficult for Germany to "rectify" its eastern frontier with Poland or to seek union with Austria. France's eastern allies, therefore, watched the Rhineland negotiations with concern, fearing that, for France, rapprochement with Germany would be rather attractive compensation for evacuation.

The suggestion that these armed forces served a peace-keeping purpose seemed to surprise and dismay officials at the Foreign Office:

What is the use of discussing disarmament when the Rhineland problem for instance is unliquidated and the occupation is regarded by a good part of Europe as a better guarantee for their own security than all Mr. Kellogg's Peace Pact? The evacuation of the Rhineland may even induce — I hope it will not — certain Powers to increase rather than decrease their armaments. The Poles and Czechs certainly showed quite unexpected interest in the Rhineland discussions.[36]

For the French, of course, this interest was not at all unexpected; Poland and Czechoslovakia were their allies, and France's position vis-à-vis Germany had a direct bearing on their national security. Even if French leaders were ever to decide that rapprochement with Germany was of greater value than alliances with Czechoslovakia and Poland, the abandonment of the eastern allies would diminish seriously France's great-power status — a heavy price to pay, particularly if Germany subsequently embarked on a campaign of eastward expansion.[37]

Britain, meanwhile, seemed very eager to evacuate, with or without assurances. For some sectors of public opinion the evacuation could not proceed quickly enough. As Walford Selby wrote to Austen Chamberlain: "the government has incurred the wrath...of the Isolationists and those who believe that the way to deal with Germany is to give her all she asks for. Lloyd George is so angry that we haven't evacuated the Rhineland without conditions that he has written to the Neue Freie Presse about it. But I am never really afraid of that criticism, it is too hollow."[38] The Foreign Office fortunately lacked Lloyd George's rashness, but the former prime minister still commanded a strong political presence, and it was quite clear that "public opinion" favored a quick settlement of the issue.

While public opinion pressed for a solution, negotiations were rendered unduly arduous by a perpetually and deliberately gloomy German delegation. Austen Chamberlain wrote of his encounter with Stresemann and Briand at Lugano in December 1928:

> ...I fear that [Stresemann] is a very sick man and his spirits and temper both showed something of the despondency and irritability caused by his illness. It is, however, the practice of the German Delegation always to profess the greatest despondency about the outlook. They refused to be anything but pessimistic up to the last minute at Locarno and they repeat these tactics at every gathering. I say tactics, for though it is due to temperament, it is, I think, also in part a deliberately chosen weapon.[39]

A French delegate had remarked to Chamberlain that Briand had to take a cure every time he met with Stresemann.

Despite his own consistently negative opinions about the Germans, Chamberlain hoped to impress upon the French the pressure in Britain for evacuation.[40] At Lugano he sensed for the first time that Briand was in a position to proceed, given a suitable agreement; himself eager for liquidation, Briand had the majority of French public opinion behind him. He instructed Tyrrell, Britain's new ambassador to France, to emphasize in his conversations with French leaders "how important British public opinion is becoming about the occupation." The Labour and Liberal parties were calling openly for evacuation of the British contingent; sections of Conservative opinion were equally emphatic. Chamberlain wanted Tyrrell to leave the impression that he was doing all he could to hold opinion at bay, but that he could only hold out so long; he would do what he could to secure concessions from the Germans, but France would have to adopt a more conciliatory attitude.[41]

In Chamberlain's opinion, however, the Germans themselves complicated the issues standing in the way of evacuation: "They are, as I told von Schubert [the secretary general at the German Foreign Office], the most difficult nation to help in the world; they were always, I said, undoing the work of conciliation which I had laboriously built up and raising unnecessary difficulties in the way of those like Briand and myself who really wanted to reach an early and friendly solution."[42] On the second last day of the Lugano meetings Stresemann had sent Chamberlain a message saying he had agreed to give the *Baltimore Sun* a statement of German views with respect to their Treaty right to evacuation. This, Stresemann said, would obviate the need for a full statement in answer to an interpellation in the Reichstag; but if Chamberlain preferred a Reichstag pronouncement, he would oblige. Chamberlain resented being confronted with this choice; he thought that any such statement might well undo any progress made at Lugano. Stresemann's violent outburst against the Polish delegate Zaleski over the issue of Germans living in Poland also had created unnecessary tension, and reinforced Polish suspicions of Germany.[43]

Tyrrell believed that Stresemann's "position is considerably weakened and that he no longer has that grasp on the direction of affairs which he has hitherto displayed."[44] Moreover he felt that Briand was overly optimistic in his assessment of French public opinion with respect to the evacuation. Though in his conversations in Paris he emphasized the impatience of the British people and a sense of moral obligation to the Germans, he found "a very strong current here running against the Germans, mainly due to their foolish speeches which have restarted French suspicion as regards the sincerity of the Germans."[45]

The Young Plan and the Hague Conferences

In February 1929 experts meeting in Paris began to hammer out a replacement for the Dawes Plan, as the American, S. Parker Gilbert, Agent-General for Reparations, had proposed. These meetings, over which another American, banker Owen D. Young, presided, demonstrated that even experts could infuriate one another: in April Hjalmar Schacht, the chief representative for Germany, seemed to include a demand for the return of the colonies and the Polish Corridor in his negotiating offer, precipitating French withdrawals from German banks the following day.[46] Despite these tensions the Young Plan emerged in June, subject to the approval of the political leaders.

The Hague Conference met in August for this purpose. Britain's new minority Labour government, with Ramsay MacDonald as prime minister and Arthur Henderson as foreign secretary, did not inspire Maurice Hankey or other top civil servants with confidence:

> I dare say the Cabinet will be in fairly frequent session during the Conference, and in that event I shall have to be knocking around. Things are not so easy as they were with the new crowd. They have odd methods of their own of doing business and I am afraid things may get in a muddle. I get on very well personally with [MacDonald], but everyone agrees he is not too easy to work with. I think all the heads of the civil service feel we are living in rather difficult times.[47]

Organization did "get in a muddle," and Hankey, called upon to restore order, became secretary general of the conference.

Hugh Dalton, the new parliamentary undersecretary at the Foreign Office, realized already in June that Chancellor of the Exchequer Philip Snowden would raise difficulties about the reparations settlement, hoping to increase Britain's share. It was, thought Dalton, "a hopeless policy! The view of his Office, and ours, is that a few millions are dust in the balance compared with the gains of an early and complete evacuation which will also certainly follow swiftly on a general acceptance of the [Young Plan]. But Uncle [Henderson], though sound on principles, is a bit afraid of P.S."[48] Snowden thus became the "worst enemy of Germany... with his anti-French passions, which may delay evacuation."[49]

France sent a "holiday government" to the Hague; for health reasons, Poincaré had retired (for the last time) in July, and Briand now served both as prime minister and foreign minister. Poincaré would be missed; letters written to him by friends around this time praised him for his work in liquidating the war. H.A. Jules-Bois, writing from New York (before the resignation), expressed his faith in Poincaré: [Y]ou are the only one who, after saving the country several times, can save it again, despite the blindness of factions."[50] Maurice Herbette, the ambassador in Brussels, wrote after the resignation: "with self-sacrifice which knows no precedent, you wanted to finish your work and to assure the general and most advantageous possible liquidation of the war."[51]

With Briand in firm control of his delegation, French cooperation was virtually assured.   Now Philip Snowden posed the greatest obstacle. Maurice Hankey, much in demand because of Snowden's intransigence, wrote to his wife on 10 August: "Today I thought he went too far.   Chéron, rather a decent old Frenchman, made a speech combatting Snowden's figures.   Snowden's reply was, practically, to the effect that all Chéron's figures were false, and the deductions he had drawn from them wrong! No arguments and no figures but merely a reiteration that they must submit to his terms.   That fairly blew the lid off."[52] This was, of course, the famous incident in which Snowden called Chéron's remarks "grotesque and ridiculous," words whose effects have been debated since, first for their appropriate renderings in French and second for their role in precipitating a run on sterling in August and September.[53] In Maurice Hankey's account, however, the "whole incident was closed amid something approaching jollity" the following day, thanks in large part to his efforts.[54]

Delegates to the Hague Conference were eager to liquidate the war, but each party also hoped to secure the best deal possible. For Briand this was a political necessity. The British delegation, generally less willing than the French to delay the proceedings, had to contend with Snowden. Hankey wrote to his son that the delegation was very poorly organized, that Henderson and Snowden added personal antipathy to disagreement over the issues to be resolved; MacDonald's despatches, publicly supporting Snowden but privately admonishing the delegation for "making a mess of it," did not help.[55] Robert Boyce has suggested that Snowden's performance marked a turning point for Britain, away from international cooperation and towards a narrower focus on British interests.[56]

Yet Hankey believed that Snowden unwittingly helped the French through his intransigence, for Briand knew how to play the situation:

> Briand is playing the game I expected.   On the political side he is displaying an
> extraordinarily conciliatory spirit, offering to abandon the Rhineland...but always
> subject to one condition, namely that there is a settlement of reparations.   In other
> words he means to get into a position to represent that the British Government in
> general, and Snowden in particular are blocking the peace in Europe for a matter of [2
> 1/2 million pounds] a year![57]

Despite this wrangling, Germany accepted the Young Plan and made exactly one payment in May 1930, notably while the Allies still had troops in the

Rhineland. The main feature of the plan was its commercialization of Germany's debt: bonds were to be sold on the world market, to be paid back by Germany over a period lasting until the 1980s. In the event, however, the bond issues were undersubscribed, and the whole plan foundered within two years.[58] The reparations issue was not settled until the Hoover moratorium of 1931 and the Lausanne Conference of 1932 finally put it to rest.

The conference intended to liquidate the war left a bitter taste. Maurice Hankey wrote to his son that he was

> disagreeably impressed with the state of Europe... The hatreds between Germans and Poles and between Germans and French are barely concealed. Once there was a bad outburst between Massigli and the German Secretary Boltze, which I had difficulty in allaying. ...I was accused by name in the Kölnische Zeitung (quite falsely as luckily I could prove) of treating Zaleski, the Polish Foreign Secretary, 'mit der grössten Entschiedenheit' [with the greatest peremptoriness]. Zaleski was attacked by all the opposition papers in Poland for standing it. After seeing Zaleski, who was very pleasant, I saw von Schubert and asked him to make the correspondent deny it. Von Schubert remarked, 'But, my friend, for treating Zaleski "mit der grössten Entschiedenheit" you will be the most popular man in Germany!' Oh! la! la! How glad I am that it is all over — for a few weeks at any rate.[59]

Hugh Dalton, meanwhile, was becoming discouraged with his own government's performance on the European scene. After discussing the Conference with Ronald Lindsay, permanent undersecretary at the Foreign Office, he wrote: "The Hague fills us both with gloom. [Snowden], he says, has created a real war mentality in this country." Dalton replied that Snowden had no experience in negotiation, which Lindsay said was illustrated by "his failure to divide the French from the Italians."[60] On the train to Geneva on August 28, Dalton wrote: "The Hague Settlement...has altered the face of my universe for the better, but still leaves a very difficult atmosphere."[61] Speaking with British officials in Geneva, he noted that all were "very gloomy [on the] effect of Snowden's behaviour. It is being said that the Labour Government is being more nationalist than its predecessor, that it has no sense of the international situation."[62] Back in Britain, however, the tabloids praised Snowden's display of gall.

The foreign secretary, Arthur Henderson, could call himself an internationalist, but he had failed to assert himself in the face of MacDonald and Snowden's intrusions.[63] Nevertheless, at a second Hague Conference the following January, negotiators reached agreement on a reduced reparations settlement and evacuation of the Rhineland. With these knotty problems apparently solved, the future looked brighter.   In Britain, MacDonald hoped to improve relations with Germany, attributing lack of progress in this area to the general inertia of Baldwin's government.   He believed that, by treating Germany well, Britain could expect reasonable behavior in return.

The Turning Point and Beyond: Rumors of War

With the nagging issues left from the war on their way to resolution, how did the future look?   The *Economist* in December 1929 saw Germany's future in the "new Europe" as hopeful, though challenging; with "final liquidation of the war in sight, the European stage is set for a new act, in which the part of Germany, though perhaps no bigger as measured in terms of 'lines' than it has been in the last ten years, will offer far greater scope for genius."[64] Gustav Stresemann's work had provided the strongest clue as to the future direction of policy.   This, at least, was the opinion of Erich Koch-Weser, leader of Germany's waning Democratic Party, who had written that Stresemann's conciliatory approach, at first seen as the only way to advance Germany's interests, was now the best means of securing German desires.   His book on postwar German foreign policy was "calculated to appeal to his countrymen and to convince the foreigner" that Stresemann's approach was the one "best calculated to further the ends which the average man has at heart."

Koch-Weser called for the sublimation of the military impulse in favor of an economic pursuit of the same goals.   Germany would therefore be pacifistic and a strong supporter of the League of Nations, albeit a League that would not be allowed to "degenerate into an instrument for the maintenance of the status quo"; renouncing her colonial ambitions, Germany would become the champion of oppressed peoples.

In the meantime, he argued, destroying economic barriers in Europe would enable the German people to channel their productive energies beyond their overcrowded homeland.   This might cause some anxiety among neighbors, but it seemed to be inevitable in these modern times:

This calls up pictures of a progressive germanisation of Europe which may seem alarming; but a moment's reflection on the penetration of almost the whole world, of recent years, by American methods and influences reveals unmistakably that it is impossible, in modern conditions, to resist the infiltration of economic and cultural influences from any country whose inhabitants have sufficient vitality to originate anything.[65]

A United States of Europe, based on political and economic cooperation, would eliminate the current barriers.

Koch-Weser's book did not skirt the four issues that stood in the way of such cooperation: disarmament, cultural autonomy for the German minorities, the eastern frontier, and *Anschluss*. From this the *Economist* surmised that, much as Germans desired concessions on these issues, particularly the latter two, "she is prepared to wait until they are freely conceded to her by the public sense of justice." Those skeptical about peaceful resolution of these problems needed only to remember that, by this logic, political boundaries would not matter much in a disarmed, open-market world. Germany, too, might be satisfied with strong cultural and economic ties with Austria. The article concluded:

> It is the very elasticity of a programme which rests fundamentally on the principle of eliminating distrust and forming the ties of friendly co-operation which makes it so reassuring. Germany wishes to create a state of affairs in which everybody will see reason. Meanwhile there is no need to decide, indeed no possibility of deciding, what that reason will dictate. We must first qualify ourselves to see it.[66]

To the "unworthy," however, the news from Germany in 1930 suggested that the basis for a conciliatory foreign policy was eroding. There had been noisy nationalist demonstrations in Germany before, but *Stahlhelm* demonstrations in the Rhineland shortly after the final Allied evacuation at the end of June 1930 had a devastating effect on French public opinion. More alarming news came on 14 September, when elections gave the National Socialists 18.7 per cent of the popular vote and 107 seats in the Reichstag, making them the second largest party.[67] Despite the great imbalances between French and German military forces, and despite the fact that France at this time was an "isle of prosperity" in an economically depressed continent, rumors of imminent war spread. While the right wing in France felt vindicated, most politicians became concerned about the highly agitated state of public opinion.

The conservative nationalist press in France first sounded the alarms. André Pironneau wrote in the *Écho de Paris* the day after the last French soldiers left the Rhineland: "Thus ends one historical period and begins another, which we cannot greet without extreme anxiety."[68] Over the following weeks the paper reported on many nationalist demonstrations and incidents of violence; with more than a hint of irony editors placed such front-page headlines as "Hitlerites Attack French Sportsman" and "Racists Redouble Pillages of Reprisal at Trier" under the kicker "The Spirit of

Locarno."[69]   On August 12, "Germany Unanimous Against the Treaty" greeted readers; on September 15, the day after the elections, headlines proclaimed that the Reich was "moving toward a régime of force." On September 28 the *Écho de Paris* reported on collaboration between the Reichswehr and the Red Army.

Towards the other end of the political spectrum, Léon Blum sought to reassure readers of *Le Populaire*. On November 19 he wrote: "How many times, during these last weeks, haven't we heard the question asked, with dread as much as in earnest, 'Do you think there will be war?... Will we be at war next spring?'" Needless to say, Blum continued, the response of politicians like Henry Franklin-Bouillon and Louis Marin, as well as the "reactionary" press, was inappropriate: "France, they say, is envied, disparaged, watched; her enemies silently are building the engines of future aggression. She must be defiant and vigilant. She must fall back, shore up the few alliances that remain, and rearm."

What the nationalists forgot, Blum argued, was that war had a vast array of causes, primarily economic, but also historical, political and personal. Collective psychology also played a major role; war became possible when the mass of opinion believed it to be possible, and inevitable if people believed it to be so. Blum believed, therefore, that there would be no war if people did not want one; a determined, collective will would render war impossible: "Every man can do his small part, repeating what Briand declared one day at Geneva: 'As long as I am there, there won't be war!' This is not a foolish, sentimental wish; it is a potent affirmation of will."[70]   Blum still believed strongly in the Socialist International, and in the ability of Germany's Socialists to keep Hitler far from power, despite his recent electoral successes. Even if Hitler took over, he would need alliances to embark on a campaign of revenge; only Hungary and perhaps Turkey would follow him on this desperate campaign. Blum believed that the disquiet over Germany was based on a memory of Germany from before the war, and not on present realities: "No, that phase of history is over, well over, and it is up to us to cast upon it the last shovelful of dirt. The power and prestige of Germany are no longer such that she could group under her shadow, as fourteen years ago, half of Europe. Neither to Hitler nor to Mussolini can one attribute such absurd or demented designs.... It is up to us to see to it that they remain impracticable."[71]

Blum's ideology helped to convince him of the perils of hypernational- ist violence. However, his faith also led him to rely on vague notions of international brotherhood and of the power of individuals to influence large events. This included faith in Germany's Socialist party, which still held 143 seats in the Reichstag, and had received 24.5% of the popular vote in the recent elections.[72] A little prewar memory might have been useful, however; as the *Revue des deux mondes* dutifully pointed out, this same party had endorsed German aggression in 1914.[73] On August 1, 1914, Hermann Müller, then a German Socialist deputy, had assured his French counterparts that it would be "out of the question" to vote for German war credits, and had received similar assurances from French Socialists; two days later 78 of 92 Socialists in the Reichstag voted for those credits.[74] French Socialists also had rallied to the colors in the end, convinced that their government had sought peace.[75]

Rumors of war also reached Sir Hughe Knatchbull-Hugessen, who, as British Minister in the Baltic States, noted in early 1931 a marked decline in the European situation over the past year. The evacuation of the Rhineland, the negotiation of the Young Plan, the relatively successful Naval Conference, signs of rapprochement between France and Germany and Briand's plan for the federation of Europe had seemed to represent a new spirit of peace. Yet anxieties persisted: Italy's ambitions were unclear, as were Germany's; and France was suspicious of both. The British worried about the potential economic effects of Franco-German rapprochement or European Union. "Old Adam," the spirit of division and conflict, appeared more frequently.[76]

Somehow the spirit of conciliation had dissipated. Knatchbull-Hugessen wrote: "In general it cannot be denied that anxiety in Europe has increased, nervousness is greater, and talk of war (however irresponsible) louder. I do not for a moment believe that there is any serious danger of war in the immediate future, but there is a growing tendency in several countries to emphasize and seek their own interests to the detriment of the common welfare."[77] War rumors, though hardly a topic for discussion at diplomatic gatherings, seemed to have some basis in the circumstances of the times.

Briand also addressed the subject of war rumors in a Chamber of Deputies debate on the effects of recent developments in Germany on French public opinion and policy. He said that recent difficulties under-scored the necessity of a conciliatory policy. French opinion should not be unduly disturbed by what was happening in Europe:

> The possibility of war is lightly talked of as if it could break out at a moment's notice, as if the nation which should resort to it   would encounter no obstacle to the commission of a criminal act of this kind. It would be a terrible thing for the nation

whose impatience should lead them to such an act; they would not only let loose war; they would bring about a social catastrophe in comparison with which war itself would be a small thing...[78]

Yet Briand began to sound a little like Austen Chamberlain as he stressed the importance of Locarno as evidence of a German pledge to play by the rules and of a British guarantee of French security. Locarno was now five years old, and its champions had produced no sequel; in Germany, meanwhile, the Rhineland demonstrations and Nazi electoral successes had been followed by obstreperous declarations from supposedly responsible statesmen and government officials.

In this same debate Tardieu, prime minister since November 3, 1929 (with a brief interruption in February), stated his opinions on treaty revision and disarmament. The treaty did provide for revision; economic and financial articles had proven to be unworkable and had been changed. Borders, however, constituted a more difficult problem:

A frontier either exists and is applied: or else it is not applied and that is war....I do not believe that the evils from which the world is suffering result from the treaties of peace; they are the result of the war....Revision means the reopening of the territorial settlement in Europe....In a few months the result would be war and revolution. The revisionist campaign has been too lightly undertaken in Germany. A Germany in constant ebullition, which is always calling into question all that [it] has signed, is a danger to the whole of the world. I believe that it is also a bad thing for Germany.[79]

Tardieu, like Briand, believed that the key to peace lay in European cooperation, and promised practical proposals for the economic organization of Europe, which would be the best protection against revisionism and Bolshevik propaganda in Central Europe.

Leo Kennedy also discussed the rumors of war in his diaries. Twenty-seven foreign ministers and representatives were gathered in Geneva in January 1931 to discuss Briand's plan for European federation. A British delegate spoke to the *Times* correspondent about a declaration proposed by Sir Otto Niemeyer and Sir H. Strakosh, "who are of the opinion that much of the malaise in Europe is due to the fear that war may break out." One of the chief purposes of such a declaration would be public relations, which was why Kennedy was consulted: "its originators were good enough to say that as far as the British press was concerned all depended on the attitude of the Times."[80]

Kennedy thought that his editor, Geoffrey Dawson, would not agree to do a leader on such an announcement, though the *Times* would report it:

"my opinion would be that we could not back this declaration very cordially. No doubt there was no deliberate intention by any Foreign Minister to make war on anybody else; but upheavals were possible, and even probable in some countries, and in some they might have repercussions across frontiers, which might lead to war." Geneva, he continued, was becoming more identified with words as opposed to deeds; if these same foreign ministers could not agree on a scheme for European Federation or a plan for disarmament, would a declaration lessen the "sense of uneasiness in Europe"? Kennedy seemed to think that this proposal might open a Pandora's box: Curtius, the German foreign minister, might "annoy the Nationalists," jeopardizing his position at home; "and if the Ministers started arguing whether or not they could sign such a declaration, it would look terribly bad!"[81]

A few days later Kennedy learned more about the short life of this proposal from Philip Noel-Baker, another British delegate. Curtius indeed had raised objections (claiming later that his annoyance was due to the lateness of the proposal), and two sentences were removed as a result: "After 'We therefore declare' this was taken out — 'that we recognize the binding obligation of our mutual agreements for the maintenance of peace, that we are convinced that war would be disastrous to all' — and...'While we are aware of the alarmist rumours that have been current we desire to say that they find not the slightest echo in our consultations, our policies or our beliefs.'"[82] "Possibility of war" was changed to "possibility of international war," which Kennedy also found significant; what remained was a wan pledge to use the machinery of the League to prevent violence.

Curtius' reaction to the pledge seemed to make German intentions "perfectly plain," thought Kennedy: "They will try the machinery of the League first, and if that does not suffice to gain them their ends, they will act by violence. And they will probably not bother to give the League overmuch time either. It was honest of Curtius to make these excisions — on the other hand, if he had agreed to the original declaration he would probably have been turned out of office."[83] The irony of this episode was that a seemingly innocent declaration intended to promote confidence seemed only to make clearer the potential sources of conflict to the few who had access to this information. Had this been an "open covenant openly arrived at," or, to put it more precisely, "an open covenant openly not arrived at," the effect on public perceptions certainly would have been harmful.

Robert Vansittart also referred to these rumors in his assessment of international relations in 1931. He focused on the economic roots of the anxiety which now appeared to have much of the world in its grip, exciting feelings of nationalism and fostering belief in force:

> For the first time since the peace people talk of war — foolishly, no doubt, blind to the facts and deaf to argument. But still they talk of it as a thing no longer unbelievable and impossible. It has become once again a vague possibility in the mind of man, and from what is possible to what is inevitable is but a step for the human imagination. This frame of mind, in so far as it has been induced by economic causes, may pass away when those causes are removed. Let us hope that this will happen. Meanwhile it is doing daily mischief, undermining the hopes and ideals of the last decade, and tempting one Government after the other to turn for security to the old weapons of militarism and alliances, to tariff walls and industrial isolation; while in the work of international co-operation and mutual assistance, although all pay lip-service to these ideals, the popular jealousies, fears and suspicions aroused by material stringencies and economic confusion make it difficult for Governments to commit themselves generously to any broad-minded and far-sighted solution of Europe's political problems.[84]

While one may argue about the relationship of political to economic factors in producing this anxiety, Vansittart believed that the depression had undone much of the political progress of the past decade. Of course the economy made a convenient scapegoat for the sins of British policy, but both British and French leaders appreciated the extreme difficulty of disentangling political and economic factors. The slump had been accompanied by a dampening of confidence in the process of liquidation as an avenue to peaceful international relations. The process itself seemed to exacerbate the tensions the powers were attempting to sweep away: for example, the Young Plan increased the volume of Germany's nationalist clamor, and the Naval Conference of 1930, though good for Anglo-American relations, had increased tensions between Italy and France.[85]

The Decline and the Persistence of Briandism

Germany's announcement of a customs union with Austria in March 1931 dealt a severe blow to the most hopeful dimension of Briand's policy, that France and Germany could develop a new and constructive economic and political relationship.[86] The French economy did not begin to feel the effects of the depression until late in 1931, giving French behavior in the reparations and financial crises of that year a bullying quality in the eyes of many. While economists have debated the causes and effects of the financial crises in Austria, Germany and Britain in 1931, the fact that French financiers were in no mood to help the Austrians and Germans made these crises worse.[87] Financial intransigence also isolated France, especially from Britain.

Initially there was some sympathy in Britain for France's perspective on the customs union matter. The *Times* stated that the "crowning blunder" of the Austrians and Germans was "the fact that they have alienated the sympathy of M. Briand by their claim to be acting in the interests of European federation."[88] While not all French opinion had panicked — the Radical-Socialist *République* had said that the damage was not irreparable, and *Le Populaire* had reassured readers that fears of a new *Mitteleuropa* were based on a prewar conception of Germany — it was "certain that those who have been most active in promoting a Franco-German *rapprochement* are much disturbed and disappointed by what has happened."[89] Even the comparatively mild-mannered *Times* had discerned a note of contempt for Briand's work in the Austro-German announcement.

In the Senate's discussion of the Foreign Ministry's budget on March 28, Victor Bérard, president of the Foreign Affairs Commission, said that the announcement was "one of those coups of Berlin diplomacy that we had thought to be the monopoly of Imperial Germany." Assigning the initiative largely to Germany, he believed that if Austria accepted this arrangement, "there would be no further possibility for peace in Europe before the complete triumph of Germanism." After an interruption of applause and words of approval from his colleagues, Bérard continued:

> [T]his opinion is shared by all of France. In the last two weeks, something has changed in the attitude, in the thoughts, even in the silences of our people. All of France…suddenly has put herself on alert again….She has recognized in the "Vienna coup" the coups of German diplomacy from 1904 to 1914: Tangier, Agadir, the coup in which the deceitfulness of preparation is equalled only by the brutality of its execution.[90]

France had suffered from this kind of diplomacy before; it resumption now determined France's policy:

> Certainly not violence, because we remain convinced that democratic France's greatest asset is a policy of solidarity and peace; yet this solidarity must be reciprocated, and if it is not accepted in good faith, respect for it must be imposed by means which will preserve our security. Friends and former enemies alike must understand our people's state of mind. They must know how, from one end of France to the other, our newspapers have instilled in the simplest of our citizens the absolute conviction that this Austro-German diplomacy is incompatible with respect for the law and founded on contempt for the most solemn pledges.[91]

Whether the French people had discovered the virtues of peace through democracy or through the horrors of war, Bérard's remarks suggest that, even as rumors of war flew, the French recoiled at the thought of another war with Germany. There could be little question, therefore, of a return to the confrontational policies of the early 1920s.

The position of Édouard Herriot, whose fortunes within the Radical Party were on the upswing at this time, represented perhaps the very center of the range of opinion. On 8 May he participated in the debate on the Customs union in the Chamber, echoing his fears expressed in *L'Ère nouvelle*; he said that the pacifists, whose intentions he admired, ought to come out the most forcefully against the *Anschluss*. French pacifists wanted to renounce the use of arms. The only guarantee of security they had, therefore, was the solidity of contracts. "If I address the Chamber to speak of my anxiety," he said, "it is because I feel that all my hopes are threatened."[92] His remarks drew applause from the left, the center and even the right, but not from the Socialists. In an editorial in *Le Populaire* the following day Léon Blum wrote about the "survival of the spirit of the war," resentment, and provocation, and these criticisms were echoed from the left fringes of Herriot's own Radical party.[93]

Herriot supported Briand's foreign policy and hoped for conciliation between France and a republican Germany, but not at the expense of national security. He opposed treaty revision, and disarmament would be possible only if it did not leave France vulnerable. At the party conference in Grenoble in 1930, which took place after the German elections, he had discussed France's role as defender of liberty in Europe: "In defending herself, France defends not only herself; today she defends all that is left of the spirit of freedom in Europe. All free nations consider her to be a magnificent caryatid, supporting with all her strength what remains of the temple of liberty."[94] The speech, concerned solely with foreign affairs, was a great success, and an important step in regaining the presidency of the party from Édouard Daladier, his chief rival.

The 1931 French presidential elections, falling in the wake of the Austro-German customs union proposal, became entangled in foreign policy concerns, for Briand was a candidate. "The apostle of peace" enjoyed the support of the Left; his lackluster opponent Paul Doumer, the President of the Senate, had the support of the right of the Chamber and much of the Senate. Before the customs union proposal Briand had been considered a likely winner if he allowed his name to be put forward, but now, given the Senate's conservatism and Doumer's place of privilege within that body,

Briand's chances were greatly diminished; Doumer won the first round by a vote of 442 to 401, and won the race with 504 votes in the second.[95] Politicians quickly asserted that the defeat was no slight on Briand's foreign policy, but Radical leaders Daladier and Herriot had to defend themselves against charges of publicly supporting Briand — whose foreign policy met with wide public approval — but privately backing Doumer.[96]

Briand's foreign policy had been approved by a vote of 551 to 14 as recently as March, an overwhelming majority even when one added 18 abstentions, mostly on the far right, and 26 absentees.[97] Nevertheless, Briand's defeat in May undermined his policy considerably; he left the Quai d'Orsay the following January in ill health, and died less than two months later.

Pierre Laval hoped to receive Briand's mantle, though he only half-believed in his mentor's ideals. The similarities between the two lay more in methods than in convictions; both relied on improvisation and intuition.[98] Already in the early 1930s, Laval began to show signs of the unsavory character he would demonstrate so amply at Vichy, contributing to the negative reputation that Briand's entourage was developing in France: Tyrrell wrote that "[Briand's] loose manner of negotiating and working, his vague speeches, and the increase in the influence and abuse of influence by various members of his circle, have caused unfavourable comment for some time, and the opinion has lately become general that proceedings and methods of this sort are dangerous to the country."[99] Both Briand and Laval sought Franco-German rapprochement: the key difference between the two, however, was that Laval did not share Briand's vision of an international order shaped by the League of Nations. As early as 1925 the socialist Albert Thomas had written that Laval was "a young man of exceptional intelligence. He advocates Franco-German rapprochement, but by other means than through the League of Nations. He does not believe in Geneva."[100]

Not believing in Geneva was common among French conservatives, but Laval had sought — and received — the favor of Briand, whose sincerity was unquestioned. Like Briand, Laval had been a man of the Left, and still had a populist streak; for that reason, he garnered the support of left-wing deputies more easily than did his rival Tardieu. Yet he played to the right as well; the right-wing veteran's league, the Croix-de-Feu, cheered him upon his return to Paris from Washington in November 1931. Radical leader Herriot suspected his collaboration a short time later when the Croix-de-Feu disrupted a November 27 meeting of the International Disarmament

Congress at the Trocadéro, attended by Herriot and many foreign representatives, including Robert Cecil and the former U.S. ambassador to Britain,
Alanson Houghton.[101] Briand's heir-apparent was a man whom Tyrrell had
characterized in 1930 as "a man of great strength and very ambitious but
with few principles; it was he who in 1925 said that in French politics it was
more important to conciliate men than principle." His succession to the Quai
d'Orsay raised fears that Britain was losing influence in France.[102]

André Tardieu, too, was quite a different man from Briand. He
hoped to transform the French political system through the rationalization
of the right into a genuine political party, and wrest control from the
complacent Radicals, whom he considered to be essentially conservative
despite their leftist rhetoric. Yet he understood that the French electorate
would not support a nationalist foreign policy in 1932. In a speech before
the Senate on March 25 he intended "to show the conciliatory nature of his
direction of French foreign policy in all parts of Europe, and thereby to
appeal to the profoundly pacific sentiment of the French electorate, which
demands wants nothing more than to 'déclarer la paix à tout le monde.'"[103]
Though he hoped to transform France domestically, he did not see fit to
change the direction of foreign policy.

The elections, however, brought a shift to the left, and Herriot
became both prime minister and foreign minister. Though his ideas were
not in conflict with Briand's, he did not have the right kind of personality
to carry his policies through. Tyrrell stressed this in his assessment of the
changes to be expected from the new government:

> The danger of the situation lies primarily in M. Herriot's weakness of character. He
> has not the force of persuasive oratory which M. Briand knew so well how to use to
> inspire and cajole; he lacks decision and is easily swayed by more determined men. He
> has a parliamentary situation of great delicacy to handle; there is impending a grave
> economic crisis requiring drastic and popular measures.[104]

Herriot faced a dilemma: in his opinion, financial problems called for
conservative solutions; yet he relied on Socialist support to remain in power.

The vicissitudes of French politics complicated the final resolution of
the reparations question. Tyrrell thought the French public had been poorly
educated about the problem; though the "vast majority of the country is
weary of questions which, so long as they remain unsettled, perpetuate the
existing sense of uneasiness and even (to the French mind) keep alive the
risk of war," no government could survive a simple cancellation.[105] France
would have to have something in return from Germany, once Germany

recovered sufficiently. If Herriot failed, a less conciliatory government might well follow.

Herriot kept a very detailed journal during 1932, from the time of the elections to his resignation in December. These provide some insights into this politician, often held to epitomize the Radical party in the 1930s in all its mediocrity. They do not reveal an sinister, ignorant or short-sighted man; these were not his shortcomings. As with so many other leaders, Herriot seemed to understand the situation well enough, but his own disposition and the political environment seemed to forestall the development of any creative solutions to the problems France faced. Perhaps the most important question left by Herriot's failure was whether events overtook the capacity of men to deal with them, or whether a more capable leader — Reynaud, for example — might have met with success.

Shortly after the elections of 1932, Herriot read the declaration of the new government. With respect to foreign policy, his government would pursue the same course as its predecessors, that of founding the peace of Europe on a "general organization" of the continent — collective security; it would do all it could to contribute to "political and economical détente" as well as the "moral disarmament" of Europe.[106] To that end, however, France could not make concessions on rights granted her by treaty and "protected by the honor of signatures"; to do so would be a capitulation to force. In maintaining these principles, the government would be defending, not its own self-interest, but universal interests. Without making concessions on issues of security, the French government would be prepared to discuss any project or any initiative aimed at greater stability. The government would seek to carry on the policies of Briand. Such a speech might well be dismissed as public relations for the new government, but it reaffirmed a truth about French foreign policy, namely that the French, while extremely unwilling to give up any of the privileges resulting from the war, were willing to consider new schemes for safeguarding the peace.

British Indecision

Despite their sense that Germany had been treated unfairly in the past, British leaders began to feel that it was time for the Germans themselves to demonstrate some good faith. Henderson even had developed an appreciation for French concerns about Germany, and had established good working relations with Briand. Few could have predicted this, as Labour party members typically displayed even stronger anti-French tendencies than did

Conservatives, but Henderson found himself taking a pro-French attitude in spite of the Francophobia of MacDonald and Snowden. Alexis Léger, Briand's right-hand man (and a well-known poet under the name Saint-John Perse) told Leo Kennedy that the two foreign ministers told each other everything, and that Henderson was a loyal friend of France. Kennedy found the transformation striking: "Remarkable how H. has come round to the exact point of view of Austen C.! Austen always used to say — take France by the arm and go forward with her to meet the others. Bring them all in. That is really now H's policy. But H. in one way is better. He is brusquer, and better able to let go of France's arm every now and again, and say 'now look here my friend, that won't do!'"[107] However patronizing, this view of Anglo-French cooperation was common among British officials.[108]

To set the tone for a meeting with the German ambassador in July 1931, Arthur Henderson asked a few newspapers to call for some kind of gesture. Leo Kennedy was to write the leader for the *Times*:

> Henderson was to see the German Ambassador today, and it would be a great help if we could have a leader, appearing this morning, pressing Germany to do something toward European rehabilitation. He was himself going to speak to Neurath in the sense that other countries had done much, at the instigation of Hoover, to help Germany; could Germany not do just something in return? He thought she could.... The help to Germany had been given unconditionally — now it was Germany's turn for a *beau geste* (Germany and a beau geste are, I fear incompatible terms! If they do anything it will be by calculation).[109]

With editor Geoffrey Dawson's approval, Kennedy wrote the leader, and a similar editorial appeared in the *Daily Herald*. Kennedy was accustomed to such requests for collaboration, though he did not "remember ever before having had a whole subject and run of the argument suggested to me by the Secretary of State"; Henderson's specific request to have the article run the morning of the meeting so that it "might appear to be spontaneous" seemed to Kennedy to be "very thin."[110]

However, even in the absence of assurances from Germany, Kennedy believed that the time had come to revise the Treaty of Versailles; he discussed this directly with Henderson:

> I urged the advantage of dishing the Hitlerites by openly stating that the British Government was in favour of bringing modifications to the Treaty of Versailles. H. said he was definitely in favour of modification, but did not think it a favourable moment to say so. I fear force may be tried first, if he leaves it too long. I said

something about bringing up revision informally and unofficially in [the *Times*], and he smiled acquiescence.[111]

Soon after, his leaders in the *Times* suggested reconsideration of the treaty, and Kennedy found Geoffrey Dawson to be "unexpectedly bold in support."[112]

In presenting this view, Kennedy believed he spoke for a large section of public opinion:

We have had many signs that informed opinion throughout the country is beginning to think that way. The [Foreign Office] however are none too pleased — though I have not come into direct contact with Henderson since. I saw Selby on Friday afternoon — just after the London [Conference] had ended — and he had been seeing the French delegation off at Victoria — and one of them had said to him — 'Nous comprenons bien que rien n'est éternel.'! Is France moving?[113]

Perhaps, but not quickly — some months later the French ambassador told John Simon that "if there is any talk of revising the political clauses, it is war!"[114]

The financial crisis of August-September 1931 brought down the Labour government and brought in an all-party National Government, with MacDonald staying on as prime minister. MacDonald worried about the effect of the crisis — and measures taken to remedy it — on Britain's international prestige. This concern was evident in a note sent to Stanley Baldwin in which he discussed the task of the newly-formed cabinet:

The present Government will last so long as it deals only with the matters immediately before us. Can we draw any line between this time of crisis and a normal condition which is to follow? I do not see any such line. Undoubtedly it would be for the benefit of the country if we stayed on a little time after the immediate trouble is over, although according to the information I have had up to this morning, that crisis is by no means over. But even the day to day work of administration is to bring us into disagreements with each other, and the late Government had so many schemes in hand — especially as regards foreign matters which were beginning or had only advanced to a certain stage — which any period of uncertainty and lack of union in the Government would destroy, with the result that our influence in the world would immediately drop almost to zero. That...is happening at Geneva at the present moment. Then, if the passing of time compels us to deal with legislation, we are in a pretty hopeless position.[115]

This could also be read as a plea for harmony on matters unrelated or indirectly related to the crisis which had led to the formation of the National Government; but much of what MacDonald wrote at this time demonstrated a concern about the effects of Britain's own difficulties on her ability to be a leader in Europe or in the world.

At the same time, MacDonald had a very low opinion of France's ability to lead, despite her relative prosperity. He wrote to Viscount Astor: "France is not yet in an international frame of mind....Our present weakness is deplorable and is very bad for the world. France's strength is equally so. I say this without being in any way anti-French, but only to express the view, which I have gathered as the result of much experience, that France is too self-centered to be a good international leader."[116] Negative views of French foreign policy were common in Britain; Oxford-educated Shiela Grant Duff would be astonished a few years later to hear from *Chicago Daily News* reporter Edgar Ansel Mowrer that "only the French, who have had to live next door to them for centuries, have the measure of the Germans." To her generation, "the wicked vindictiveness of French policy had been a byword in all English accounts of post-war history."[117] Yet, as Viscount D'Abernon had observed, "France was at her worst when England's foreign policy was at its most indecisive."[118]

After the public affirmation of the National Government in the elections of October 27, MacDonald chose as his foreign secretary John Simon, a Liberal with impressive credentials in domestic and imperial affairs; he had served most recently on the India Commission. Simon's transition to foreign affairs was facilitated by a Foreign Office memorandum, prepared at the request of his predecessor, Lord Reading, discussing the "changing conditions of British foreign policy." The document, which Victor Wellesley wrote in Vansittart's absence, reflects the deep sense of crisis felt at the time:

> The present world 'confidence crisis' can be analysed as a series of interlocking problems, ranging from the purely financial and monetary problem at the one end to the purely territorial problem created by the Peace Settlements at the other end. The links in the chain fall together more or less in the following order: the monetary crisis leads inevitably back to the economic chaos in Europe. The economic chaos, and all attempts to deal with it, involve in their turn the political questions of reparations and war debts. These are linked by the United States with the question of disarmament, and the latter, in the eyes of the French Government, depends on the problem of security. The problem of security in its turn raises the question of the territorial status quo in Europe (e.g., the Eastern Frontier question), which brings us to the conflict between the maintenance or revision of the Peace Settlements. We thus have a whole range of interlocking problems, and, no matter at what link we touch the chain, we cannot find any satisfactory halting place until we have resolved this whole series of problems.[119]

Given this tangle of problems, British leaders could agree on an objective if not on how to go about achieving it. Simon, who had a lawyer's mind for detail, understood complexities but could not decide on a policy.

While economic factors complicated the current political difficulties, and leaders emphasized them, the reverse also was true, that political tensions exacerbated economic and especially financial problems. Leaders hesitated to acknowledge their shortcomings, of course, but others willingly brought them to light. Sir Arthur Salter, delivering the Burge Lecture at King's College in London in 1932, put forth the thesis that, while politics had not played a prominent role in bringing about the economic crisis of 1929, they certainly had helped to bring about the financial crisis of 1931. He observed that the continuity of loans to countries like Germany and Austria depended heavily on the intangible concept of confidence; confidence in turn depended upon political stability. Salter argued that the dissipation of the spirit of Locarno had revealed a Europe still bitterly divided. In this Europe, countries that could help — France, for example — hesitated to support needy nations whose politics were unsavory.

A keen advocate of disarmament, Salter marked the current political deterioration from the failure of the 1927 Naval Conference, and regarded the "spirit" of Locarno as ephemeral; once the period of war exhaustion passed, the tensions left over from the war manifested themselves once again. The evacuation of the Rhineland in 1930, an occasion which might have marked the end of the war, produced instead talk of another:

> [The occasion] was used...as an expression of xenophobic nationalism and enabled the opponents of Briand to weaken his position by showing him how ill a response met concessions of treaty rights. In the following winter Paris began to speak of the danger of imminent war; and the atmosphere was more febrile and apprehensive than it had been since 1914. It might have been a passing mood, but early in 1931 the question of an Austrian-German Customs Union was launched in a way which led France to believe, rightly or wrongly, first that it was only a cover for a complete *Anschluss*...and, secondly that it was the beginning of a deliberate policy of tearing up the Treaties by unilateral action. The very seriousness of the situation changed the mood of France; men no longer spoke recklessly of immediate war, but became more deliberately convinced of the real danger that existed — and exists — that policies were being initiated, a course of action being set in motion, which not at once, but within a few years would again make war inevitable.[120]

Visiting New York in May and June of 1931, Salter met with nervous investors, who asked questions like "Can you say something about the European political situation, and if possible say that we are not on the verge of another war?" From this Salter concluded that "the fears of France had crossed the Atlantic, and in the form which they had taken six months earlier in Paris — a feverish, unreasoning fear of an immediate outbreak. These fears gave the last blow to the credit structure; confidence collapsed; new lending stopped, short-term advances were called in; they could not be paid; the financial crisis came."[121] From Austria, the crisis spread to Germany, and then to Britain. The moral of the story was that "[r]umours of serious war if widely entertained are always liable to bring the whole fabric tumbling about our heads."

The solution lay in governments taking charge of the situation; planning, both national and international, would not threaten individual freedom and enterprise, but "save them from suicide."[122] Of course a great deal more could be said about the background to the 1931 financial crisis, as Salter himself admitted, but his stress on the need for planning reveals a frustration with what appeared to be anarchy in the area of international relations, both political and economic. Governments appeared to have control only of their own narrowly defined political concerns. Salter's ideas on world government did not draw much attention from the National Government, but his views were influential among the educated public.

While the complexities of the European situation presented MacDonald with increasing difficulties, he had succeeded brilliantly in Anglo-American relations where Baldwin had failed, first by his visit to the United States in October 1929, then by the successful London Naval Conference of 1930. In a letter to Secretary of State Henry Stimson in January 1932, MacDonald wrote of the difficulties of managing crisis at home and in Europe and at the same time meeting debt payments. Plans for a financial conference were being held up by in France, where a struggle was underway to see who would succeed Briand. The main problem, however,

arises out of the state of Germany. If that country is to pay no more or to pay a mere fraction...we will be unable to meet our obligations which we undertook in the Balfour Note assumption. No Government here will be able to impose further taxation upon our people in order to provide large sums to be transferred abroad. If our neighbours would only face the facts and come to an agreement with the rest of us, we could then produce some scheme with which we could reasonably ask you to concur. But I am being baffled at every point. Those neighbours of ours insist on putting their own...narrow and temporary national interests first. They have created a war-in-peace mentality amongst their own people and will not now boldly face the consequences, grapple with it and bring an international reasonableness to bear upon what is primarily an international problem.[123]

Given the unruliness of the continental powers, Britain and America had to cooperate to prevent disaster: "We will...have to come together somehow, and by mutual help try and save something so big, so deep and so high that we can only call it the civilisation of our time."[124]

MacDonald took an active role in foreign policy, often upstaging Henderson and later Simon. His controlling disposition toward both Simon and the French government is evident in this note of November 1931:

The French Government has begun negotiations with the Germans regarding...what is to be done when the Hoover Moratorium comes to an end. I think you ought to see Laval yourself. Briand is getting old and ineffective, but Laval is very approachable. Impress upon him that every day is a day nearer to a very serious crash in which every European nation will be involved, not only financially but politically. Unless we can keep things going, the whole of the political and economic fabric of Europe will be cracking and crumbling as under an earthquake.[125]

Mixed metaphor notwithstanding, the note conveyed MacDonald's sense of crisis. Yet he could not shake his distrust of his French counterparts. After meeting with Tardieu in April 1932, he wrote: "I do my best to have confidence in the French, but am always defeated....The diplomacy of France is an ever active influence for evil in Europe."[126]

The actual danger, however, came from Germany, as a letter to the editor of the *Times* in June 1932 from the League of Nations Union suggested: "the almost universal feeling that civilisation is threatened with imminent danger has been intensified by recent events in Germany." Signed by Austen Chamberlain, Norman Angell, Robert Cecil, and Gilbert Murray, among others, it called upon leaders to address the outstanding problems of the day, for the dangers could still be addressed: "We are not yet...in the condition of Christian in the City of destruction. He was 'for certain informed' that fire from heaven would consume himself, his wife and his innocent children, because he could not find the way out. On general lines the world now does know the way out."[127] The solution lay in cooperation among the former allies.

Fears were high as the powers moved towards the Lausanne Conference to be held in June. Sir Robert Horne, a member of Parliament, wrote to MacDonald in almost apocalyptic terms of the deep concern felt in the business community:

I hope you can forgive me for troubling you with this letter. I can only excuse myself on the ground of my very deep anxiety as to the present situation. World conditions, as you know, are becoming steadily worse; but perhaps you do not know how the heart of the business community is being broken and how steadily initiative is being destroyed. I said in the House a month ago that the Statesmen who go to Lausanne have nothing less than the fate of the modern world in their hands. To some that may have sounded a rhetorical exaggeration although, in fact, I was not stating anything more than I know to be the strict truth.[128]

Horne's anxieties were confirmed, he believed, by an eminent economist with a world-wide reputation, Professor Gustav Cassel, who had said that the world was "now threatening to end in complete disaster," and "We have no security that our society can survive. Beware lest the days of our civilisation are numbered. Never forget that the hours left for constructive action may be short."[129]

Cooperation among the former allies in 1932 had only a limited effect; the prospects for a lasting peace dimmed. The atmosphere, though not untroubled in 1928, had deteriorated mainly because of developments in Germany. One could claim that economic distress spread gloom among leaders, but the fear of war arose from the fact that Germans wanted more than the cancellation of reparations and the evacuation of foreign troops. Resolution of these issues only increased the clamor; the National Socialists won elections using "the excess of patriotic feeling" as a "great moral wedge" to win the support of "the confused and troubled middle class," in the midst of their economic distress.[130] Whatever the state of mind of Germany's citizens as they cast their votes in the early 1930s, the authoritarian and violent Nazi party had made its impression. The changes taking place in Germany demanded close attention from Britain and France; war was unthinkable, but it had to be thought about.

Notes

1. HNKY 3/37, Maurice to Adeline Hankey, from the Conference at the Hague, January 18, 1930.
2. S. Marks, "The Myths of Reparations" in *Central European History* 11 (1978), p. 250; J. Jacobson, *Locarno Diplomacy: Germany and the West, 1925-1929* (Princeton, 1972), pp. 143-202; 279.
3. For example, French output of crude steel in 1913 was 4.7 million tons, compared to 17.6 million tons for Germany; in 1929 France produced 9.7 million tons (highest figure for the decade), compared to Germany's 16.2 million tons (less than 100,000 tons below the peak year 1927); Mitchell, *European Historical Statistics*, p. 421.
4. Dalton I/13/28-29, December 7, 1929. Goldsworthy Lowes Dickinson (1862-1932), a political theorist, was a fellow at King's College and lecturer at the London School of Economics. In the 1920s he served on the Labour Party's Committee on International

Questions. B. Pimlott, ed. *The Political Diary of Hugh Dalton, 1918-1940; 1945-1960* (London, 1986), p. 7.

5. Wohl, p. 106; Barnett, p. 428.

6. Angus Calder's introduction to Charles Madge, *Britain by Mass-Observation* (London, 1939), p. ix. In the United States, George Gallup began using random sampling techniques to do market research in 1928, and soon branched into politics. Henry Durant established the British counterpart to the American Institute of Public Opinion in 1936, and Gallup conducted the first polls in France in June 1939.

7. The October 1933 East Fulham by-election, for example, was interpreted as a sign of public opposition to increases in military expenditures. Mowat, p. 422. In Britain, the 1928 Representation of the People Act gave women and men aged 21 and over equal voting rights (the 1918 law had given the vote to women 30 and over); in France women were enfranchised only in 1944.

8. Fussell in *The Great War and Modern Memory* (Oxford, 1975) and Correlli Barnett in *The Collapse of British Power* (London, 1972) consider these war memoirs from different angles. Fussell examines their considerable literary merits; however, he seems to assume, along with most of the writers, that the broader political context is irrelevant to the individual experience of war. In his discussion of imperial decline, Barnett considers the effects of these works on Britain's resolve and ability to protect herself and her interests. He challenges the myth that the war itself had caused Britain's decline, though he does argue that the psychological effect was great. He takes the writers to task for helping to create the myth of a "lost generation": though many young members of the "governing class" had been killed, many more had not (pp. 426-436).

9. R. Wohl, *The Generation of 1914* (Cambridge, 1979), pp. 106-107.

10. N. Branson, *Britain in the Nineteen Twenties* (Minneapolis, 1976), p. 242.

11. Wohl, p. 106.

12. G. Craig, *Germany, 1866-1945* (Oxford, 1978), pp. 489-493; Wohl, pp. 55-60. Remarque's works were included in book burnings all over Germany on the night of May 10, 1933. K-D. Bracher, *The German Dictatorship* (New York, 1970), p. 259.

13. F.L. Carsten, *The First Austrian Republic, 1918-1928* (Aldershot, 1986), p. 164.

14. Branson, p. 242.

15. At least 45,000 copies of the play were sold in 1929. Barnett, p. 429.

16. Ibid., p. 243.

17. Ibid., p. 244.

18. *Halliwell's Film Guide* (sixth edition, London, 1988), p.245. The same producer remade the film in 1939.

19. Chamberlain never saw the film. MAE, series Z (Europe 1918-1929) Great Britain 42/13-14, Aimé de Fleuriau, French ambassador in London, to Briand, n.d. (late February 1928).

20. Transcript of House of Commons debate, printed in the *Times* (London), February 28, 1928, reported in MAE, series Z (Europe 1918-1929), Great Britain 42/16-19.

21. The *Times*, February 11, 1928, p. 10; February 22, p. 14.

22. The *Times*, February 28, 1928.

23. Ibid.

24. See especially R.S. Cockett, *Twilight of Truth: Chamberlain, Appeasement, and the Manipulation of the Press* (New York, 1989) and P.M. Taylor, *The Projection of Britain: British Overseas Publicity and Propaganda, 1919-1939* (Cambridge, 1981).

25. Wohl, pp. 29-30 and n. 48. The memoirs attracting the most attention during this time were those of top leaders: Clémenceau's *Grandeur et misère d'un victoire* (Paris,

78   *Democracies at the Turning Point*

1930); Marshal Foch's two-volume *Mémoires pour servir à l'histoire de la guerre* (Paris, 1930); and Joffre's *Mémoires 1910-1917*, volume 2 (Paris, 1932). The view from further down the ranks in many cases took much longer to appear. For example, Marc Bloch's *Souvenirs de Guerre* appeared 25 years after his death (Paris, 1969). Other personal testimonies appeared only in the 1970s: L.Bathas' *Les carnets de guerre, 1914-1919* (Paris, 1978); A. Kahn *Journal de guerre d'un juif patriote* (Paris, 1978); and P. Reybaut *"Les raisins sont beaux."* *Correspondance de guerre d'un rural* (Paris, 1977). See Carole Fink's introduction and postface in her translation of Bloch's *Memoirs of War* (Cambridge, 1988), pp. 15-73; 179-180.

26. FO 408/51/41, Crewe to Chamberlain, Paris, May 22, 1928.
27. J. Giraudoux, *Siegfried*, ed. G.V. Banks (London, 1967), act 3, scene 4, p. 93.
28. Ibid., act 4, scene 3, p. 106.
29. Giraudoux's 1935 play, *La Guerre de Troie n'aura pas lieu* (translated by Northrop Frye as *Tiger at the Gates*) was much less hopeful. In it, Hector, an advocate of peace, brings war upon Troy.
30. FO 408/51/41, Crewe to Chamberlain, Paris, May 22, 1928.
31. PHPP (Phipps papers) 2/15/67-68, Phipps to Tyrrell, Paris, February 1, 1928. Phipps was minister plenipotentiary in Paris at this time; Tyrrell, still permanent undersecretary at the Foreign Office, succeeded the Marquess of Crewe as ambassador to France later that month.
32. PHPP 2/7/66-67, R. Lindsay to O. Sargent, Berlin, March 29, 1928.
33. PHPP 2/15/69-72, Phipps to Tyrrell, Paris, February 3, 1928.
34. PHPP 2/15, Phipps to Tyrrell, Paris, February 17, 1928.
35. PA AP 217/7/120-128 (Massigli papers), memorandum on the subject of a general plan for negotiations leading to the evacuation of the Rhineland.
36. FO 800/263/41-47, Selby to Chamberlain, Foreign Office, October 2, 1928.
37. For an overall assessment of France's relations with Poland and Czechoslovakia, see the conclusion to P. Wandycz, *The Twilight of French Eastern Alliances, 1926-1936* (Princeton, 1988), pp. 448-477.
38. FO 800/263/41-47, October 2, 1928.
39. FO 800/263/107-109, Chamberlain to Tyrrell, Foreign Office, December 18, 1928.
40. Jacobson, pp. 125-126.
41. FO 800/263/107-109. Despatch cited above.
42. Ibid.
43. See C. Fink, "Defender of Minorities: Germany in the League of Nations, 1925-1933" in *Central European History* 5 (December 1972), pp. 344-352.
44. FO 800/263/116-118, Chamberlain to Rumbold, Foreign Office, December 19, 1928; FO 800/263/126-128, Tyrrell to Chamberlain, Paris, December 21, 1928.
45. Ibid.
46. Kindleberger, p. 65.
47. HNKY 3/36, Maurice to Robin Hankey, July 3, 1929.
48. Dalton I/10/135-136 (Diary), June 17, 1929.
49. Dalton I/10/137-138, June 24, 1929.
50. Poincaré IV, n.a.fr. 15995/20, H.A. Jules-Bois to Poincaré, New York, June 24, 1929.
51. Poincaré XIII, n.a.fr. 16004/88-89, Maurice Herbette to Poincaré, July 27, 1929.
52. HNKY 3/36, Maurice to Adeline Hankey, Scheveningen, August 10, 1929.
53. Kindleberger, pp. 68-69. Kindleberger writes that Britain's gold losses went to New York, where the Federal Reserve discount rate finally had been raised.

54. HNKY 3/36, Maurice to Adeline Hankey, Scheveningen, August 11, 1929.
55. HNKY 8/27/1-9, Maurice to Robin Hankey, Seaford, September 5, 1929.
56. See *British Capitalism at the Crossroads, 1919-1932* (Cambridge, 1987), pp. 207-212.
57. HNKY 3/36, Maurice to Adeline Hankey, Scheveningen, August 9, 1929.
58. E.W. Bennett, *Germany and the Diplomacy of the Financial Crisis, 1931* (Cambridge, MA, 1962), p. 6; R. Binion, *Defeated Leaders: the Political Fate of Caillaux, Jouvenel and Tardieu* (New York, 1960), p. 290.
59. HNKY 8/27/1-9, Maurice to Robin Hankey, Seaford, September 5, 1929.
60. Dalton I/10/182-183, August 22, 1929.
61. Dalton I/13/1-2.
62. Ibid.
63. D. Carlton, *MacDonald versus Henderson: the Foreign Policy of the Second Labour Government* (London, 1970), p. 55.
64. December 7, 1929, p. 1068.
65. Ibid.
66. Ibid., p. 1069.
67. L.S. Stavrianos, *The World since 1500: A Global History* (Englewood Cliffs, N.J., 1982), p. 419.
68. *Écho de Paris*, July 1, 1930, p. 1.
69. *Écho de Paris*, July 10, 1930, p. 1.
70. *Le Populaire*, November 19, 1930, p. 1.
71. *Le Populaire*, November 23, 1930, p. 1.
72. Stavrianos, p. 419. This was down from 153 seats and 29.8% of the popular vote in the May 20, 1928 elections.
73. See its uncharitable obituary of Hermann Müller on March 22, 1931, which stated in its first paragraph "Although he had none of the gifts of a true statesman, circumstances called on him to play a historical role in memorable events."
74. Most recently, Müller had been Germany's chancellor between June 1928 and March 1930. Craig, pp. 524-533.
75. Bernard and Dubief, pp. 3-6.
76. KNAT 1/7/3-8 (Diary), February 5, 1931.
77. Ibid.
78. FO 425/406/14, W. Tyrrell to A. Henderson, Paris, November 14, 1930.
79. Ibid.
80. LKEN 10 (Diary), January 20, 1931.
81. Ibid.
82. Ibid.
83. Ibid.
84. VNST 1/3, An Aspect of International Relations in 1931.
85. Roskill, *Naval Policy Between the Wars*, volume 2, pp. 37-70.
86. See below, chapter 5.
87. Kindleberger, pp. 144-158.
88. The *Times*, March 25, 1931, p.14.
89. Ibid.
90. JO, Sénat, session ordinaire, 1931, volume 114 (2), March 28, 1931, p. 761.
91. Ibid.
92. Quoted in M. Soulié, *La vie politique d'Édouard Herriot* (Paris, 1962), p. 335.
93. Ibid, p. 336.

94. Ibid., p. 330.
95. Oudin, p. 544.
96. Ibid., p. 337.
97. FO 425/407/40, Tyrrell to Henderson, March 5, 1931.
98. F. Kupferman, *Pierre Laval 1883-1945* (Paris, 1987), p. 76.
99. FO 425/407/46, Tyrrell to Vansittart, Paris, May 14, 1931.
100. Kupferman, p.76.
101. Soulié, pp. 341-342.
102. FO 425/405/20, Tyrrell to Henderson, Paris, April 14, 1930; FO 800/274/257-263, Poliakoff to Vansittart, August 4, 1931.
103. FO 425/409/52, Tyrrell to Simon, Paris, April 2, 1932.
104. FO 425/409/67, Tyrrell to Simon, Paris, June 28, 1932.
105. Ibid.
106. PA AP 89 (Herriot)/26 (Journal)/93, June 7, 1932.
107. LKEN 10 (Diary), May 23, 1931.
108. J. Cairns describes this love-hate relationship, often described in romantic terms, in his article "A Nation of Shopkeepers in Search of a Suitable France." *American Historical Review* 79:3 (June 1974), pp. 710-743.
109. LKEN 11 (Diary), July 9, 1931.
110. Ibid.
111. LKEN 11 (Diary), July 13, 1931.
112. Ibid., July 27, 1931.
113. Ibid. "We understand well that nothing is eternal."
114. To which Simon replied: "Well, in view of the present division of forces, you shouldn't have too much difficulty." LKEN 12, January 13, 1932.
115. PRO 30/69/1176/33-36, MacDonald to Baldwin, September 5, 1931.
116. PRO 30/69/677/54-55, MacDonald to Viscount Astor, October 4, 1931.
117. S. Grant Duff, *The Parting of Ways: A Personal Account of the Thirties* (London, 1982), p. 73.
118. J. Cairns, "A Nation of Shopkeepers...", pp. 729-730.
119. CAB 27/476/497-507, November 26, 1931.
120. Salter, *Political Aspects of the World Depression* (Oxford, 1932), p. 16.
121. Ibid., p. 17.
122. Ibid., p. 20.
123. PRO 30/69/678(4)/679-685, MacDonald to Stimson, January 8, 1932.
124. Ibid.
125. PRO 30/69/677/367, MacDonald to Simon, November 14, 1931.
126. Quoted in Marquand, *Ramsay MacDonald*, p. 717.
127. PRO 30/69/1442/748, letter to the *Times*, June 3, 1932.
128. PRO 30/69/1442/430-436, Horne to MacDonald, London, June 2, 1932.
129. Ibid.
130. W.S. Allen, *The Nazi Seizure of Power* (Chicago, 1965), pp. 275-277.

3

Old Adam: Perceptions of
Germany, 1928-1933

One thing is surprising in the middle of a situation so complex, and that is how little Germany seems to concern herself with the economic crisis, with unemployment, with the breakdown of its public and private finances....[T]hese problems are not solved. The government of tomorrow, whatever that may be, quickly will feel their painful sting.
— André François-Poncet[1]

As British and French leaders worked with their German counterparts to liquidate the war, they hoped also that the intensity of German revisionism would diminish. Instead, as Britain and France retreated on issue after issue, passing recriminations back and forth, German revisionism became the dominant force in European politics. Observers pinned the fragile hope that reason would prevail in Germany on such "responsible" leaders as Stresemann and Hindenburg, for the disintegration of the Versailles order left no structure within which to contain the former aggressor.

Stresemann's Last Years

Anyone who knew anything about Germany in the 1920s knew that revisionism was a powerful force; but Gustav Stresemann, as foreign minister from 1923 to 1929, gave it a relatively friendly face. With solid conservative credentials, Stresemann guided German foreign policy through the settlement of issues remaining from the war, maintaining his nationalist goals while cooperating with the former adversaries. While Stresemann was in power, Germany would not embark on a foolish campaign to reclaim lost territory. But, as Henry Kissinger has most recently pointed out, personality could not fill the void which the former allies created by failing to establish a deterrent to future German aggression.[2] Indeed, Stresemann's cooperativeness acted as a wedge between British leaders eager to normalize relations with Germany and their more cautious and suspicious French counterparts.

For Horace Rumbold, arriving in Berlin in 1928 as Britain's new ambassador to Germany, the atmosphere compared favorably to that of 1914. Just before the war he had been a counsellor at the same embassy;

now he found that "[t]he noisy self-assertiveness and bumptiousness of the pre-war Germany had completely disappeared. The people seemed quiet and even silent and it was quite clear that they had been thoroughly chastened. I should not like to say that there has been a change of heart. Perhaps it would be more accurate to describe the change as one of method."[3] Rumbold was sure that, among the vast majority of Germans, the experience of the war had discredited any attempt to dominate Europe by military means; as proof he pointed out that some of the most powerful political parties had opposed the construction of one of the four armored cruisers permitted by the Treaty. Yet the German people did not intend to accept the status quo: "they are far too great a nation to be content with a subordinate position in Europe and, unless I am mistaken, they mean to have, and will attain, the leading place in Europe, though by economic means."

Like so many of his compatriots, Rumbold placed a great deal of faith in personalities, and his first meeting with Stresemann caused him concern: "Opinions differ as to his state of health. He looks a very bad colour. His friends say that he ought to go very slow or else he will break down completely. It will be a disaster, in my mind, if he did break down. For Germany needs two men, i.e., Hindenburg and Stresemann, for the next four or five years, by which time the reparations problem will presumably have been settled, the Rhineland evacuated, and Germany [will] have definitely turned the corner."[4]

Both Britain and France moved toward reconciliation with Germany in the late 1920s, but the former allies did not act in concert. British politicians found their French counterparts to be excessively nervous about Germany, and therefore inflexible in negotiations aimed at resolving outstanding problems. At the same time, the French did make efforts to live in peace with Germany, and the popularity of Briand's policies indicated that the French people genuinely hoped for an end to the enmity.

But British officials focused on lingering French fear, and the construction of the Maginot Line appeared to them to be its most powerful manifestation. Walford Selby of the Foreign Office wrote in November 1928 that

> [t]he great majority of Frenchmen, while they recognise that guarantees such as the occupation of the Rhineland must in due course disappear, continue to view the future with misgiving, and the haste and energy which France is now displaying to develop her scheme of fortifications on the eastern frontier of France is sufficient proof if that were needed of the scepticism of France and Frenchmen as regards the pacific intentions of the new Germany and the change of mood and outlook of her people.[5]

Despite the accomplishments of Briand and Stresemann to that point, the French government still sought security in tangible form. This French agnosticism exasperated British officials. As Robert Vansittart pejoratively wrote, "materialistic French logic" forbade that the ideals of the League and its methods "should ever be examined as end in themselves or ideals to be sought for their own sake."[6]

British officials in Germany, however, could attest to the validity of French concerns. Whether or not Germans harbored dreams of a war of revenge, they certainly stood to dominate Europe by other means. The British consul at Mainz, in the Rhineland, had written that he was

> unable to see any diminution in that craving for expansion and for world recognition on the part of Germany which was so noticeable a feature in Germany before the war. [The consul] admits to a change in method, the military scheme having ostensibly...been discredited, but concludes that it may be possible that Germany is once again heading for the leadership of the new Europe, and refers to French anxieties with which he feels it impossible not to sympathise.[7]

The British representative on the Rhineland Commission even more pessimistically thought that the "new Germany will probably not lose much time in claiming the rewards of her economic leadership and superior efficiency very much on the lines with which we were acquainted before the war."[8] The war had not damaged German industry; in crude steel production, for example, Germany remained Europe's leading producer throughout the 1920s, second to Great Britain only in the disastrous year 1923.[9] Rumbold himself believed that France "was caught between the spectre of German militarism and the even more substantial ghost of German economic domination."[10]

For France, logic suggested reconciliation with Germany in the face of this unequal competition, particularly since French industrial might was concentrated in the vulnerable northeast region of the country. Work on the establishment of a new basis for Franco-German relations progressed smoothly in 1928, despite the swing to the right in the spring legislative elections. In December the Chamber of Deputies discussed the outlook as they prepared to vote on the Foreign Ministry's budget. Édouard Soulier, speaking for the conservative "Union républicaine démocratique," the largest single group within the ruling majority, asserted the essential unity of French foreign policy, "a policy of peace, of defense, and of vigilance."[11]

Of course French officials exercised particular vigilance with respect to Germany, and in this debate Soulier remarked that certain functionaries in Germany perpetuated an atmosphere "unfavorable to détente by blaming France for Germany's inability to accomplish her desires." One matter on which France indeed stood in the way was on the question of *Anschluss* between Austria and Germany. "In the summer of 1928," said Soulier, "manifestations [of pro-*Anschluss* sentiment] were more numerous, and were also more pronounced, provoking much commentary in the European press."[12] France, therefore, had to remain alert.

Nevertheless, said Briand in the same debate, Locarno had created a possibility for lasting peace between France and Germany. Speaking after a long speech by the Socialist deputy Bracke, who expressed misgivings about the viability of a peace based on inequalities among nations, Briand asserted that French policy was based on the peace treaties, and that the system created by the settlement was the basis for the postwar European order. The implication was that Germany had to be integrated into this system; the basis for discussion would not be a list of German grievances, but assurance of Germany's intention to work within the system.

Stresemann did not provide this assurance. Pierre de Margerie, the French Ambassador in Berlin, spoke with Stresemann a few days after Briand's speech in the Chamber, and felt compelled several times to combat the pessimism with which Stresemann viewed the present state of relations between Britain, France and Germany, especially in the light of Austen Chamberlain's recent remarks on the subject of the Rhineland. Stresemann took particular interest in Briand's comments on the *Anschluss* question, contesting Briand's distinction between the right of a people to self-determination and an unacceptable right to commit suicide. In his view *Anschluss* would be in no way an Austrian suicide, but in any case it was not a live issue at this time. To this de Margerie replied that it was precisely for that reason that France protested against this pointless agitation which only served to poison and alarm public opinion.[13]

British relations with Germany, meanwhile, were not entirely smooth, either. According to the official assessment, Germany continued to protest the $33\frac{1}{3}\%$ tariffs on many of their exports to Britain by the Safeguarding of Industries Act.[14] Most of the discord, however, stemmed from matters relating to the settlement of the war:

> There has also been an unpleasant and increasing tendency in Germany to call in question the motives underlying the actions and supposed policy of His Majesty's Government, the recent instances of which were the outbursts which followed the revelation of the existence of the Anglo-French naval pact, and the participation of a British Cavalry regiment in the French manœuvres in the Rhineland. The conclusion

of the 'Pact' and the manœuvres were roundly declared, absurdly enough, to be violations of the British obligations to Germany, and to mark the British abandonment of the Locarno policy. The regrettable desire to believe the worst where the ex-Allies...are concerned were most recently illustrated by the behaviour of the German Government and press over the forged treaties published by the 'Utrechtsch Dagblad'"[15].

The evacuation of the Rhineland and reparations continued to dominate Britain's relations with Germany in 1929. Sir Hughe Knatchbull-Hugesson, a counsellor at the British embassy in Brussels, believed that a fair settlement would bolster democracy in Germany:

> A settlement on these points, which while safeguarding the essential rights of the Allies, gives Germany decent conditions would really be the climax of British policy. Since the war British policy has struggled for...'conciliation' and for support for the democratic element in Germany. All our trouble with France up to 1924 was because we saw her going too much in the direction of suppression and repression....Our original hopes of nursing the young democratic plant in Germany had suffered and dwindled considerably during the period ending with the Ruhr occupation and it may still remain to be seen how far the elements hostile to democracy in Germany have been strengthened by the treatment meted out to the Reich up to 1924.[16]

Kellogg-Briand Pact notwithstanding, Germany's future course remained unclear, he thought, perhaps even to the Germans themselves. "But I think it is too much to expect that when anything to her own advantage turns up, she will not seize it," he wrote. After the reparations settlement and evacuation, one could expect Germany to take up the *Anschluss*, the Corridor and Silesia, through "peaceful penetration."[17]

Yet German militarism remained. Horace Rumbold downplayed the significance of the patriotic associations, which he regarded as a "psychological safety-valve to German military enthusiasms."[18] The Reichswehr was another matter, but even it seemed to be in no condition to wage war. Stresemann had told him that

> he could not conceive how anybody could imagine it to be a formidable instrument of war. He contrasted the physique of the soldiers in it with that of the pre-war army soldiers, and there I am with him as far as Berlin is concerned. He instanced the great number of suicides in the Reichswehr owing partly to the feeling that the men enlisted can not leave for ten years and have little prospect of promotion. What could the Reichswehr do against Poland for instance? In a war in the East, the Poles would invade Germany. But I hardly like to pass over Stresemann's remark in silence and yet the position is rather awkward.[19]

What of the Republic itself? Clearly elements remained within Germany that were hostile to the new constitution. In June 1929 a rather strange situation arose in the Reichstag itself. In July 1922 the German parliament had passed a "Law for the Protection of the Republic," instituting legal safeguards to prevent the ex-Kaiser from returning to Germany. The law, renewed in 1927 for two years, was due to expire on July 22, 1929, and the government therefore asked for another two-year renewal, but a vote on June 27 failed to obtain the needed two-thirds majority. Harold Nicolson, then a diplomat at the Berlin Embassy, wrote that, due to the government's withdrawal of an agrarian reform bill, the Economic Party had voted with the Communists and nationalists, defeating the motion and allowing the law to lapse.[20] This created an awkward situation, which passed unnoticed for the most part. Arthur Henderson, the new British foreign secretary, replied to Nicolson that if French authorities asked him about the British government's position on the matter, he would "take a similar line to that followed by His Majesty's Government at the time of the return of the Crown Prince to Germany and deprecate any undue importance being attached to the potential dangers of the ex-Kaiser's return."[21]

British military experts, examining the question of German industrial and military potential, discounted reports alleging German industrial preparation for war. Colonel P.W. Gosset, a military expert at the Berlin Embassy, responded to a work by G. Whitham entitled *The Industrial Mobilization of Germany* by saying that, though it gave the impression that Germany was rapidly rearming and therefore constituted a threat to the peace of Europe,

> this is not the case. Although there may be alleged manufacture of war material in Germany and although she may have begun to study and to organize Industrial Mobilization, the results of the war and of the work of the late MIACC [Military Interallied Control Commission] have been such as to render some years of preparatory work necessary. The danger is, therefore, not immediate, unless the stupidity of the extreme Nationalist section of the nation leads to a premature explosion, which would bring about its own defeat. Let us hope that, during the intervening years, more moderate councils will prevail and that Germany will learn to cooperate with other nations without wishing to dominate them.[22]

The fact that, in the present circumstances — i.e., without the necessary armed forces — Germans would be foolish to embark on an aggressive course, was often invoked. These circumstances might change, but in the meantime many hoped that the German people would come to appreciate the advantages of peaceful economic and political cooperation.

With respect to Germany's armed forces, Gosset had written earlier that he believed that the present government "would limit itself to the absolute minimum as regards the execution of the military clauses, but it may be anticipated that, under a government containing representatives of the German Nationalist Party, 'infractions' would assume serious dimensions and possibly lead to a crisis in international relations."[23] Gosset believed that the peace of Europe depended upon the restriction of German armaments, but that this in turn depended on German cooperation: "It appears essential, therefore, to secure this cooperation by encouraging the existing desire for peace amongst the masses of the population and by keeping the German people and, more especially, the Republican parties informed, as far as possible, of all infractions by Germany of the military clauses and of the obvious consequences that must ensue if such infractions are continued and carried beyond a certain point."[24]

Peace depended both on a German desire for it and on the willingness of Britain and France to see that the provisions of the Versailles treaty were enforced.   The Quai d'Orsay kept careful records of violations of the Treaty, though the reliability of French intelligence reports was open to question, sometimes by French officials themselves.[25] The British also kept a close watch, however; the military attaché in Berlin, James Marshall Cornwall kept the Foreign Office well informed of circumventions and violations.[26]   While Germany's capacity to fight has been the subject of some debate, the main fear of both British and French observers remained Germany's ultimate intentions, which they could not know.[27]

Stresemann's death in October 1929 meant the loss of an advocate of cooperation.   Rumbold wrote to Lord Stonehaven that

Stresemann's death is really rather a disaster. Two props have sustained Germany in recent difficult years, i.e. Hindenburg and Stresemann. Now one is gone and the other, though still very vigorous, is an old man of 82 who cannot, in the nature of things, last many years more. The German is not, as a rule, gifted with political instinct, and that was a gift which Stresemann had in a very high degree. His policy will be carried on, but by men of inferior calibre to himself. In some ways Stresemann was the biggest statesman who has arisen since the war. The tributes paid to him by foreign statesman and the press have been very flattering and soothing to German self-esteem. The Germans feel that they must have some value to have thrown up a statesman like Stresemann. The confidence of the nation itself has been restored, and the only danger is that, given the German character, self-confidence may degenerate into arrogance. We shall see.[28]

Stresmann's personality-driven formula for success, striking a balance between nationalism and international cooperation, accompanied him to the grave. The future of German foreign policy was unclear, but the days of lying prostrate before the Allied victors had long passed.

Revisionism Unleashed

Germany's new foreign minister, Julius Curtius, struck Rumbold as "a quiet, conciliatory and level-headed man, but it is obvious that he neither has nor can have at the present moment the same national and international prestige as his predecessor had."[29] The absence of a powerful voice for moderation at the Wilhelmstrasse was worrisome; such a benign figure as Curtius increased the danger that control of foreign policy might shift to more assertive elements. In the event, however, Curtius himself was largely responsible for what Peter Krüger has called the "fall from grace" (*Sündenfall*) of Weimar foreign policy, the Austro-German customs union proposal of March 1931, which marked the end of the policy of fulfillment and conciliation, and a capitulation to domestic revisionist pressures.[30]

In France, Stresemann's death did not produce a change of policy, and Briand's conciliatory approach to Germany continued to enjoy wide support. At the end of the December 1929 debate on the estimates for the foreign ministry, 343 deputies voted for the government, and only 17 voted against.[31] The opposition, with an articulate spokesman in Henry Franklin-Bouillon, focused its attack on France's weak response to German revisionism. Franklin-Bouillon said that from Germany's perspective Locarno was a foot in the door to treaty revision; Stresemann himself had told a group of businessmen in Dresden just days after the end of the conference that the renunciation of armed force formulated in the treaty was dictated by reality, by the simple fact that for the moment Germany did not have armed forces. Locarno, he had concluded, signified that the world war had produced no winner. The Bavarian premier had explained the rationale for Locarno in this way:

> after all that the German people has had to put up with from France over the past years, I can understand that the German people would want to rise up and oppose by force this kind of policy. But since an act of this sort is impossible, probably for another generation, it would be foolhardy to threaten without having the force to carry it out. I therefore prefer a policy that conceals a clenched fist, in order to pull it out one fine day.[32]

Franklin-Bouillon concluded: "There isn't a single German, whatever his party, who accepts without reservation the current boundaries of the Reich. If we lose sight of that fact for a single moment, our whole foreign policy will be ruined. We will move from illusion to illusion and from error to error, on to certain disaster."[33] One of his colleagues commented that Franklin-Bouillon was "a voice crying in the wilderness."[34]

Paul Reynaud, a rising star in the Chamber, advocated a more pragmatic approach when he spoke for the *groupe d'action démocratique et sociale* the following day. He could understand Germany's response to defeat; what concerned France was security, specifically the assurance that Germany would not launch a war of revenge. The solution, he believed, lay in industrial cooperation, which would integrate their economies, rationalize production and make war impossible. He had begun to examine the possibilities for such cooperation in 1923, concluding that it was too soon; but now circumstances had changed.

Trying to recast the debate, Reynaud rejected distinctions between "good" and "bad" Germany. French Socialists and Radicals believed that the "good" Germany was left-wing Germany; but they had to acknowledge that until recently cooperation had come from a conservative foreign minister.[35] Nor could one speak of German industry as being "good" or "bad": the Hugenbergs and Thyssens, leaders of heavy industry who could rely on German resources, tended to ally themselves with the agrarians to raise tariff barriers; but those whose industries required resources from abroad were more internationalist in temperament and outlook.[36] A much more solid basis for peace between France and Germany was the realization in Germany that Stresemann's policy of fulfillment was in Germany's best interest; as Curtius had stated recently: "our policy is not that of a humbled and conquered [country]. It is in our interest to recognize partisans of entente and of peace."[37] There was no "good" and "bad" Germany, concluded Reynaud. There was no "eternal Germany" that knew only force. There was only a modern Germany, infinitely complex and constantly changing. "The first of our duties is to take up contact with this Germany, to study it, to understand it, and to dissociate hostile elements from a policy of peace."[38]

Meanwhile, however, in Germany the National Socialists were making gains in local elections. Rumbold wrote to Arthur Henderson on December 17 that "[t]here is evidence that political circles here are not merely puzzled by the unexpected successes of the National Socialist party, but a little uneasy at the manner in which a capricious electorate continues to shower favours on these noisy newcomers."[39] Harold Nicolson had described such successes already in November, but "[n]ow come further reports of local elections of Bavaria and Thuringia announcing fresh successes for the same party, successes which continue to be won mainly at the expense of the German Nationalists, though the other *bourgeois* parties, with the exception of the Centre party, have also contributed."[40]   In Bavaria the social democrats and the Catholic Party had held their ground, but the *bourgeois* parties and, notably, the Communists, had lost ground.

Rumbold made no reference to economic distress as a possible reason for National Socialist gains. Economic distress was present in 1929 already; Kindleberger writes that labor tensions in the steel industry in the last months of 1928, followed by a severe winter and tight credit conditions produced clear signs of depression by summer.[41] However, while economic hardship might have helped to create a predisposition among German voters to consider political extremes, the National Socialists won votes, not by presenting a clearly articulated economic agenda, but by playing on common prejudices and a sense of Germany's having been wronged and betrayed.

In 1930 Robert Vansittart returned to the Foreign Office after a two-year absence, as permanent undersecretary. In "An Aspect of International Relations in 1930" he attempted to describe the mentality of the time in European nations, "as reflected by its press and statesmen." Though he asserted a faith in human progress, he said that the purpose of the memorandum was to describe the extent to which "the old Adam" again stalked Europe — in other words, the degree to which the "pre-war system of European alliances and balance of power" was reemerging at the expense of "the spirit of the League and disarmament."[42]

Vansittart's views on Germany were not startlingly prescient, but he did present its revisionist agenda clearly.[43]   Since the end of the war, Germany had sought "to re-enter the comity of European nations on a footing of equality with the other Great Powers" and also "to modify the penal provisions of the peace settlement which has galled her pride and hampered her national development."[44] Modification included the restoration of colonies, *Anschluss*, rearmament, and adjustment of the border with Poland, in increasing order of importance.

These goals were clear, Vansittart wrote, but how would the Germans seek to accomplish them? They could address the questions of Poland and rearmament openly and directly, or they could wait until their own country was more stable internally, in the meantime participating in such international organizations as the League and (if it came to pass) Briand's federation without committing themselves politically. Vansittart hesitated to guess which route Germany would choose: "On the whole, one would be inclined to suppose that she would go slow. There is much which needs doing to put her house in order. In fact, after economic rationalisation, it is now the turn of political and financial rationalisation. It is, moreover, evident that thus reorganised, with her political influence and prestige established, she will be in a far better position than now for extorting settlements satisfactory to herself on both issues."[45]

A great deal depended on who controlled German foreign policy. At present Germany had no outstanding personality to guide it and to "moderate and educate public opinion," although Dr. Curtius could be relied upon to steer the course Stresemann had mapped out. However, without a powerful personality in control, foreign policy could become the "sport of irresponsible extremists." Though the fortunes of Hugenberg's National People's Party had fallen, "[t]he degree of sympathy still aroused by Nationalist denunciations of the Treaty of Versailles should not be underestimated." Vansittart also did not wish to exaggerate the significance of the recent electoral success of the National Socialists: "These, under the leadership of the half-mad and ridiculously dangerous demagogue Hitler, make the best or worst of both worlds, preach a combination of militant socialism and militant nationalism, with uncompromising hostility to the peace settlement and the policy of fulfillment."[46]

Vansittart assessed the danger cautiously, but he believed that something had to happen. The "liquidation of the war" accomplished by the Hague Conferences marked the end of an era. Germany had entered a new phase, and the direction of her policy would affect all of Europe: "The very uncertainty as to its trend cannot fail, on the one hand, to excite the fears of those countries which hope for stability and security, and, on the other, the expectations of those whose circumstances are such as to make policies of adventure, or at least fishing in troubled waters, seem profitable."[47] The Germans themselves might choose the methods of the old diplomacy if they found that the new methods of conciliation, arbitration and disarmament could not achieve their objectives.

The German elections of September 1930 brought the sense of unease implicit in Vansittart's "Old Adam" memorandum into clearer focus. Capitalizing on the increasing economic distress and resentment at the position of Germany in Europe, the National Socialists became the second-largest party in the Reichstag.[48] Chancellor Brüning, already having taken a step away from democracy by resorting to rule by decree, called upon

Hitler for consultation.[49]   The National Socialist gains strengthened the position of Briand's opponents in France.   Already in January, Austen Chamberlain (no longer Foreign Secretary) had written to his sister that Briand's "star has paled rather before Tardieu's." Though Tardieu left Briand in charge of the Quai d'Orsay, his own disposition was more like Poincaré's.   Poincaré, now retired, wrote a series of articles in the conservative newspaper *Figaro* during the summer of 1930, asserting that the policy of entente with Germany was based on a false understanding of the German spirit, which in fact was bent on the restoration of lost territories and world domination.[50]

Foreign observers now had to take stock of Hitler. Austen Chamberlain spoke to the former ambassador to Germany, Viscount D'Abernon, who "was very gloomy about Hitler — not dangerous, he thought, if there were a *man* to fight him, but since Stresemann's death Germany had no man. What a troubled world it is! I hear from Fleuriau [the French ambassador in London] that Briand's position is much shaken in France by Hitler's success. And wherever you look there is distress, unrest, suspicion. What will happen next?"[51]   Chamberlain's outlook was and would remain very pessimistic. Though in hindsight this fits very well with the deterioration of the European situation during this time, Chamberlain's views were shaped to some extent by ill health and a propensity to criticize the work of his successors at the Foreign Office.

If British observers could not predict what would happen in Germany, they could at least count on the French reaction.   J.L. Garvin of the *Observer* wrote on October 5 that "the French reaction to the Hitler phenomenon develops as expected.   The irony is familiar.   While M. Briand, the man most congenial to Germany and to Europe, is weakened, M. Poincaré is strengthened.   He has begun by scoffing at the general impulse to peace by disarmament, and has publicly claimed for France something better than what he cheaply calls "international anthems".[52]   An Italian correspondent who sent a clipping of this article to Poincaré wondered whether or not peace would depend on French and not German wisdom once "Prussianist" Germany reemerged.

William Tyrrell, reflecting wishfully on his efforts to keep opinion in France moderate, wrote to the prime minister that the initial response of alarm in France had given way to a

realisation of the very serious financial repercussion that the German elections may have upon the world in general. This impression I am using in order to make them realise here that it is in the interest of the French franc to take a calm and dispassionate view of the Fascist party in German as it would only be playing their game if the programme tempted France into a relapse and into the pursuit of an anti-German attitude.[53]

Tyrrell believed that powerful business interests would pressure right-wing politicians to keep calm. He found such a calm attitude in Philippe Berthelot, the secretary general at the Quai d'Orsay: "[he] dreads above all the economic consequences of the German elections at a time when all are suffering from economic depression, but he did not conceal from me that he thought Briand's position was seriously shaken."[54] The public, he feared, had concluded that Briand's policy of conciliation had failed.

By this time the effects of the economic slump were being felt over much of Europe, but not in France, where the economy was less tied to the world economy and the devaluation of the franc by Poincaré in 1928 had made French goods attractive to foreign buyers. The French ambassador in Washington, the Catholic poet and dramatist Paul Claudel, saw this as an opportunity for closer Franco-American cooperation; the situation "places special tasks of solidarity on the two states that maintain a strong economic and political position." He believed that speculation and the Wall Street crash were not the deepest causes of the slump: "The truth is that the whole world is gravely ill, of a malady that is beginning to manifest itself everywhere, for example in political troubles in South America, but from which large regions of the globe, enormous markets of consumers like China and Russia, have been suffering for twenty years."[55] Americans therefore ought not to be completely demoralized by the manifestations of this illness in their country, but ought instead to try to use their power and influence in the world to provide intelligent leadership.

One area where the United States could help was in Germany. The ambassador spoke to many American journalists while returning by boat from Europe. "They all professed that they were alarmed at the force and magnitude of the movement sweeping Germany towards a demand for release from all contractual obligations, be they financial, military, or territorial." They similarly doubted the ability of Stresemann's heirs to block this trend. In this respect the editors of the large newspapers, anxious to reassure public opinion and especially the many holders of German bonds, did not represent the opinion of the best-informed people in their editorials. To the bad news coming from Germany could be added rumors of a crash in Italy, "economic aggression" from the Soviet Union, unrest in the Balkans, revolutions in South America (where there was much American investment), economic disaster in Japan due to the collapse of the silk market. Indeed, in light of this situation, electoral invitations to optimism emanating from time to time from Washington took on a bitter irony. The sense was that this worldwide crisis had not yet reached its culmination, and that the winter ahead would be difficult.[56]

September 1930, therefore, marked a turning point not only for Germany; for foreign observers the Nazi victories seemed to cast other European and world problems in a different, more somber light. The evil effects of economic misery had produced potential political dangers. Maurice Léon, a French financier living in New York, wrote to Poincaré in October that he had spent eight weeks in Germany and left September 17 for the United States, stopping only briefly in Paris to see Paul Reynaud and André Tardieu:

> I summarized for both of them my impressions: the economic situation, bad everywhere, has lent itself to the demagogy of the extreme right as well as the extreme left. The other parties are divided and timid. The consequence of this melee very probably will be a dictatorship of partisans of revenge which, if not discredited from the start by effective preventive measures, will be able to launch a war which in the end would benefit bolshevism.[57]

Economic and financial cooperation could correct the world crisis "relatively easily": "the world economic crisis, the basis of the political malaise, could be attenuated, encouraging the forces of order in the whole world."[58]

Pierre Cot, a Radical deputy (who later became Daladier's Air Minister), returned from Germany in October and wrote to Poincaré asking to see him: "I am just back from Germany and I find the economic and political situation of that country extremely serious. My opinion is that French public opinion understands poorly the dangers to which upheaval and revolution in Berlin would expose us."[59] Few who visited Germany at this time could fail to appreciate the dangers posed by this surge of nationalism, fueled by economic distress, but what could be done? Were leaders able to think of ways to alleviate the conditions which seemed to them so ominous?

If the deteriorating situation called for outstanding leadership, the circumstances did not produce it. Ramsay MacDonald, Britain's prime minister from June 1929 to June 1935, presided over a foreign policy of retreat and capitulation before the advancing dictatorships. In March 1930 he wrote from London to the ambassador in Madrid, Sir George Grahame: "There is little going on here, except the drudgery of the Naval Conference and the troubles created at point after point by the French. The European situation is anything but comfortable, and the outlook is not promising.

Somehow or other Great Britain seems to have lost its grip. The change between 1924 and 1930 is very marked."[60] Writing later that year to Arthur Balfour about the deepening economic crisis in his own country, he said that "What alarms me most is the state of mind into which the country is getting, and the incapacity of so many of the business men whom we come across."[61] But throughout his tenure as prime minister MacDonald himself was unable to lead his country — or Europe — out of that "state of mind."

Leaders knew that they faced a dangerous situation, but not knowing what shape these dangers would take made planning difficult. At the end of 1930 Major-General J.R.G. Charles delivered a lecture at the Senior Officer's School, presenting a "military appreciation" of the current world situation; Maurice Hankey, whose "own mind [had] been working very much on these lines," sent a transcript to MacDonald. Charles began by saying that "The more immediate problems confronting this country are bound up with the general situation in Europe to a greater extent than is perhaps generally realized, with the result that whilst naturally pre-occupied with our own Imperial problems further afield, we may be in danger of ignoring or somewhat minimizing the complexity and gravity of the situation with which we are faced nearer home."[62]

Britain's efforts at securing the peace were running aground. Besides the enigma of Russia and the animosity between revisionist and status quo powers, three factors threatened the peace of Europe, and all three concerned Germany: its recent elections, the disarmament question, and the Polish Corridor. In the September elections, "eleven million Germans (out of an electorate of thirty four millions) voted for violence and the repudiation of all international agreements in one form or another." These voters "have turned to the self-styled parties of Youth and Courage, whose avowed policy is the denunciation of the Peace Treaties, and a flat refusal to continue the payment of Reparations." As long as he lived, Hindenburg would maintain order, but his death "would almost certainly precipitate a crisis as might easily draw all Europe, and incidentally ourselves, into a vortex of universal conflagration."[63]

The crisis demanded an assessment of the military situation in Germany, including "the reactions of the Army to the present political situation, and the potentialities of that Army as a fighting machine when all restrictions have been removed, as is visualized in the near future by the ever-growing ranks of the extremists, and to no small extent by the military leaders." Germany had an army of 100,000 men, to which could be added 200,000 whose terms had expired. In addition three million others had war experience or post-war training. Germany's true strength lay, however, in "her industrial organization, which, as regards capacity modernization, and extremely centralized control, is second to none in Europe."[64]

One of the purposes of the Treaty of Versailles had been to reduce Germany's ability to wage war, but

> [it] would be idle to pretend that the enforced disarmament of Germany has been either completely or permanently carried out, although the Commission of Control, which was withdrawn in 1927, achieved considerable success in enforcing the military restrictions of the treaty. In drawing attention to the various ways in which the Treaty restrictions are being evaded, it must be emphasized that such military preparations as are undoubtedly being made, are designed with a view to future rather than to present requirements. The existing German Army is, in fact, regarded by its leaders as an interim organization, and is therefore being trained as a cadre on which will be built up the army of the future. With the removal of all restrictions, Germany would be free to train the whole of her manpower in the way she considers most suitable, and to perfect her existing plans for the adaptation of her industry to war requirements.[65]

Charles listed the ways in which the restrictions were being violated: the limits on the size and training of staffs was being circumvented; short terms of service increased the number of reserves, as did assistance to such illegal paramilitary organizations as the *Stahlhelm* and the deployment of "defence detachments" along the eastern frontier; and police training was essentially military in character.

Of the various paramilitary groups, the largest and most powerful was the *Stahlhelm*, which its leaders described as "a strategical reserve behind the political Right flank, to be thrown in should the need arise." The organization was losing many members to the National Socialists, and was itself threatened by a split within its ranks over methods. The leadership and "moderate" members wished the organization to retain its essentially military character, that of a reserve to the Reichswehr, while the extremists wanted it to assume a more political role in line with the National Socialists. Either way, the *Stahlhelm* would remain a dangerous instrument of revision.

The Reichswehr also had ties to the extreme nationalists. Charles believed that many junior officers were "entirely sympathetic" to the National Socialists, and that they were working to assure army neutrality in the event of an attempted coup d'état. The Higher Command had taken steps to thwart such intrigue, and as long as Groener remained Minister of War the army would remain loyal to the government, but, if someone like Kurt von Schleicher took over, he might strike a deal with the National Socialists. "It is important in all this to note for how much personalities count and how the death or removal of a strong and incorruptible man like Hindenburg or Groener might precipitate a crisis...such as might lead to indescribable chaos."[66]

In addition to training as many men as possible, Germany experimented with forbidden weapons, such as tanks, heavy artillery and airplanes:

> As far as secrecy allows, and there are indications that all pretence at secrecy may be thrown aside in the near future, this training is carried out not only in Germany, but also probably in a more intensive form in Russia. Expenditure on material has steadily increased and is now on a most extravagant scale. There is little doubt that large sums, shown under other headings in the Budget, are in reality devoted to subsidizing commercial enterprises, with the object of fostering and gaining control of a vast munitions industry.[67]

Chemical weapons were easily derived from commercial products, making obvious the military advantage gained through Germany's leading position in Europe's chemical industry. Germany led Europe also in civil aviation, which the government heavily subsidized.

With respect to disarmament, Charles believed that Germany would use the ambiguities of the Treaty of Versailles to justify a demand for her release from the restrictions on her armed forces, once it became clear that France, Italy and the Little Entente had no intention of reducing theirs. A rearmed Germany serious threatened the peace:

> Germany could then rapidly become the dominant military state in Europe as she was before the late War, and, having forged the sword, the wish to use it might soon manifest itself. What the attitude of the French Government would be in the event of such action, remains to be seen. In her present mood, France would undoubtedly proceed to re-occupy the Rhineland. It would be difficult to reconcile the re-occupation of the Rhineland with the Treaty of Locarno, while the question as to the action to be taken by Great Britain, with her combined obligations under this Treaty and the Treaty of Versailles, would be a political and juridical problem of an extremely delicate nature.[68]

The third threat to peace involving Germany was the "open sore" of the Polish Corridor: "There can, in fact, be no peace in Eastern Europe until this is readjusted." Though the Corridor had been part of Poland before the partition of 1793, the fact that it currently separated East Prussia from the rest of Germany made it incompatible with a "reawakened" Germany: "Germany has promised in the Locarno Treaty never to attempt to readjust this frontier by force of arms, but there is little doubt that, after she has shaken herself free of some of the more disagreeable clauses of the

Peace Treaty, she will make such an attempt." Charles believed that European conditions were deteriorating rapidly. The nations of Europe fell into two categories, one of "virile nations with martial instincts, good powers of organization, and a highly developed state of civilization," the other of "effete or decadent nations, who, through no inherent virtue of their own, have acquired territories and prestige to which they are certainly not the natural heirs." He concluded on a grim note:

> It has been said that Peace Conferences have always been the grave of reputations and the womb of future wars. If the future of Europe is as dark as it appears to be, will the verdict of history be any different as regards the initial settlement after the Great War? ...[W]hatever may be the solution of the problem of Europe, the position of the British Government is bound to become one of increasing and almost intolerable difficulty.[69]

Charles' somber outlook had many echoes in Britain. Hugh Dalton hated the prospect of meeting his constituents in the first days of 1931: "It is all so tragically different, so far as economic questions go, from what one hoped and dreamed a Labour Government would be like. And, even in the international field, there is fear in Europe, and Old Adam stalketh in the noonday. We go on signing new bits of paper, but who believes in the undertaking they enshrine?"[70]

Austen Chamberlain shared the belief that Britain's influence in European affairs had declined in recent months and years. Pondering the possibility of once again becoming foreign secretary in a new Baldwin government, he did not believe that another stroke as dramatic as Locarno could be dealt in these circumstances. He wrote to his sister:

> ...talking of the future, we may speculate about it but it seems to me that all prophecy is at present futile... I see a terrible recrudescence of trouble and unrest and it is easier to see the perils that beset peace than to find a remedy. Mussolini's attitude has changed and not for the better; Germany lacks the strong guiding hand of Stresemann and France, frightened by Hitler's success and Mussolini's flirtations with Hungary and Bulgaria has reacted violently against the policy of appeasement. There is good work to be done at the [Foreign Office] but there is no easy success and perhaps no success at all to be reaped.[71]

Though he had little confidence in his successor at the Foreign Office, Chamberlain also believed, along with many of his colleagues, that economic and imperial problems diminished Britain's ability to play a remedial role in European affairs.

Arthur Henderson's most obvious problem was his own prime minister. *Times* correspondent Leo Kennedy, speaking with Chamberlain about Henderson's failure to reach an understanding with Briand over Grandi's proposal for a shipbuilding holiday for 1930, thought "it was partly because he did not feel sure enough of himself. And this arose, in part, from his not feeling sure enough of his PM's support. MacD is always butting in, and Henderson doesn't quite know where he is sometimes."[72] Speaking with Henderson himself after the German elections, Kennedy found him to be "thoroughly depressed about the general European situation, as well he may be. He believes however that the Social Democrats will come into the German Government, and that gives him a little hope."[73]

Though many British politicians despaired at their inability to play a decisive role in a deteriorating situation, career diplomats stressed the importance of British involvement. In Paris Kennedy spoke with Tyrrell, whom he found to be "a most analytical talker, and illustrates and supports his opinions by the diplomatic events of the last 30 years with which he has been so closely associated." Tyrrell's first point was that

> Great Britain *must* continue to interest herself in Europe. I [Kennedy] had noticed (I said) a tendency to leave Europe alone and concentrate on the Empire — yes, so had he, he said, but that would be fatal to Europe: and to ourselves, eventually; for they would mess things up and then we should be drawn in. We are the arbiters, the balance-holders, the nation whom others trust — let us not throw away our influence, to the general loss.[74]

Tyrrell went on to suggest that the last war might have been prevented, had Britain not opted for "splendid isolation" in the years preceding it.

Tyrrell also stressed the need for close cooperation with France. Treaty revision was impossible without French assent, and "if we side with Germany and try to force her into revision nothing whatever will be done — unless it be by war."[75] Tyrrell had said the same to Henderson a few days earlier, and "Henderson agreed — this is back entirely to the [Austen Chamberlain] policy! and quite right, I think. Though public opinion in England is so favorable to Germany now, that it is difficult to carry out."[76]

As for Germany, Tyrrell decried what he saw as the stupidity of its politicians, but recognized the potential menace. Of the Nazi leader, he thought "Hitler was a bit cracked, but a great force. In a great hall in [southern] Germany Hitler had once shot two revolver bullets up through the roof and said, 'Those will be two historical marks in the history of Germany'!"[77] Tyrrell also worried about Britain's tendency to become "terribly tangled up in pacifist treaties," and Kennedy agreed that it would be disastrous to rule out fighting in any circumstances.

1931 was the first year in which Adolf Hitler appeared of the British embassy's "List of Leading Personalities", a compilation of about 80 short biographies of Germany's leading politicians, scientists, industrialists, and financiers. The writer described Hitler's success since 1929:

> In 1929 Hitler, who had gradually penetrated northwards from Bavaria into Thuringia, found himself suddenly carried forth on a fresh wave of popularity. The youth of the country rallied to his banner. Large numbers of students, who found on graduating that there was no opening for them owing to the wave of economic depression then setting in, joined the Nazi leader. A year later Dr. Brüning, by a pardonable miscalculation, gave Hitler his chance by dissolving the Reichstag when the tide of unemployment was rising rapidly. To Hitler's great surprise he found himself at the head of a party of 107 delegates. Being a foreigner he was ineligible for election himself and consequently had to appoint a deputy to head his party in the Reichstag. His views soon became less extreme than those of his lieutenants. A note of hesitancy crept into his speeches. He hedged when asked if he would repudiate the debt settlements outright. Hitler's speeches are merely strings of platitudes delivered with unexpected emphasis. To the German ear his foreign (Viennese) accent sounds attractive and helps to rivet the attention.[78]

This account portrayed Hitler's success to that point as almost accidental. While his movement was still small he was undoubtedly a firebrand, but now, with this unexpected propulsion into a position of national prominence, his tone had become more moderate. Like many others, Rumbold hoped that the responsibilities of public office and success within the Weimar system would soften the rhetoric of the National Socialists. In any case, they were not yet in control.

In February 1931 Sir Hughe Knatchbull-Hugessen enumerated the troubling developments in Germany over the past year. A year earlier Foreign Office opinion held that the future of Germany would depend on whether or not a strong nationalist movement would emerge. Subsequently the elections in September had produced an "active state of public opinion." Now even those in office openly attacked the Young Plan and disarmament, and made demands about the eastern frontier. This agitation, along with Germany's economic problems, produced anxiety in France and criticism of the government: "Of course those in office do not intend to give way to this, but the position of the Government is so shaky that they cannot stand out against it."[79]

However, Brüning and Curtius were not yet doomed, he continued, and "one must hope that in course of time the ultra-militant side of National-Socialism will discredit itself."[80] In the meantime, however, Germany remained a serious threat to the stability of Europe:

> ...it is a serious consideration that, once again after securing modifications, Germany has not paused to draw breath before demanding more. She did this after Locarno and has always done so. The outcry about the Eastern frontiers (evidently the next 'étape' for Germany) is loud and sustained and reacts in France and everywhere throughout Europe, while the outcry against the Hague settlement affects credit and creates anxiety — although of course it reacts in Germany too. Events like the Stahlhelm demonstration at Coblenz seem to be worthy of nothing but condemnation. The exclusion of 'Im Westen nichts neues' [*All Quiet on the Western Front*] is another uncomfortable sign....
> [A]t long range there can be no deception about German designs and policy (which are at least intelligible and natural) but one fears that, with the present spirit in Germany the Government will not be strong enough to resist any temptation which may crop up and with Europe in its present condition temptations would not be very surprising.[81]

Europe at this time seemed particularly vulnerable to the kind of difficulties Germany was creating. Though the economic condition of the country seemed to make war an unlikely choice, it seemed quite clear to this observer, and presumably his colleagues at the Foreign Office with whom he discussed these matters, that Germany would resort to war if she could.

Planning for a Dangerous Future

French observers had little difficulty believing in the dangers Germany posed to peace in Europe. Indeed, planning for a German campaign of revenge had never ceased. While efforts at conciliation and cooperation continued even after the customs union fiasco, too many signs of the "old" Germany had resurfaced for the hopes of the late 1920s to be maintained. While construction continued on the Maginot Line in 1932 and 1933, Herriot, Paul-Boncour and Daladier sought assurances from Britain, which MacDonald refused to provide.[82]

André François-Poncet, who had arrived as ambassador to Germany in 1931 hoping to broaden the economic entente, gave up on the Weimar Republic in July 1932. On July 20, Chancellor von Papen deposed key members of the Prussian government, including the Socialist prime minister, and imposed martial law on Berlin and Brandenburg. A few days later, Kurt von Schleicher had given a radio address in which he was "unfriendly, if not hostile" to France.[83] On the 28th, three days before the Reichstag elections in which the National Socialists won 230 seats, François-Poncet wrote to Herriot that the 20th had marked an important moment in postwar history: "It has become obvious that the aristocracy, landed, military and bureaucratic — that is, the class that formerly governed Prussia and Germany — intends to govern once again, after it has driven out liberalism and socialism."[84]

The Disarmament Conference, beginning in February 1932, openly demonstrated the dismal state of European international relations. The German demand for equality of armaments stirred French fears, though in a note on 29 August the German Foreign Office sought to reassure French leaders of the "sincere and moderate character of German intentions," while increasing the pressure on them to make the concessions.[85] In his journal Herriot noted that in Germany there had recently been a republican youth rally against rearmament and war, but the "best" commentary on the note had come from Berlin: "The celebrations at the Stadium on the third demonstrate what Germany means by *Wehrsport*; the exercises performed for the public were maneuvers....The uniform, the command, the equipment were military. All that was missing was the carriage and use of firearms." The following day the *Stahlhelm* had demonstrated at the Tempelhof airport, 160,000 to 180,000 strong, "in front of the former crown prince, the old princes, the chancellor and ministers of the Reich....They speak not of the *revenge* but of the *liberation* of Germany."[86] For much of the year 1932, French observers feared a return of the reactionary forces that had driven Germany to war in 1914; in many ways this prospect was more frightening than that of a National Socialist government, of which Germany and the world had no experience. Indeed, Hitler and other National Socialist leaders sought to assure French contacts of their pacific intentions, and they would continue to do so after January 1933.[87]

British leaders had not anticipated that German revisionism would become so menacing so soon. For Maurice Hankey, developments in Germany warranted reconsideration of Britain's defense policy. On November 21, 1930, two months after the first major National Socialist electoral victories, he had a conversation "of a rather private nature" with Robert Vansittart, the purpose of which was to "communicate...the misgivings I feel about the state of Europe, more particularly as bearing on the assumption on which Imperial Defence preparations have been based since July 5, 1928, that at any given date there will be no major war for ten years." What concerned Hankey was not so much the success of Hitler, "which might or might not be an ephemeral development," but rather "the fact that nearly all the parties in Germany now stood for a revision of the Treaty of Versailles, as affecting the Eastern Frontiers, as well as of the Young Plan." German demands would confront the League of Nations with "problems that were insoluble on any principles of mere justice and right, as I had learned at the Paris Peace Conference."[88]

Hankey doubted that the League would be able to handle a peaceful revision of Germany's eastern frontier, because Poland and France would oppose it. Yet Germany would not accept the status quo indefinitely. His citation of examples from the nineteenth century suggested that, in his opinion, the advent of the League had not altered the nature of international relations fundamentally; while the League served the interests of status quo powers, other states might still use force to settle their disputes:

> If the League could not settle them, how were these questions likely to be settled? Most of the wars of the century preceding the Great War had arisen out of irredentism in Italy, Greece and other Balkan States. These were the root causes not only of Balkan wars but of larger wars such as the Crimean War and the Russo-Turkish War of 1878, in addition to the Italian part of the war of 1866. A formidable nation like Germany was not likely to be content to be turned down year after year by the League of Nations.[89]

Similarly, Hankey saw little hope in disarmament. France would not disarm to Germany's level; nor would she allow Germany to rearm to her level. Germany, in any case, would retain a capacity to rearm quickly, given the efficient nature of the armed forces she did have, not to mention her industrial strength. A rearmed Germany would put an end to whatever stability existed in Europe.

The split between France and Italy might provide the occasion for Germany's rearmament, and also for the division of Europe into two camps: Italy, Bulgaria, Hungary, Austria and Germany against France, Yugoslavia, Poland, Romania, and Czechoslovakia. "In these circumstances," wrote Hankey, "it appeared to me that the outlook in Europe was much worse than it had been ten years before the late War, and to base our Imperial Defence on a ten-year date advancing from day to day appeared to me to be living in a fool's paradise."[90] He considered it his duty to so inform the prime minister, but not before consulting with Vansittart at the Foreign Office.

Vansittart told Hankey that the Foreign Office had not endorsed the assumption that year. Generally agreeing with Hankey as to the condition of Europe, he viewed the situation with "misgiving," but not "anxiety." The Foreign Office had refrained from endorsing the Ten Year Rule in its memoranda to the Chiefs of Staff Committee and the Imperial Conference, but hesitated to press for a reconsideration of the policy. His "Old Adam" paper was to be revised the following spring, but possibly earlier, now that Vansittart was aware of Hankey's concerns; Vansittart suggested to Hankey that this revision "would provide an opportunity for a review of the ten year assumption if I then still desired to raise the matter."[91] Hankey therefore decided to wait until the appearance of that memorandum to raise the matter with the prime minister.

Hankey was not so much concerned with the extremes of German politics as he was with the mainstream. One of his correspondents concluded from Rumbold's reports in November 1930 that the "German Fascists have rather missed fire"; people who had met Hitler decided that "though he is a useful 'tub-thumper' he is not a 'big' man in the sense that Mussolini is."[92] Hankey feared the words of such "responsible" politicians as Dr. Wilhelm Kaas, leader of the German Center Party:

> Dr. Kaas says there is 'danger in delay'. There is still hope in Germany, at any rate in those circles which have so far supported the policy of understanding and form the responsible majority. The critical phase for Europe will begin 'when Germany ceases to hope'. It has been the aim of German foreign policy to exclude this tragic possibility. They remain true to this policy, but one thing is clear: 'the physical and psychic endurance of every people has its limits. The German Samson will not allow himself to be tied for life to the treadmill of Versailles'.[93]

Germany portrayed her difficulties as tragic but in fact was beginning to turn the screws. In January Hankey suggested that the assumption of 1928 be reexamined.

Hankey argued that since 1587 Britain often had been unprepared on the eve of great conflicts: "How foolish a Government would have looked that had reaffirmed an assumption of ten years of peace during the early part of 1914! And yet there was less talk of war on the Continent then than now, and the outstanding problems were less acute."[94] There might not be a war in the next ten years, but "no other Great Power has adopted any assumption for its defensive preparations comparable to our own." France had reorganized her army and was spending twenty-six million pounds on frontier and anti-aircraft defense. Many other nations were taking precautions or preparing for war:

> The writer personally has seen something of the activities on either side of the Franco-Italian frontier. Belgium is just embarking on a new scheme of frontier defence. Russia's activity in armaments is notorious. All the leading countries, including the

United States of America, are preparing plans for the mobilisation of the nation for war. In Poland a gas-mask has been placed on sale by the Government, which civilians are invited to purchase, and facilities are provided for instruction in its use. In Russia, Poland, France, and even in disarmed Germany, anti air-raid rehearsals have recently taken place in various towns. Without attaching exaggerated importance to the not un-natural anxieties of nations which bore the brunt of the Great War in an even more acute form than this country, it may be said that the attitude of the Land Powers is quite different from our own. We are disarmed morally and to a great extent materially. The same cannot be said of the land powers.[95]

Hankey felt Britain to be in a very different position from the Continental powers: "Even if, in later years, we see ourselves heading for war, it will be extremely difficult for us to bring our defences up to the proper standard, since this will oblige us to give our reasons to the League in circumstances of great international publicity, thereby tending to precipitate the very situation which we wish to avoid."[96] Taking the high moral ground might yet exact a high price from an Empire that had to be concerned not only with Europe, but also with potential or actual crises in India, Afghanistan, China, Iraq, Egypt and Palestine. Nevertheless Hankey acknowledged that the League remained the greatest hope for the maintenance of peace on a continent in which there was no effective balance of power.

Action on the ten-year assumption was delayed, however. The Austro-German customs union proposal in March 1931 greatly alarmed France, but it also pressed diplomatic forces into action, and the visit of Brüning and Curtius to Chequers in June raised hopes of an improvement in the European situation. Hankey therefore hesitated to embark on a full review. A speech he wrote for the prime minister reflected a more hopeful outlook:

We attach no small importance to the steps that have lately been taken towards the strengthening of the machinery of peace. The recent visit of the German Chancellor and the Foreign Secretary, the coming meetings in Berlin, and the contemplated meeting of French and German Ministers in Paris, are all steps in the direction of improving the situation. And in the last few days the European atmosphere has been greatly improved by the initiative of the President of the United States; and we hope — indeed we anticipate — that this will be followed by other gestures of appeasement which will facilitate and culminate in the Disarmament Conference of next year, on which so much must necessarily depend.[97]

The improvement did not prove to be a turning point, however. For many British leaders the crises of August and September which led to the formation of the National Government and the abandonment of the gold standard further diminished Britain's prestige in the eyes of the world. Meeting with MacDonald at Chequers on November 21, 1931, Hankey discussed British policy's "want of grit." Britain's attitudes towards disarmament were perceived abroad as weakness, as was her inability to fulfil strategic commitments. But Hankey's affirmed the present course of policy:

> In most respects, of course, our policy is fundamentally right, even if it is in conflict with the views held abroad. To a considerable extent it has been forced on us by the inexorable course of events. In many matters also we are so far committed along the road on which we have started that we must see the policy through. Nevertheless it is submitted that the National Government, if it is to regain the confidence of foreign countries, should make a practice of weighing the effect of its decisions (including more especially its publicity) abroad as well as on our own people, and that the key-note of its policy should be the restoration of confidence and the rehabilitation of our old reputation for sturdiness.[98]

Once a courtesy, consideration of foreign opinion now was a necessity.

Hankey focused on accomplishments rather than failures in his comments on Vansittart's December 1931 memorandum on changing conditions in foreign policy. To a large extent, he wrote, disarmament had been achieved with America and Japan, reducing the risk of war with these powers "almost to zero" — three months after Japan's invasion of Manchuria. Progress on reparations and war debts was slow, but likely to continue under the pressure of world events. The time was probably not right for disarmament, however, and as for Europe: "Instead of entangling ourselves more closely with military commitments in a Europe torn to distraction...a more helpful approach towards at least a partial solution of the world's problems appears to lie in the direction of arrangements with our own Dominions and perhaps with countries that have adhered to sterling....The stage appears set for some advance in our economic relations with our kinsmen overseas."[99] The impulse to withdraw from Europe was intensified by the barrage of seemingly intractable problems.

Addressing British policy's "want of grit," the Committee of Imperial Defence cancelled the Ten Year Rule in March 1932, on the recommendation of the Chiefs of Staff Sub-Committee. However, the cancellation did not produce a change of policy; no one in the Cabinet expressed disapproval of the move, but "recognised...that this must not be taken to justify an expanding expenditure by the Defence Services without regard to the very serious financial and economic situation that still obtains."[100] The Cabinet also felt that the subject was related to that of disarmament, and "required further exploration," with the result that Hankey could write to MacDonald ten months later that "at present no-one quite knows whether the rule stands or not, and the whole position is vague and unsatisfactory."[101]

Germany achieved another victory against Versailles in June 1932 at the Lausanne Conference, which in effect cancelled reparations, on the meaningless condition that, as receivers of reparations forgave Germany's debt, the United States would forgive her debtors. Hankey wrote to Ramsay MacDonald that the Germans ought now to be satisfied:

> The Germans have within the last few years vastly improved their status as compared with the Treaty of Versailles. They are recognized as a first-class Power by virtue of becoming a Permanent Member of the League of Nations. They are protected against aggression by the Locarno Treaty, as well as by the Covenant. They secured the evacuation of the Rhineland 5 or 6 years before the appointed date. Finally at Lausanne they have rid themselves of reparations, provided they do nothing foolish before a debt settlement enables the Powers to ratify Lausanne. Here is the strongest ground — the ground of self-interest — for urging them to do nothing rash or provocative....It is their interest, no less than ours, to avoid upsetting Europe at this juncture with inevitable reactions on America.[102]

MacDonald was very pleased with the results of Lausanne, and he wrote: "when it is carefully studied I think it will be found the prettiest bit of work which has been done in international politics for a long time."[103] Even the French premier Herriot was relieved that a step had been taken to restore confidence and bring France out of isolation, albeit at a high price.[104]

Meanwhile, however, the Disarmament Conference sent out alarming signals. In September 1932 Hankey wrote down some of his own observations on the meaning of Germany's demand for equality in arms. On one level it made perfect sense for a member of the Council of the League of Nations to want to arm herself, for defensive purposes, just as the other great powers did. Put that way, the demand seemed reasonable, but of course there remained the "history of events leading to the Great War." None of her neighbors had aggressive designs against her; even if they did, the Covenant and Locarno protected Germany. Financially she was in no position to rearm. Why then, did she wish to?

> To discover a motive it is only necessary to remember that the principle aim of German foreign policy is to release herself from the shackles of the Treaty of Versailles and to recover all that she has lost. Part of her desires have been accomplished....The next item in the political programme is the readjustment of the Eastern frontier. This is a much harder nut to crack. There is not the smallest reason for Germany to hope that she can recover the Polish 'corridor' or the Silesian mines, or Posen, by purely peaceful means, since to Poland the territorial cessions involved signify a national disaster of the

first magnitude, the loss of that direct access to the sea which, rightly or wrongly, is regarded in Poland as indispensable, and economic assets essential to the financial structure of the nation....Yet, according to all accounts, official and unofficial, the readjustment of the Eastern frontier is the supreme desire of every good German.[105]

This, then, was the sticking point; appeasement had taken care of the problems of reparations and the Rhineland occupation, mainly at the expense of the powers making the concessions. Germany's next demand was for the life-line of a nation. This memorandum suggested that, while Britain had not committed itself to Poland, it could not ignore a German attack.

Hankey knew that Britain needed a policy, but he suggested the League of Nations rather than a military commitment as the solution:

Before our policy is finally and irrevocably decided, it appears important to obtain an appreciation, based on the best information available...as to the trend of Germany's military policy. An attitude that is well-suited to a country whose statements can be relied on at their face value may be wholly inappropriate to a Germany that is meditating an aggressive policy on her Eastern frontier....For an unrepentant Germany it might be necessary to consider a much more drastic policy: not war, or the use of force, but steps such as bringing her before the Hague Court and exposing her attitude to the force of the League's main weapon, namely the full glare of the public opinion of the world.[106]

Ultimately, however, the problem demanded Anglo-French firmness:

There is probably only one way in which the German ambitions to rectify the Eastern Frontier, which are such a danger to the peace of Europe, could be permanently checked, and that is by very drastic and loyal concerted action by the United Kingdom and France. We should have to say very firmly to Germany: 'You were put in a short-waistcoat at the Treaty of Versailles because you started the war of 1914, and to prevent you from repeating the process. So far as we can judge you are threatening to do the same all over again....We quite admit that the Treaty of Versailles cannot last forever and that sooner or later it must be superseded. In principle, therefore, we are in favour of your claim to equality, but in the interests of peace we simply dare not concede it until your people show a change of heart.'[107]

To back up such words, Britain would have to be prepared along with France to reoccupy the Rhineland. However, British public opinion would not tolerate "that kind of action, or indeed any firm action."

In these circumstances, Hankey's advice to the Chief of the Imperial General Staff was ambiguous:

For the maintenance of peace...there is only one nation that is sufficiently detached and sufficiently detached and sufficiently respected to act effectively. Everyone really knows, after the experience of the last War, that the side on which the United Kingdom throws its weight must win. So long, therefore, as we keep clear of entanglements we may be able to act as a balancing force to maintain the peace. For that, however, we must maintain our weight and our strength. Consequently, though no doubt we will do our part in any Disarmament Treaty that may be entered into, we ought at least to ensure that, within whatever limits of strength are assigned to us, our forces are fully efficient. To put it brutally, I rather hope that you will tell them not to let the services down too far and not to starve whatever force we have, as we have been starved in recent years.[108]

Faced with an increasingly threatening Germany, Hankey wavered between reliance on the moral force of the League and reliance on armed forces.

Despite the growing need for Anglo-French cooperation, the former allies remained divided. In December 1932, the Chamber of Deputies rejected Herriot's proposal that France pay its war debts to the United States; wondering whether France would "ever... realise her responsibilities to enable Europe to settle down," MacDonald wrote to Tyrrell:

I give you no official instructions, not even advice; but...you should talk to somebody of importance, like Herriot, and say that during the last twelve months the self-centered policy of France, with elections and defeats of governments and so on, at such a time has been a cause of the greatest disquiet to the very best friends of France on our side, and is giving us increasing difficulty both as regards public opinion outside and the more-or-less mischievous sections of the Opposition....The delay in Disarmament, the jeopardy in which Lausanne has been put, and the almost supreme futility of the more recent conversations at Geneva, have all been owing to France. That is undoubtedly the view of growing numbers of the people in this country, and if cordial co-operation is to remain France really ought to take steps to put an end to all these uncertainties.[109]

Tyrrell replied that his hope did not "lie so much in the sermons delivered to the politicians" as in France's growing financial problems: "when the franc is in danger France will become sane and give up her narrow insular policy of isolation and take her share in the rebuilding of the world." He did have to admit, however, that "at present her tactics are inducing the Americans to become less rigid in the extraction of their pound of flesh."[110]

Even if many in Britain had recognized the German danger and the need for cooperation with France, a diversity of opinion still existed. T.P. Conwell-Evans, a university professor teaching in Königsberg, East Prussia, wrote to Ramsay MacDonald that his observations led him to believe that war was very likely: "I am convinced myself that unless a complete change occurs in the relations of the Great Powers which gives Germany hope of peaceful revision, a clash is inevitable. Until I came here, I was beginning to believe, after my studies of the League, that war was very improbable. I now regret to think that it looks a *most probable contingency*. The Germans will never 'give in' on the Corridor question."[111]

Security for Britain, however, lay not in cooperation with France, but with the Germans, with whom the British shared greater similarities:

> The Entente Cordiale is to-day, as it was from 1904-1914, a most illusory means of security. It merely helps to support a jerry built status quo. I firmly believe that a close understanding between Britain and Germany is a much more effective means of security. It would at once weaken the disastrous French influence in Eastern Europe, and give emphasis to the Anglo-German ideas of federalism as opposed to centralised state principles so dear to the French. The Germans are honest, reliable and truthful, they have great ability and energy, they have a great future; we would benefit greatly commercially and otherwise in a common understanding. The League of Nations will never work without such a change in relations. The Germans distrust it absolutely as a French institution.[112]

The First World War had done little for Anglo-French relations, as Robert Graves attested in *Good-bye to All That* (1929). A feeling of antipathy towards France, practically a feature of British political culture, operated at the highest levels. The feeling would have been mutual for the French, save for the fact that those French who felt an even stronger dislike for the Germans recognized the need for Anglo-French cooperation.

While the evidence was sufficient to convince policy makers of the need for such cooperation in the early 1930s, the German situation remained unpredictable. For those who sought them, "glimmers of hope" appeared, even in late 1932. The *Economist* reported one observer's impression that Germany was "once more travelling on the up-grade." While this would not be perceptible among Germany's poor, who constituted a majority of the population; the change was more noticeable among the middle and upper classes. Increased buying power for the Reichsmark was one reason; but the German bourgeoisie was also, for the first time in three or four years, "seeing a glimmer of economic light."[113] The article reasoned that sensible, politically-aware Germans were very keen to foster these signs of recovery; fearful of the "social menace" of unemployment, the chief goal of any government — and all social classes — had to be to restore jobs, a goal which for the moment superseded the traditional capitalist pursuit of profits. To that end, the appointment of General von Schleicher was reassuring: "On the whole, then, the present mood of the German people and the German chancellor is a mood of sober common sense; and this is a psychological asset of inestimable importance, not only for Germany, but for the world."[114] Of course, certain thorny problems remained — *Gleichberechtigung*, rearmament, the Eastern borders — but such political questions needed to be set aside for the moment:

> In Germany, as in the rest of the world, the problem of depression and unemployment puts all political problems into the shade. But if Germany and the world recover, these awkward political questions will re-emerge. If we are wise, we shall show sufficient faith in the prospects of recovery to prepare for its awkward, as well as for its desirable, consequences in good time. The folly of attempting to discriminate against a great nation in perpetuity must be undone while there is still time to do it peaceably.[115]

In other words, appeasement of Germany ought to take place now, while the risk of war was low.

The reader may detect a certain amount of wishful thinking in this article, for example, a tendency to assume that ultimately the German middle classes, like their British counterparts, would act sensibly. Indeed, in late 1932, the Nazis' fortunes were waning somewhat.[116] The article also underscored the point that in December 1932 Germany's future was as uncertain as ever. Hitler became chancellor just one month later, but he did not yet represent what observers most feared about Germany. Their greatest concern remained that those forces which had controlled the country before the Great War would regain control of an economic and military giant. They did not see Hitler as "Old Adam" incarnate; his relationship with the guardians of that spirit was not clear to them, and in most cases they underestimated both his potential and his power.

Notes

1. *Documents diplomatiques français 1932-1939* (hereafter DDF), series I, volume 1, no. 76, François-Poncet to Herriot, Berlin, July 28, 1932, p. 732.
2. *Diplomacy* (New York, 1994), p. 276.
3. Horace Rumbold papers (HR) 36/79-84, Rumbold to King George V, Berlin, October 24, 1928.
4. HR 36/96-102, Rumbold to Lord Stamfordham, Berlin, November 15, 1928. In this letter Rumbold also disagreed with Stamfordham's suggestion that the French disliked the British even more than they did the Germans.
5. FO 800/263/67-72, Walford Selby on the European situation, November 23, 1928.
6. Vansittart Papers (hereafter VNST) 1/1, "An Aspect of International Relations," May 1930.
7. Ibid.
8. Ibid.

9. Mitchell, *European Historical Statistics*, pp. 421-22.

10. VNST 1/1.

11. JO, Chambre, session extraordinaire, tome unique, p. 630, December 4, 1928.

12. Ibid.

13. MAE, series Z (1918-1929), Austria 82/43-50, P. de Margerie to A. Briand, Berlin, December 6, 1928.

14. FO 425/403/87, Memorandum: the Foreign Policy of His Majesty's Government, April 8, 1929; Mowat, pp. 132, 166.

15. FO 425/403/87 (Memorandum cited above).

16. KNAT 1/5/1-9 (Diary), January 1, 1929.

17. Ibid.

18. HR 36/145-150, H. Rumbold to R. Lindsay (secret), Berlin, January 3, 1929.

19. Ibid.

20. FO 408/54/1, Nicolson to Henderson, Berlin, June 28, 1929.

21. FO 408/54/19.

22. WO 32/3591, note by P.W. Gosset, Berlin, October 16, 1929.

23. FO 840/6/5/8, Report by Col. F.W. Gosset, Berlin, August 9, 1929, sent by Nicolson to Henderson.

24. Ibid.

25. E.W. Bennett, *German Rearmament and the West, 1932-1933* (Princeton, 1979), pp. 78-85.

26. M. Gilbert, *Sir Horace Rumbold: Portrait of a Diplomat* (London, 1973), pp. 231, 322-329; F.L. Carsten, *Britain and the Weimar Republic* (New York, 1984), pp. 233-236, 258-262.

27. Based on F.L. Carsten's work in the German archives, published as *The Reichswehr in Politics, 1919-1933* (Oxford, 1966), Neville Waites suggests that the Germany was not sufficiently rearmed before 1933 to pose a threat to European security. G. Castellan's *Le Réarmement clandestin du Reich* (Paris, 1954), presenting French secret service documents attesting a German danger by 1930, is less accurate. N. Waites, ed. *Troubled Neighbours: Franco-British Relations in the Twentieth Century* (London, 1971), p. 155.

28. HR 37/67-72, H. Rumbold to Lord Stonehaven, Berlin, October 10, 1929.

29. PRO 30/69/675/259-61, Rumbold to MacDonald, Berlin, December 13, 1929.

30. *Die Außenpolitik der Republik von Weimar* (Darmstadt, 1985), p. 533.

31. FO 425/404/23, William Tyrrell to A. Henderson, Paris, December 29, 1929.

32. JO, Chambre, sessions extraordinaires, tome 2, December 24, 1929, pp. 1576-7.

33. Ibid., p. 1577.

34. Ibid.

35. Ibid., 2e séance, December 24, 1929, p. 1600.

36. Ibid.

37. Ibid.

38. Ibid.

39. FO 408/54/128 Rumbold to Henderson, Berlin, December 17, 1929.

40. Ibid.

41. Kindleberger, p. 103.

42. VNST 1/1, p.3.

43. N. Rose, *Vansittart: Study of a Diplomat* (London, 1978), pp. 89-90.

44. VNST 1/1, p.4.

45. Ibid., p. 5

46. Ibid.

47. Ibid., pp.5-6.

48. A.J. Nicholls, *Weimar and the Rise of Hitler* (London, 1968), p.148.

49. Brüning did so largely to push the National Socialists into a position where they would reveal that, like everyone else, they could not solve Germany's problems. H. James, "Economic Reasons for the Collapse of the Weimar Republic," in I. Kershaw, ed. *Weimar: Why Did Democracy Fail?* (New York, 1990), p. 51.

50. Poincaré XXII, n.a.fr. 16013/76/7, S. Pichon to Poincaré, August 19, 1930.

51. AC 5/1/515, to Ida, September 20, 1930. Sisters Hilda and Ida were Austen and Neville's closest confidantes, at least as far as their correspondence was concerned.

52. Poincaré XXI, n.a.fr. 16012/68 bis, clipping sent by R. Pazzini to Poincaré, October 6, 1930.

53. PRO 30/69/752/267, Tyrrell to MacDonald, Paris, September 25, 1930.

54. Ibid.

55. MAE, series Z (1930-1940), Germany 713/16-20, Claudel to Briand, Washington, D.C., October 7, 1930.

56. Ibid.

57. Poincaré XV, n.a.fr. 16006/412-413, M. Léon to Poincaré, New York, October 10, 1930.

58. Ibid.

59. Poincaré VI, n.a.fr. 15997/319-320, P. Cot to Poincaré, October 22, 1930.

60. PRO 30/69/676/591, MacDonald to Grahame, March 31, 1930.

61. PRO 30/69/673(1)/50-51, MacDonald to Balfour, October 2, 1930.

62. WO 32/4079, "Some Problems of the World Situation: A Military Appreciation", delivered December 18, 1930.

63. Ibid.

64. Ibid.

65. Ibid.

66. Ibid.

67. Ibid.

68. Ibid.

69. Ibid.

70. Dalton I/13/208-209 (Diary), December 29, 1930.

71. AC 5/1/520, Austen to Hilda Chamberlain, November 9, 1930.

72. LKEN 9 (Diary), June 18, 1930.

73. Ibid., September 24, 1930.

74. Ibid., October 10, 1930.

75. Ibid.

76. Ibid.

77. Ibid.

78. FO 408/57/11, Rumbold to Henderson, Berlin, January 23, 1931.

79. KNAT 1/7/3-8, Note on the European situation at the beginning of 1931, February 5, 1931.

80. Ibid.

81. Ibid.

82. E.W. Bennett, *German Rearmament and the West*, p. 509.

83. DDF, series I, volume 1, no. 65, François-Poncet to Herriot, Berlin, July 27, 1932.

84. DDF, series I, volume 1, no. 76. François-Poncet to Herriot, Berlin, July 28, 1932.

85. DDF, series I, volume 1, no. 128, annex. Note submitted to François-Poncet by the Baron von Neurath, August 29, 1932.

86. PA 89 (Herriot)/29/44, September 3, 1932.

87. For example, MAE, series Z (1930-1940), Germany 713/82-96, Conversation with Major Wittmer, April 27, 1932. Wittmer assured his French interlocutor: "France has nothing to fear from us."

88. CAB 63/43/108-112, November 21, 1930.

89. Ibid.

90. Ibid.

91. Ibid.

92. CAB 63/43/113, C.F.N. Macready to Hankey, November 21, 1930.

93. Quoted in CAB 63/44/3-15, Hankey, The Basis of Service Estimates, January 9, 1931.

94. Ibid.

95. Ibid.

96. Ibid.

97. CAB 63/44/91-107, Brief for the Prime Minister's speech on Disarmament, June 29, 1931 (written by Hankey, June 26). The word 'appeasement' leaps out at today's reader; Hankey used it, of course, without any negative connotation. The French term 'apaisement' was used to describe the policy of Briand, again with the connotation of pacification and conciliation.

98. CAB 63/44/187-200, Note on the task of the National Government, November 21, 1931.

99. CAB 63/44/212-224, notes by Hankey, December 5, 1931.

100. Quoted in CAB 63/46/60-61, Hankey to MacDonald, January 16, 1933.

101. Ibid.

102. PRO 30/69/678(1)/114-122, Hankey to MacDonald, August 22, 1932.

103. PRO 30/69/754/1104, MacDonald to Lillian Wald, July 11, 1932.

104. PA 89 (Herriot)/26 (Journal I)/340-341.

105. CAB 63/45/150-155, memorandum by Hankey, secret, September 29, 1932.

106. Ibid.

107. CAB 63/45/168-174, Hankey to Sir G. Milne, Chief of the Imperial General Staff, October 17, 1932.

108. Ibid.

109. PRO 30/69/678(4)/730-731, MacDonald to Tyrrell, December 16, 1932.

110. PRO 30/69/678(4)/732-734, Tyrrell to MacDonald, December 19, 1932. The U.S. rejected Britain's token payment offer. Duroselle, *France and the United States*, p. 129.

111. PRO 30/69/678(2)/270-274, Conwell-Evans to MacDonald, Königsberg, January 2, 1933.

112. Ibid.

113. *The Economist*, December 24, 1932, p. 1185.

114. Ibid.

115. Ibid.

116. Harold James suggests that the National Socialist movement had been in trouble for a few months when Hindenburg named Hitler chancellor. He also writes that the trough of the depression in Germany was the summer of 1932, so the economy was indeed on the "up-grade." in I. Kershaw, ed., *Weimar: Why did Germany Democracy Fail?*, pp. 51-53.

4

Britain, France and
the League of Nations

Benesh made one capital remark, that the League would be much better when it did not live in constant enthusiasm.
— Leo Kennedy[1]

The Great War hardly had begun when Theodore Roosevelt, outraged by Germany's violation of Belgian neutrality, wrote that "the time ought to be ripe for the nations to consider a great world agreement among all the civilized military powers to *back righteousness by force*. Such an agreement would establish an efficient world league for the peace of righteousness."[2] The same moral imperative drove the efforts of his political rival, Woodrow Wilson, towards the establishment of the League of Nations at the end of the war. Yet the organization that emerged from the peace talks played an ambiguous role in European and world politics, and certainly never wielded a big stick. That ambiguity finally destroyed an organization which had aspired to take on the most fundamental role of government, to protect citizens against aggression.

To succeed the "new diplomacy" would need the support of all the world's major powers. But the United States never joined, and Soviet Russia did not join until 1934, by which time Japan and Germany had quit. Britain and France therefore controlled the League. Though they shared an interest in maintaining peace and stability in the world, their resources were finite, and the use of these resources remained governed by their own national and imperial interests. Leaders also clashed over the purpose and methods of the new diplomacy.

Exactly how the League would preserve peace remained a question throughout its existence, even to its strongest advocates. For Radical and Socialist French politicians, schooled in the spirit of positivism, the League had to provide security in material form, confronting would-be aggressors with the prospect of punishment by sanctions and military force. However, for Robert Cecil and many of his colleagues in Britain's League of Nations Union, the League confronted would-be aggressors with the deterrent force of "world public opinion"; members would think twice before shaming themselves in the eyes of the world, while all nations reaped the benefits of an inexpensive, non-military security system.[3] These conflicting visions of the League coexisted, creating a system of flexible response on the one hand, but guaranteeing no one's security on the other.

Nevertheless, during the 1920s, the League successfully managed relations among the successor states lying to the east of Germany and Italy. Britain and France shared an interest in stabilizing the region, and the fact that the League was a conduit for loans to many of these fledgling states enhanced its authority.[4] In November 1927, for example, it forced Poland and Lithuania to end the war between them.[5] The League also restrained Hungary and Romania from fighting over disputed territory. It could claim success even in a dispute involving a larger power, the case of Italy's aggression against Corfu in 1923.[6]

The great test of the early 1930s, however, was Japan's aggression against China. The crisis tested the machinery of the League as well as its claim to be a world organization; the League failed on both counts. First, the conquest of Manchuria and the violence in Shanghai discredited the belief that decent and responsible League members honored their solemn pledges; confronted by "world public opinion" — albeit with little talk of sanctions, let alone force — Japan, instead of withdrawing from Manchuria, withdrew from the League. Secondly, the League could not handle this problem alone; Japanese expansion threatened British and French interests in the Far East, but it also affected the United States and the Soviet Union.

As for the impact of the Manchurian crisis on Europe, Christopher Thorne has refuted the arguments of those who have argued that the League's failure to punish Japan gave the green light to Mussolini and Hitler.[7] True, a system of collective security and close vigilance might have stopped them, but such a system did not exist before or after the crisis. In any case, Hitler and Mussolini did not believe in the League. Their plans had to anticipate the likely reactions of Britain and France, not the League.

Japan's actions coincided with final preparations for and the beginning of the long-awaited Disarmament Conference. The League Covenant itself implied that the arms races led to war, and that unscrupulous private manufacturers engineered wars for their own personal profit.[8] The Central Powers had been disarmed at the end of the Great War, with vague assurances that the Allies would follow suit eventually. Preparations for the Conference began in the happy days following the Locarno agreements, but, by the time the conference finally began — six years later — neither Britain nor France could subscribe to the League philosophy. British leaders already had allowed imperial defenses to fall to a state where certain colonies, such as Singapore, lay quite vulnerable. Even in France, which took the German threat much more seriously, domestic pressures also threatened military budgets, and military leaders struggled to maintain an adequate, albeit exclusively defensive, posture.

The League of Nations, insufficiently empowered to carry out its chief task, became an obstacle in the process of securing peace in Europe. Many politicians and diplomats did not share, let alone trust, Geneva's perspective on European and world politics. Yet no one could attack an organization founded for such noble purposes, and Britian and France participated actively in the League's work. The League's "righteous" approach to international relations created divisions among important sections of opinion, however; advocates of this "new style" of diplomacy looked askance at the "old style" which nonetheless remained the default mode for diplomacy.

The Machinery of the League

During the interwar years, the League may have represented righteousness (albeit in a chauvinistic or circumscribed form)[9], but it failed to confront potential aggressors with a plausible deterrent. The root of this problem lay not so much in the language of the League's Covenant as in the apparent unwillingness of its members to clarify and follow the outlined procedures. The organization attempted to make nations liable for their actions in the international arena; to that end, article 10 of the League's Covenant called on members to "respect and preserve as against external aggression the territorial integrity and existing political independence of all members of the League." Member nations pledged to submit disputes for arbitration or judicial settlement, as described in articles 12, 13 and 15. Finally, article 16 called for economic sanctions against members that resorted to war in violation of the Covenant; it also allowed for military, naval or air action to be taken to "protect" the Covenant.[10] Yet French efforts to give the League "teeth" — to develop the actual means by which force would be brought to bear — had met with strong resistance throughout the 1920s, most significantly from Britain. The League's most attractive quality was its goal of preserving peace. Yet the desire to prevent another major war — which many believed would destroy civilization — blunted the instrument by which a just peace was to be maintained: collective security.

Related to the problem of enforcement was the problem of the League's place in the complex of international relations. The League of Nations was an attempt to bring order to an "anarchical society"[11]: a world in which sovereign nation-states interacted with one another but were responsible to no higher authority. The League's obvious failures overshadowed the progress it made toward what Hedley Bull described as the "international society": those aspects of human activity and a general sense of common interests that transcend national frontiers.[12] It did valuable work in such areas as assistance to refugees and the establishment of international standards for working conditions. In an era of nationalism and hypernationalism, the League suggested, however timidly, an alternate path.

But confidence in the League and the new style of diplomacy for which it stood was incomplete. Therefore, despite the negative cast "secret diplomacy" had been given by Wilson's Fourteen Points, the diplomats of the League's larger members, Britain, France and Germany, carried on much of their work in the old style, even in Geneva. The League obviously could not handle every dimension of international relations, but diplomatic successes such as Locarno, despite polite nods in the direction of Geneva, detracted from any League claim to be the sole way of peace.

Britain and the League

In April 1928 Sir Eric Drummond, secretary general of the League since the post had been created, wrote to Robert Cecil that he hoped the Kellogg Pact discussions would result in "good things for the League," because "otherwise the general outlook does not seem to me to be very bright, and I fear that we may be in for a period of stagnation, if not re-action, in international affairs generally. If so, I do not think that we can do anything better for the League than just go on."[13] From his own experience, he knew how little of the work of liquidating the war had been entrusted to the League.

Drummond himself and the position he occupied reflected the reserve with which the League's founders had framed the organization. They originally had planned to establish a chancellorship to be filled by a worthy head of state, but, fearful of what a charismatic figure might be able to do with such an office, they reduced the title to "secretary general" and sought to fill it with a high-ranking civil servant. Maurice Hankey received the first offer, but he chose not to give up his considerable influence in Britain for a position with powers yet untested. The position went to Drummond, a competent but uninspiring figure.[14]

British attitudes towards the work of the League were divided, but not entirely along party lines. Conservative governments in Britain had rejected initiatives in 1923 and 1924 that would have given the League greater resources with which to back up the "force of world public opinion." They resisted French-led efforts to create a "sanctionist" League, stressing instead the League's role as a forum for conciliation.[15] This caused some embarrassment to more enthusiastic supporters, particularly since the 1924 initiative had been an attempt by the short-lived Labour government to make amends for Britain's rejection of the Draft Treaty of Mutual Assistance. Yet Ramsay MacDonald himself was uncomfortable with the Geneva Protocol, which allowed for the use of League-controlled force as a last resort.[16]

Robert Cecil, a Conservative but also a spiritual father of the League, resigned from the Cabinet in 1927 over what he perceived to be a philosophical difference of opinion over disarmament. His departure drew criticism of the government from small-power delegates to the League; looking to the Great Powers to create a secure world, they charged Britain with "dilatoriness on matters of disarmament."[17] But Britain's vacillations extended beyond matters of disarmament. Austen Chamberlain had explained Britain's relationship to the League in a speech before the assembly: "He said that his devotion to the League, great though it was, could never supersede his devotion to that older League, the British Empire, recalled the magnitude of the obligation undertaken by Britain at Locarno, and added that it was asking the impossible to invite Great Britain to take for every country and every frontier the guarantee given at Locarno."[18] The speech repudiated the principle of collective security, which without British participation would be a good deal less collective. Despite British resistance, the League established a new security commission, and the Council set about asking each member nation what forces they could contribute if the League found it necessary to combat aggression.[19]

Though it refused to make the League an instrument of collective security, Britain had become its greatest financial power. Between 1923 and 1927, Britain provided major loans to Austria, Hungary, Greece, Bulgaria, Estonia and Danzig through the League. France's financial instability before 1926 kept it from issuing similar loans; but even after Poincaré stabilized the franc, Bank of England governor Montagu Norman suspected that French financiers pursued "a separate policy of political loans in Europe." By 1932, Britain had lent £40 million, compared to France's £2 million.[20]

Continuing to act as lender of last resort until its own financial crisis in 1931, Britain used the League as a proxy.[21] The benefits for the prestige of the League were obvious, but the Bank of England's motives were not entirely idealistic.[22] In contrast both to the desire to dissociate Britain from European politics and to its own pre-war insularity, the Bank sought to foster international contacts, especially with U.S. financiers, in order to hasten the financial and economic reconstruction of Europe. Britain's economic health depended upon European recovery, i.e., the revival of international trade and the linkage of European currencies through the gold standard. By providing loans through the League, Britain minimized the risk of arousing jealousies; the League thus provided an ideal forum for central bank cooperation. The fact that the United States was not a member of the League did not hinder American financiers, many of whom shared an interest in Europe's financial recovery.[23]

However, objections to increases in League expenditures dampened the effects of British generosity. Austen Chamberlain, for example, had complained about an increase of £1,500 in the budget of the Health Organization.[24] In 1928 British delegates joined forces with their Italian colleagues in an attempt to cap the League's total annual budget at £1 million.[25] In the midst of the difficulties raised by the Disarmament Conference and the Manchurian crisis, Ramsay MacDonald's National Government raised yet another protest over the high cost of international organizations; it "viewed with anxiety" the increase in the combined budgets of the League, the International Labor Organization, and the Permanent Court at the Hague, which in fact had increased from $5 million in 1923 to $6.33 million in 1931.[26]

In the absence of wholehearted support from His Majesty's Government, the League found its most enthusiastic British support in a private organization, the League of Nations Union. With about 600,000 members in 1928, the Union was the largest and best-organized pro-League movement in the world, but its influence on Whitehall and Westminster was small.[27] In part because civil servants and politicians paid little attention to the Union, inconsistencies of philosophy among its members went unchallenged. No one dissented from the view that the chief purpose of the League was to prevent war, but opinions varied as to how this was to be accomplished. Key members, including Robert Cecil, would change their opinions over the years. Cecil acted as Britain's moral conscience, but few leaders possessed the patience to engage him on specific issues.

In October 1928, Gilbert Murray, Regius Professor of Classics at Oxford University and Chairman of the Union's Executive Committee, wrote to Ramsay MacDonald about the dangers that another Conservative government would pose to the peace of Europe: "It makes me miserable to see your friends and mine so eagerly cooperating to put the Tories back. I fear they will succeed, and then God help Europe!...I don't think the Tories can bring about a war in the next five years, but I do think they may reduce the League to a sort of diplomatic Concert of the Great Powers, and start an economic conflict that may be almost impossible to stop."[28]

MacDonald's reply echoed Murray's concern: "You are of course right in thinking that there cannot be another war within the next five years, but I am back from the Continent very distressed about the general militarist tendencies there for which we are mainly responsible."[29] But MacDonald himself felt little enthusiasm for the League. That the Labour government of 1929-1931 drew nearer to the League than had its Conservative predecessor was due to the efforts of its foreign secretary, Arthur Henderson, who often found himself at odds with MacDonald and the Chancellor of the Exchequer, Philip Snowden.[30]

Though inexperienced in the conduct of foreign affairs, Henderson had a clear sense of what he hoped to accomplish as foreign secretary. He faithfully applied Labour party doctrine in his work: a commitment to the ideal of world government, to be achieved gradually through the rule of international law; support for the resolution of disputes by judicial means; and a commitment to disarmament as a means of reducing the dangers of war, though states were entitled to defend themselves, collectively if necessary.[31] Members that failed to cooperate with the process of compulsory arbitration would be subject to economic sanctions. Military force could be used as a last resort, but only by a League force that pooled the resources of largely disarmed members.[32] Henderson came closer to sharing the French vision of the League than any other major politician in Britain.[33]

On September 19, 1929 Henderson signed the Optional Clause, by which signatories promised to submit disputes that could be resolved judicially to the Permanent Court at the Hague.[34] He did so with the reservation that disputes within the Empire would not be subject.[35] Henderson was an unexpected success at Geneva, where the tenth Assembly had begun with an address by MacDonald, whose speech displayed a typical British coolness toward the League.[36] Henderson's policies enjoyed considerable public support, but his alacrity was not representative of the government as a whole, and he could do little else to strengthen the League during these comparatively peaceful years. If MacDonald left Henderson to his own devices in Geneva, he did so knowing that the extent of Britain's commitments were clear.[37] Britain, with its own imperial and world interests to defend and a declining capacity to do so, would not commit itself to vital League interests unless they coincided with its own perceived vital interests. With a burgeoning independence movement in India and similar troubles in Egypt, British leaders did not wish to see their authority diminished through the further empowerment of international tribunals.

Henderson took Cecil, still officially a Conservative, into the Foreign Office as chairman of the Committee on League Affairs. Philip Noel-Baker, another Union member, became Henderson's personal private secretary, and Hugh Dalton, also a friend of Cecil, became parliamentary undersecretary. This core of League support within the Foreign Office was isolated, however, from politicians and civil servants alike. The personal animosity between Henderson and the prime minister diminished the effect of his efforts. Snowden was overtly hostile to Cecil and the Union. The armed services also showed little regard for the League. The Union, meanwhile, distrusted Maurice Hankey, the most influential member of the Civil Service.[38] Among the Foreign Office professional staff, Robert Vansittart, appointed permanent undersecretary by Henderson in 1930 (under pressure from MacDonald), was an improvement on his predecessor Ronald Lindsay, who had infuriated Henderson by communicating with MacDonald behind his back; Vansittart, though, occasionally did the same.[39] After leaving the Foreign Office, Henderson became president of the Disarmament Conference. For his efforts, Henderson would win the Nobel Peace Prize in 1934, even though the conference had failed.

Even though Arthur Henderson and Robert Cecil, bolstered by the prestige of high government office, promoted the League, British support for the League remained narrowly circumscribed. The League's fortunes did not seem to improve with greater support from a few important British officials. In October 1930 the *Economist* took stock of the League's difficulties, after the Eleventh Assembly adjourned with a pessimistic speech by Cecil.[40] The League, the article said, faced the most difficult political task of all time:

> The supreme difficulty of our generation — a difficulty which underlies the war problem, the unemployment problem, the gold problem, and every other problem with which we are beset — is that our achievements on the economic plane of life have outstripped our progress on the political plane to such an extent that our economics and our politics are perpetually falling out of gear with one another. On the economic

plane, the world has been organised into a single, all-embracing unit of activity. On the political plane, it has not only remained partitioned into sixty or seventy sovereign national States, but the national units have been growing smaller and more numerous and the national consciousnesses more acute. The tension between these two antithetical tendencies has been producing a series of jolts and jars and smashes in the social life of humanity, and the smash which pushed us into founding the League — the Great War of 1914-1918 — was not a unique catastrophe.[41]

The League had been founded to prevent another such catastrophic war, in which national political interests had been allowed to overtake the greater interest of international economic efficiency and prosperity. Yet it seemed unable to control these passions.

The League's chief failure in its first ten years of existence, and the grounds for its current pessimism, was that "it has certainly not eliminated the danger of war between Great Powers, that is, it has not made life safe against the only kind of war which is capable, nowadays, of bringing catastrophe upon the world at large." The problem lay in the general outlook of its members. The writer faulted the French specifically for obstructing the "League's activities in every sphere":

The ground for pessimism lies rather in the general temper and outlook of the statesmen and parties who are in the ascendant in certain great countries. The symptom that is really alarming is the persistence, or recrudescence, of the belief that national interests can best be served by a policy of 'sacred egoism'; and the most ominous instance of this attitude is its prevalence in France. We can understand it in Germany and Italy, whose statesmen would like to see drastic changes in the present political disposition of the world. In a country which has everything to lose by change and everything to gain by the establishment of a political world-order which rules out change by violence, a nationalist policy is such a piece of perversity that it becomes a rather terrifying portent.[42]

Particularly troubling, he wrote, was French opposition to efforts at enabling the League to suppress slavery. In the area of economics and humanitarian causes the League had a strong record, and "was swimming with the tide" of international cooperation. The French attitude was therefore more damaging than might initially appear to be the case: "a small setback for the League in its humanitarian and economic work may be a ground for greater disquiet than a much more sensational setback to its efforts after peace and disarmament."[43]

Yet France could not afford to ignore the League, the article continued. The League's rivals in 1920 — the Supreme Council of the Allies and the Conference of Ambassadors, Prime Ministers and Foreign

Ministers — had since yielded to Geneva. But while the League had become the forum for the discussion of international politics, the Covenant had hardly been expanded. Little had been built upon the foundations: "When we measure the growth of the League during its first decade we cannot help being disappointed to find how small this has been, or disturbed to see how vigorous and wide-awake the opposition is apt to be nowadays whenever any question arises of completing the original plan."[44]

The *Economist* did not speak for the British government; its criticisms of French behavior at Geneva no doubt reflected reality, though it might just as well have levelled similar criticisms at its own government. The League was a product of British and French policy; more specifically, it reflected the difficulties in Anglo-French relations in the 1920s. Unable to agree on a mutually satisfactory formula for postwar order, Britain and France both were dissatisfied or disenchanted with the League by the end of the decade.

Nevertheless the League was a fact of international political life. Old-school diplomat Horace Rumbold's assessment of the German-Polish border dispute demonstrated little faith in the League's capacity to handle serious problems:

> It has been common knowledge for many years past that Germany will try for a revision of her eastern frontiers at as early a date as possible. The question is how is such a revision to be effected, since the Germans have undertaken to abstain from endeavouring to bring it about by forcible means. One way would be recourse to the Council of the League, but any recommendations on the subject would require unanimity and I do not yet see the Poles consenting to a revision of the Treaty arrangements concerning the corridor and Danzig.[45]

First of all, German membership in the League reinforced the hope that Germany would not seek to solve its dispute with Poland by force. Secondly, Polish membership on the League Council would prevent that body from resolving the problem. Though the League clearly was a factor, it was not part of the solution Rumbold envisioned: "...only direct negotiations between the interested parties could bring about such a revision and there is nothing inherently improbable in the Germans eventually trying to rope in France with a view to the latter applying pressure to Poland to be accommodating on the subject."[46]

The formation of the National Government ended Henderson's tenure as foreign secretary. Neither Lord Reading nor Sir John Simon shared his enthusiasm for the League; both made clear from the beginning their firm opposition to the application of sanctions against Japan.[47] Two of the

League's great trials, the Manchurian crisis and the Disarmament Conference, combined to make 1932 that organization's *annus terribilis*; they will receive special attention later in the chapter.

France and the League

One of the League's main problems was that a pure version of internationalism did not exist. While the League obviously had its detractors both in Britain and France, even supporters of the League could not cast off the perspectives ingrained in them by education and experience in their own countries. Thus while men like Briand, Joseph Paul-Boncour, Joseph Avenol and René Massigli spoke strongly on behalf of the League, many in Britain saw the French as obstructing the work of the League, particularly in the area of disarmament, and manipulating it to their own ends. To these charges the French could reply that Britain had rejected moves toward making the League the instrument of collective security that would make disarmament possible.

Whereas British leaders pleaded imperial preference in defining Britain's relationship to the League, their French counterparts felt no need to distance themselves in this manner. They were not alarmed by periodic rumblings in Algeria and Indochina, their largest colonies. The colonies did receive attention from the press, particularly as the conquest of Algeria reached its centennial in the early 1930s, but right-wing papers, for example, merely wondered how agitators could be so blind to the benefits of French civilization.[48] Meanwhile, more tangible threats to French civilization existed on their own borders.

The broad coalition supporting Briand's foreign policy during these years embraced the League of Nations as a potential instrument of collective security. Speaking for the Radical and Radical-Socialist groups in the Chamber of Deputies on November 30, 1927, Jean Montigny asked "How can our hopes to consolidate the peace not take refuge in Geneva, when those who are contemptuous and skeptical [of the League] offer us only bloody balance-of-power politics and old diplomatic routines that a hundred times in history have demonstrated their bankruptcy?" The League had yet to be perfected, but Montigny argued that France had signed the Optional Clause already in 1925, and its delegates were now pursuing the question of disarmament, "asking, according to France's logical and constant policy, that security precede disarmament."[49]

In his speech to the Chamber, Briand defended both the Quai d'Orsay and the League. Like Montigny, he explicitly rejected the thesis that disarmament itself would bring peace: "Don't worry about security, they tell us. If you begin by tackling this problem, you'll never get results. Begin by disarming. Let the whole world disarm. As the ministers of national defense disappear, so also will disappear all troops of every form." For Briand, however, this scenario presented the problem of verification. How could each nation be sure that other countries also were disarming? Who would take the bold and risky first move? Briand singled out Soviet Russia for some ironic comment: "I know one country which is completely in favor of disarmament and which M. Cachin [a Communist deputy] presents as the best qualified to regulate this question." Maxim Litvinov had just proposed complete disarmament to the Preparatory Commission; yet in recent months the Red Army had held maneuvers involving 700,000 men. Referring to recent celebrations of the tenth anniversary of the October Revolution, Briand pointed out that armies had marched with their weapons: "they are not ashamed of this army. They have shown it, and they have said to us: 'See its power! See its beauty!'" How, then, could France disarm? "If one disarms under such conditions, what a handicap for nations of good faith, and what an encouragement for those with ulterior motives!"[50] Briand's remarks drew lively applause.

Nevertheless, Briand believed that the League would one day find a formula for peace combining disarmament and security. Clearly he regretted the need both for a hard stance on disarmament and the continued use of traditional forms of diplomacy. He assured the deputies that, if he could reveal to them every dossier and detail concerning the difficult issues of the day, they would see that French efforts were entirely guided by a desire for peace: "With England, who remains [France's] friend (*lively applause*), to whom she remains devoted from the heart and out of gratitude; with Germany, who, I must say, remains faithful to the Locarno accords (*applause from the left and the extreme left*), in all circumstances, France, in this diplomatic collaboration, has worked for peace."[51] Indeed, since the war France had registered every treaty with the secretariat of the League, with the exception of the secret military alliance with Belgium in 1920 (which became public in any case). Though not openly arrived at, French covenants were open.[52]

Briand's assessment of Britain's approach to the League made a virtue out of what he otherwise might have criticized: "The egotism of Great Britain — what is it, other than that national egotism without which a country is lost in international talks?"[53] One could not establish peace among nations, he continued, by seeking to obliterate "everything which gives humanity its character and beauty (*applause*)": "I was moved, I confess, in Geneva, when I saw my dear friend Sir Austen Chamberlain, so loyal, so generous, so devoted to our country...explaining with such frank simplicity the difficulties which the adoption of the protocol would present for that miniature league of nations that is the British Empire."[54] That Chamberlain explained this position before an assembly of forty-seven nations was further testimony to the "beauty of the institution." Briand concluded his speech by stating his confidence that the League would be able to "dissipate the current clouds."[55]

With Briand as director of foreign policy, supported by a solid parliamentary majority, the French government supported the League more enthusiastically than did Britain's Conservative government. Liberal internationalism might work for France in ways which old alliance diplomacy had not, and France was in no position to stand alone in European (let alone world) politics. Given these exigencies, France was less likely than Britain to claim imperial responsibilities as an obstacle to full cooperation with the League.[56] Unlike the British, the French looked beyond their own frontiers for security, and collective security seemed to be a worthwhile experiment in a time of elusive alliances. The French understood that whatever "hegemony" they enjoyed was temporary; visionaries like Briand saw no future in chauvinism for a dependent power, and sought to establish an international basis for peace. Internationalism, thus defined, coincided with national self-interest.

By the beginning of the Disarmament Conference, however, the League had failed to become the guarantee of security that the French had sought ever since the war. German demands for equality of rights alarmed French leaders, who were now being asked to make reductions in their own armaments. An exhausted Briand left the Quai d'Orsay in January 1932, and before the end of that year France had four foreign ministers: Pierre Laval for five weeks, André Tardieu for fifteen weeks, Édouard Herriot for seven months, and finally Joseph Paul-Boncour, who would retain his post through Hitler's first year in power. Each pledged to continue the policies of Briand — even Tardieu, although in his case independent-mindedness and lack of diplomatic skill harmed his credibility. Throughout the troubled years of the early 1930s, French leaders appeared genuinely concerned with the fate of the League; ironically, this concern led them to attempt to keep the Manchurian issue away from the League.[57] As for disarmament, fiscal constraints were beginning to suggest the desirability of cuts in military spending; but German behavior simultaneously suggested that such cuts might be an unaffordable luxury.

Disarmament

The Disarmament Conference took place at a time when the partly sunny skies of the late 1920s had long since darkened: "'Tis cold, 'tis cold, and clouds shut out the view" wrote Ramsay MacDonald to French premier Herriot in September 1932.[58] League supporters asserted that arms races, sponsored by avaricious private manufacturers, caused wars; disarmament, therefore, was the foundation of security. Many British and French leaders (not to mention their potential adversaries) had difficulty accepting this faith. How, for example, could France disarm when the political situation in Germany was deteriorating, and their army remained the best (and perhaps only) means of guaranteeing security? The League was not yet a reliable instrument of collective security, but it proceeded as if it were. For Britain, too, the Disarmament Conference occurred just as leaders began to recognize a need to bolster rather than reduce defenses.

With the question of disarmament, the League penetrated the realm of its members' national security. Between 1925 and 1933, disarmament was at the top of the League's agenda. In December 1925 the Preparatory Commission on Disarmament had begun to address the task mandated by article 8 of the Covenant.[59] To examine the work of this commission between 1925 and the beginning of the Disarmament Conference in February 1932 would be a monumentally dull exercise, but a survey of attitudes towards disarmament and expectations of the upcoming conference evokes the mentality of the time. The length of the preliminary negotiations was in itself a bad sign; moreover, during this time the political situation in Europe deteriorated to the point where the Conference, which could not simply be cancelled because of the great expectations felt by public and politicians alike, took place in a grim environment, amidst metaphors of darkening skies and gathering storm-clouds.

The Preparatory Commission met intermittently in sessions lasting about a month, but repeatedly failed to come up with a draft convention agreeable to all member nations. The November 30, 1927 session was notable for the arrival of outside participation from the United States and the Soviet Union. The Soviet delegation, headed by Maximilian Litvinov, promptly proposed the abolition of all weapons, armed forces and military organizations, a plan attractive for its simplicity but which was fatally "relegated to the commission's next meeting."[60] Advocates of disarmament were embarrassed by the proceedings; in April 1928, Philip Noel-Baker wrote to Cecil that the last meeting had been "a complete and possibly disastrous fiasco. The world was presented with the spectacle of the Great Powers resolved to do nothing..."[61]

Finally, however, a Draft Convention was completed in 1930. Without discussing numbers, the Preparatory Commission established a formula for arms reduction and agreed on the definitions of a number of terms which could be variously interpreted.[62] Negotiators had taken four and a half years to reach this point. Agreement on a formula did not commit powers to reductions and limits; the final numbers would, however, and the arduous process of deciding what those numbers should be had not yet begun.

Preparation had begun not long after the celebratory fireworks at Locarno; by the time the actual conference began in February 1932, a different spirit had taken hold in Europe. The *Times* was not hopeful:

> There looms before the League this year a problem with an even wider spread [than Manchuria]. The nations are to send their delegates to Geneva to a Disarmament Conference, from which much is hoped and which for many months has occupied a large place in the public mind....French insistence on security, then, as often, set forth, is a relic of France's memory of two great wars. This, together with the reciprocal anxieties of other nations, contributing to the general fear, forms the obstacle which the peoples of the world, probably without exception, would rejoice to see removed.[63]

The *Times* saw French anxiety as a "relic" of the old warlike mentality which impeded progress towards universal peace. At the same time, it overlooked the warlike behavior of revisionist powers which occasioned that anxiety. The *Times* even mentioned the growing Nazi movement in Germany, as well as the war in China: but it did not ask whether Germans who voted for National Socialist candidates did so in order to remove those unfortunate suspicions that persisted among the peoples of Europe; and Japan's invasion of Manchuria merely demonstrated an impulse with which Britain and other colonial powers could identify. The chaos in China was "embarrassing to nations with substantial interests" in that country. Japan therefore "felt bound to protect by force both her prestige and her material concerns," presenting the League with "an awkward problem."[64]

Many of those who arrived in Geneva for the conference commented on the atmosphere they encountered there. In happier days, the outlook from this cosmopolitan city had helped to convince Briand of the possibility of European Union. British Air Minister Londonderry could not describe what was different about the place: "I find the complete League of Nations atmosphere very interesting, but I am fully conscious that it is quite a different atmosphere to any other, and I should say that there is always the danger of getting a disproportionate view."[65] Perhaps it was a sign of the times that the atmosphere at Geneva inspired caution instead of hope.

Le Temps made the French position clear, stating that the conference was beginning "in an atmosphere not exactly favorable to the absolute mutual confidence" necessary for a positive outcome. With China and Japan at war, powers with Far Eastern interests had to protect their nationals. Closer to home, Hitler's agitation had "poisoned the international atmosphere." Germany's actions in 1931 — the announcement of a customs union with Austria, the refusal to pay reparations, the campaign against the military clauses of the Treaty of Versailles and the campaign for revision of the eastern borders — made it necessary for those who were the "most confident in an organization of the peace to take up the question of disarmament only with the greatest circumspection....Disarmament must be and can be only a consequence of established security."[66]

André Tardieu arrived confidently in Geneva as a delegate to the Conference, having become War Minister in January after André Maginot's death. This visit was his first to the League of Nations, but he threw himself into the work of the conference with characteristic aplomb; inspired by cold logic, he drew a plan for an international force which would make disarmament possible. He had little patience for the Geneva "style": Paul-Boncour later remembered that "his temperament was rather averse to the slowness, to the oratorical precautions, to the somewhat pious phraseology in use there."[67] He accused the Assembly of too often having taken the "course of least resistance," and proposed that disarmament be accompanied by the creation of a "preventive and defensive" army.[68] Only then could the League provide security for its members. The response was enthusiastic, but only briefly; delegates "were not *that* serious about disarmament."[69]

Leo Kennedy of the *Times* met Sir John Simon in the hallway at the Hotel Beau Rivage, "and a few words with him showed me that he was against [Tardieu's] project, though he doesn't feel inclined to say so."[70] A few days later they spoke on the train to Paris, and again Kennedy was struck and bothered by Simon's extreme reluctance to draw conclusions:

[Simon] said 'if I liked, I could simply annihilate [the supranational army idea] by criticism' — he proceeded to do so, merely taking up 2 or 3 points, but showing conclusively how impossible the scheme is. Yet he didn't say 'we can't have it', or commit himself against it. All the train of his thought, however, was hostile to it. He pointed out many absurdities, and although the League of Nations Union apparently bombards him with requests to consider it favourably, he believes...that public opinion...would not accept it. I certainly have done my best to give him this impression.[71]

Kennedy, of course, wanted Simon to reject the idea forcefully, and he apparently had few qualms about seeking to influence the foreign secretary.[72] Yet he understood that outright rejection might ruin the chances of getting the French delegation to agree to any measure of disarmament.

Tardieu's logic may have been unassailable, but his proposal was unlikely to solidify the Entente between France and Britain which he claimed had been reestablished. British delegates faced the problem of rejecting the French proposal without destroying the possibility for some reductions at least. Kennedy wrote that "Simon definitely does not want to be identified with French policy every time," and suggested to Henderson that the time had come for Britain to stand up to France. Henderson replied that as long as France had a right-wing government such an approach would be useless.[73] Indeed, delegates eagerly awaited the French elections in May, which were expected to result in a swing to the left.[74]

British delegates were keenly aware of the fact that America was watching; they still had war debts to pay, and Americans had justified their insistence on payment by contending that the Europeans were spendthrift warmongers. The delegates therefore sought anything that could be called a result, but they had come to Geneva without any bright ideas. After talks with Herriot, Painlevé and Paul-Boncour, MacDonald decided that significant cuts were unlikely; he wrote to Baldwin that the choice was now between a "gesture which we know to be nothing but a gesture and get a good deal of popular applause" or significant discussion of bombing.[75]

However, his colleague and personal friend Lord Londonderry gained notoriety among advocates of arms reduction for his opposition to a ban on aerial bombing. In February he conveyed to Stanley Baldwin his conviction that the League had to be maintained; to that end Britain's role would be crucial;[76] yet he opposed an agreement outlawing bombing, arguing that in war reliance could not be placed on artificial laws. Strongly influenced (along with many others) by the views of Giulio Douhet, he strongly believed that air power would determine the outcome of future wars: "Can anyone reasonably question the theory that the next war, when it occurs, will largely take place and be decided in the air?"[77] This same point of view would inform Baldwin's famous "the bomber will always get through" speech the following November; given the fact that people could not protect themselves against aerial attack, a country could defend itself only by being more powerful in the air and better able to destroy the enemy than vice versa.[78] Nevertheless disarmament advocates hoped that an agreement could be reached; but Sir John Simon, though he felt "rather strongly" on the matter, according to Leo Kennedy, "gains dialectical points over [Lord] Londonderry (not v[ery] difficult) and then gives in to him."[79]

Despite France's apparent obstinacy on the question of disarmament, some sought to accommodate. Pierre Cot, in the midst of the 1932 election campaign, wrote to Robert Cecil that "the state of our finances will encourage wisdom."[80] Tardieu's fusion of the three ministries (War, Marine, Air) into a Ministry of National Defence had been a step toward greater economy. The Minister himself, François Pietri (a former Budget Minister), had expressed the need for restraint in military spending on a number of occasions.[81]

To the satisfaction of disarmament advocates, the elections produced a shift to the left. For a time, however, Cot feared that Herriot and Paul-Boncour would yield to Weygand, whose views on disarmament did not change.[82] "Je ne désarme pas," the Chief of the French General Staff told Leo Kennedy; "I am responsible for the defense of the country."[83] At the moment, he said, France had two growling dogs on its borders, Germany and Italy. Weygand was impervious to Kennedy's talk about the unjust peace and the need to forgive; he believed that Britain had an important role to play, and ought to play it.[84]

For Herriot, arriving in mid-June as France's new prime minister and foreign minister, the atmosphere in Geneva had changed greatly since the last time he had been there as Premier, in 1924: "...on this stormy June day, the air is charged with electricity. In the conference room there are large windows but they are closed. Here and there one senses reserve, sometimes duplicity. The experiments in internationalism have not changed mankind."[85] The conference ground to an impasse as it became clear that, even with an electoral swing to the left, France was unwilling to make large-scale reductions in the only wholly reliable source of security they possessed. The Germans, meanwhile, continued their demands. The British, refusing to take sides, could not break the deadlock.

Geneva offered little hope for improvement in the European situation in 1932. During the summer of 1932, however, a conference taking place at Lausanne, only 63 kilometers to the east and still on Lake Geneva, achieved a result which contemporaries would once again label the "liquidation of the war": the final settlement of the reparations problem. Proclamations of support for the League could not mask the fact that old diplomacy was at work here. The four recipients of reparations even concluded a secret "gentleman's agreement," making cancellation contingent on U.S. cancellation of war debts; in addition MacDonald and Herriot assured one another of the importance of Anglo-French consultation on the important issues of the day. French leaders had long sought Anglo-French cooperation, but for MacDonald the chief objective was to control French behavior. The results of the conference demonstrated how much the French were willing to pay for closer ties with Britain: Germany was freed of its reparations obligations but agreed to pay a lump sum, which its negotiators had whittled down from 4 billion marks to 2.6 billion.[86]

Meanwhile, Germany's demand for equality of rights in armaments — *Gleichberechtigung* — exacerbated the tensions in Geneva. British delegates hoped to sooth French fears and warn them of the dangers of German extremism; at the same time they intended to remind the German delegates of the difficulties they created, to the detriment of their own cause. However, Maurice Hankey wrote that the intransigence on both sides did not conceal the fact that the "real risk [of war] lies on the Eastern frontier of Germany." Hankey recognized the potential for "tremendous mix-up" should a conflict start there and draw France into Germany in apparent violation of Locarno and the Covenant: "I do not think the Chiefs of Staff want to suggest that there is risk today of war with France," he wrote, commenting on a recent memorandum, in which the British vulnerability to French air attack had been outlined.[87]

MacDonald expressed frustration with the Germans in a letter to Robert Cecil. They had known from the beginning of the Conference in February that they would eventually get what they wanted:

The Germans know perfectly well that in our view the time has come to end the armaments prohibitions of Versailles. They also know that there would not have been the least difficulty in getting their claim to liberty recognised by every power. Very early in the year at Geneva we had started conversations which made this clear beyond doubt. Those conversations, however, also made it clear that further exchanges of views on the question of how that liberty should be immediately used were necessary....The Germans were begged from time to time and by various mouths not to put unnecessary difficulties in their way by making declarations which had better be discussed privately to see if an agreement could be come upon them before announced publicly when accommodation would be vastly more difficult.[88]

Nevertheless the German government, led by the extreme nationalist Franz von Papen since Brüning's resignation on May 30, did make such a peremptory demand, which now threatened to scuttle the conference.

MacDonald blamed both France and Germany for this turn of events:

> Two things are true: the first is that for ten or twelve years France has had an opportunity of pursuing a policy which by now would have enabled the release of Germany from the armament provisions of Versailles to be made without any danger or trouble. The other is equally grave and true: Germany within the last month or two, in spite of her knowledge of the favourable opinion of other Powers, has handled her case in such a way as to rouse a maximum of fear in Europe, and to make it both appear on paper and sound when uttered as a return to the militarism which was in office right up to the War. The outlook is deplorable. Quite apart from this last mishap, the waste of time and the bad organisation of the Conference at the beginning enabled enthusiasm to ooze out, and I am very unhappy about the results.[89]

Despite the observations of top officials like Vansittart and Hankey, MacDonald continued to view Germany as having been wronged and France as the intransigent oppressor of Germany.

In late August German leaders hoped to collect on British sympathy; they pressed the French ambassador in Berlin, François-Poncet, on the matter of arms equality, asserting that France was the only power at Geneva that had failed to approve this concession. Suspecting that the Germans were taking liberties with the British position, Herriot asked Fleuriau, the ambassador in London, to call on British leaders to find out if this was so.[90] The episode revealed the disarray within the British delegation. Personal animosity exacerbated the problem, according to Leo Kennedy:

> The PM and Simon do not get on at all well, and the latest row is over this German claim....When Bernstorff was saying to Simon the other day that he understood that the Brit[ish] Gov[ernmen]t was favourable in principle to the German claim, Simon cut him short, [and] said he had no right to assume that. But MacD. had said that both to Brüning, at Stimson's villa outside Geneva, [and] to von Papen at Lausanne — so naturally Bernstorff had the right to assume it.[91]

Simon's discomfort when MacDonald was in Geneva was "ocularly visible"; according to Kennedy, MacDonald used aides to gather opinions about Simon. While some were careful not to express opinions, others, like Sir

Eric Drummond, did not hesitate; "to any League man Simon is taboo, for he has no convictions and little sincerity."[92] However, MacDonald did not like Drummond, either; he found him to be too representative of the old diplomacy.[93]

For all their bitterness towards France, British leaders could harbor no illusions about Germany's violations and circumventions of the current restrictions, which rendered suspect the demand for equality of rights. James Marshall-Cornwall, the highly competent British military attaché in Germany, had kept a close watch between 1928 and 1932.[94] Despite surprisingly backward tactical methods and training techniques, the Reichswehr contained the nucleus of a "very formidable fighting organization," he had written in 1928.[95] In Stockholm (he was also military attaché for the embassy there) he had found German engineers working at a munitions factory; in the German press he had found obituaries for German pilots and tank officers killed in Soviet Russia; and from his own observations of maneuvers he found that the Reichswehr regularly violated the provisions of the peace treaty.[96]

To delegates and journalists in Geneva in 1932, Germany's clandestine rearmament was common knowledge. Kennedy knew of German munitions factories in Holland, Sweden and Russia. The revelations did not alter his basic sense that Germany had been wronged after the war; nor did they produce sympathy for French security concerns. The only possible solution to the disarmament impasse was to grant Germany the right to make samples of forbidden weapons. Giving in to the reality of the situation, he continued that "we cannot prevent them by force — so it is best to give them the right by agreement and try to control the numbers, which may be possible now, but will not be later."[97] He also questioned French opposition to Germany's demand for a militia, which he believed would lure German youth away from such paramilitary organizations as the *Stahlhelm*.[98] Kennedy appeared to give primary consideration to the possible benefits of compliance with German demands, while discounting the possible negative consequences. This same tendency would render appeasement towards Germany ineffective throughout the 1930s.

Kennedy argued his case with Czechoslovak foreign minister Beneš in Geneva in October. Beneš feared that the new German chancellor, Kurt von Schleicher, had damaged greatly the cause of democracy in Germany; the effects would last at least five years, during which time Schleicher would militarize the country.[99] Because of this turn of events, Beneš believed that Germany ought not to be allowed to rearm, though it should be granted "theoretic" equality. Kennedy rightly wondered how that might be accomplished. He told Beneš that, since Germany would rearm anyway, the other powers ought to strike a bargain with her. Beneš envisioned a European system in which all alliances would be merged into a collective security arrangement including Germany.[100] England might join as well. Kennedy agreed that it might, "if all countries were really contented and had not the sense of injustice which they at present have."[101]

By December, the Conference had failed to achieve any results. MacDonald held out little hope for success: "a very powerful case could now be put up...that the League of Nations has become a menace to the tranquillity of the world," he wrote to Baldwin.[102] On December 11, a compromise declaration according Germany some semblance of equality was an attempt to lure Germany back to the Conference, but the talks would not resume before Hitler had taken office in Germany. Though the National Socialists asserted their pacific intentions in the early days of the new regime, their participation in the Disarmament Conference was an odd spectacle and produced no results.

Manchuria

A great deal has been written about the crisis which began with an explosion on the Japanese-owned South Manchuria Railway on September 18, 1931.[103] The subsequent conquest of the Chinese province of Manchuria by the Japanese army, completed by the following February, presented the League with a dispute between two major powers and tested the body's capacity to deal effectively with the violation of international law, in this case both the League Covenant and the Kellogg-Briand Pact. The outcome of the crisis is familiar: the League appointed a five-man commission to investigate; headed by the Earl of Lytton, the commission examined the claims of both China and Japan and in October 1932 recommended Manchurian autonomy under Chinese sovereignty. By that time, however, only voluntary withdrawal by Japan or military action by its opponents could change the fact that Japan controlled the region. The League followed the American example of not recognizing the puppet regime of Manchukuo; it did not use sanctions or force to expel the Japanese, who demonstrated their contempt for the League by rejecting the Lytton Commission report and withdrawing from the League in March 1933.

Perhaps no other crisis could illustrate so well the weakness of the League as a world organization. While French leaders hoped, with some reason, that the League would not take up this dispute, the League could not afford to ignore a major conflict between two of its members. But neither the United States nor Soviet Union were members; these two powers had Far Eastern interests comparable to those of Britain and France.[104] For liberal internationalism to triumph in this situation, the League would have had to include at least all the major powers; because it did not, the tendency for League policy to reflect the policies of Britain and France was exacerbated.

How did the League's failure in the Manchurian crisis affect the prospects for European peace? Though the League had failed to deal with aggression in Asia, would its European members not act more quickly in a European crisis to protect their most vital interests? Or were the major questions of European politics not for the League to decide in any case? The League's failure contributed to a sense of malaise, and contemporaries certainly lamented this failure, but revisionist powers could not conclude from this experience that the League or its members would stand by should they attempt to redraw the map of Europe.[105]

For British leaders, the potential danger to British Far Eastern interests vastly outweighed concern for the future of the League. Japan's actions produced a stronger reaction among British leaders than they did among the French. Initially the morality of the situation was not clear; indeed, Britain herself had sent troops to Shanghai as recently as 1927 to protect trading interests.[106] All powers with interests in China shared an exasperation with the chaos that had reigned there since the 1911 revolution. For Maurice Hankey, the long-dreaded moment had arrived when Britain had to countenance a threat to its interests without having the military forces in place to defend those interests. The League offered little solace; indeed, in the eyes of some, it was partially to blame for this state of affairs, having instilled a false sense of security among the public at least.[107] Politicians, however, could hardly plead this excuse, having strenuously avoided committing Britain to the League in such a way as to make the latter a genuine substitute for a traditional security system.

In any case, the Manchurian crisis and Japanese violence in Shanghai enabled Hankey and the Chiefs of Staff Sub-Committee to persuade the Cabinet to terminate the Ten Year Rule on March 23, 1932. However, Neville Chamberlain, Chancellor of the Exchequer and the second-most powerful figure in the Conservative party, argued for restraint: "the fact is that in present circumstances we are no more in a position financially and economically to engage in a major war in the Far East than we are militarily."[108] The argument shaped policy for much of the decade.

The crisis also took Britain's League of Nations Union by surprise, and, indeed, few could be sure what was happening there at first. However, Robert Cecil, as Britain's substitute representative on the League Council, suggested that sanctions might be necessary if Japan's motives were aggressive. Lord Reading asked him to drop this suggestion.[109] As the crisis developed, Union members failed to reach agreement on how the League might handle the problem, and drew different conclusions from the outcome. For those who wished to believe that world peace could be preserved without resort to force, events conformed themselves to the faith. Union membership, however, began to decline.[110] Leaders still did not dare to "oppose the League openly"[111]; but in the tensions between those who believed Britain needed to rearm and those who continued to argue for strict economy, the welfare of the League was not of paramount concern.

For France the Manchurian crisis was an unwelcome distraction from European problems. *Le Temps*, acting as a mouthpiece for the Quai d'Orsay, from an early date insisted that the League would do more harm than good in attempting to handle the problem.[112] This opinion was important, for, realistically speaking, "the League of Nations amounted to England and France."[113] If France did not want to do anything about Japan's activities in China, chances were slim that the League would be able to do anything, no matter what the sentiments of its smaller members. Few believed that Japan posed a threat to their Far Eastern interests.[114]

Part of the reason why the League would be unable to handle the dispute between Japan and China was that it had never become the instrument of security France had asked for in the 1920s. Yet the Quai d'Orsay also informed British diplomats that Briand knew that the dispute "could not be treated exactly as if it were a dispute between two European powers."[115] Many in France disputed the notion that it was in fact a great test for the League; in fact, many approved of Japan's actions, which they believed would bring order to a long-troubled region. Such was the French response that rumors circulated of the two powers having struck a secret deal whereby France would defend Japan's actions in return for Japanese cooperation in blocking moves towards disarmament. No such intrigue had taken place; while the Quai d'Orsay wanted to maintain good relations with Japan, alignment with Britain and the United States in the face of a growing German danger was the top priority.[116] What was a dilemma for the Committee of Imperial Defence — whether Germany or Japan posed the greater long-term threat to imperial interests — was, for French leaders, an easy choice. Economically, French relations with Japan were not of great concern; while Japanese expansionism might threaten Indochina, France could count on Britain and the United States being at least as concerned for their own interests in the region. The Quai d'Orsay recognized the danger of a German-Japanese alliance, but this prospect paled by comparison to France's European problems.[117]

Nazi electoral success in 1932, followed by Hitler's accession to the chancellorship in January 1933, dimmed the League's prospects further. Stanley Baldwin wrote to Robert Cecil in March 1933: "I don't think an Archangel could do much at Geneva at the moment."[118] The European atmosphere had deteriorated rapidly since the German elections, he continued: "The French are in a panic: the Germans won't go to Geneva, and my unhappy colleagues are faced with an almost impossible situation. The Americans are so immersed in their own trouble as to be completely useless in international matters."

By the end of 1933 the League of Nations had failed two fundamental tests. The Covenant had mandated arms reduction in order to create a lasting peace in Europe. Now the Disarmament Conference was in ruins, even as the League was demonstrating its inability to provide security for its members.[119] Japan and Germany had left. The London Economic Conference of the previous summer also had failed, "handicapped from the start by the refusal of President Roosevelt to allow War debts or tariffs to be discussed."[120] In July, Philip Noel-Baker had written that the League had "never sunk to so low an ebb in influence and prestige."[121]

In conversation with Leo Kennedy, the new secretary-general of the League, Joseph Avenol, took a defensive stance. He argued that the League ought to be maintained, and that "the last two years should not be taken as a criterion."[122] These times were particularly stressful both politically and economically; Kennedy wrote that Avenol "confided to me that he regretted very much that the Assembly had been called to settle the Sino-Japanese dispute." By an "unfortunate accident," the Disarmament Conference was in session when the crisis arose. Otherwise, Avenol thought, the League would not have been consulted. Kennedy concluded that "all one could hope for would be to build up a cooperative system at Geneva as well as one could, just using the present institutions of the Council Assembly and Secretariat for what they were worth."[123]

No one could give the League a ringing endorsement at the end of Hitler's first year in power. Hitler's own rejection of the League demonstrated his contempt for the "new diplomacy," which in any case had failed to take hold as a new paradigm for international relations. The events of 1931 to 1933 made it impossible to maintain much hope of using the League as an instrument of collective security. Whether of necessity or for lack of faith, British and French leaders had not invested the League and the new diplomacy with sufficient powers. The Disarmament Conference presented troubled Europe with the problem of a runaway League agenda; falling when it did, it merely exacerbated tensions. Meanwhile the Manchurian crisis demonstrated that the League was no more than the sum of its diverse, indecisive parts.

Notes

1. LKEN 6 (Diary), September 13, 1928.
2. J. M. Cooper, Jr., *The Warrior and the Priest: Theodore Roosevelt and Woodrow Wilson* (Cambridge, Mass., 1983), p. 279.
3. C. Thorne, *The Limits of Foreign Policy* (New York, 1972), p. 107. Cecil's position on the use of sanctions and force was ambiguous; he was willing to contemplate the use of economic sanctions. In reference to revisionist elements in Germany, he wrote to Sir Norman Angell on January 16, 1931 "What I want to have delicately insinuated to them is that if they ask for force and violence, sooner or later they will inevitably get it, and they must not count in such a case on British reluctance to war to keep them out of it." BL MS 51140/12-13.
4. Baldwin papers 119/119-123, Bank of England note on loans, May 12, 1932.
5. "The *Times* Review of the Year 1927," December 31, 1927, p. iv.
6. See J. Barros, *The Corfu Incident of 1923: Mussolini and the League of Nations* (Princeton, 1965).
7. Thorne, pp. 404-408.
8. See Article 8 in S. Fischer-Galati, ed., *Twentieth Century Europe*, p. 39.
9. American and British negotiators had rejected a Japanese proposal to include in the Covenant a declaration of equality of all nations and peoples. R. Sontag, *A Broken World* (New York, 1971), p. 14. The mandate system, by which Britain and France took over German colonies and parts of the former Ottoman empire (inhabited by "people not yet able to stand by themselves") was justified by the "principle that the well-being and development of such peoples form a sacred trust of civilization." See article 22, Fischer-Galati, p. 45.
10. Fischer-Galati, pp. 36-47.
11. The term is Hedley Bull's, from *The Anarchical Society: A Study of Order in World Politics* (New York, 1977).
12. Bull, pp. 13-20.
13. BL MS 51111/101-102, Drummond to Cecil, April 24, 1928.
14. J. Barros, *Office Without Power: Secretary-General Sir Eric Drummond 1919-1933* (Oxford, 1979), pp. 10-15.

15. Arnold Wolfers wrote that this essential difference between French and British attitudes was rooted in their respective attitudes towards Germany. French policy sought the establishment of strict League restraints on Germany's revisionist impulses towards Eastern Europe. For Britain, a more flexible League might allow for eventual peaceful revision of the Treaties. *Britain and France between Two Wars* (New York, 1940), pp. 383-384.

16. F.M. Leventhal, *Arthur Henderson* (Manchester, 1989), pp. 127-130.

17. "The *Times* Review of the Year 1927," December 31, 1927, p. iv.

18. Ibid.

19. Ibid.

20. Baldwin papers, 119/119-123, Bank of England note on loans, May 12, 1932.

21. Charles Kindleberger develops the idea of "lender of last resort" in *The World in Depression, 1929-1939* (Berkeley, 1986).

22. R.S. Sayers, *The Bank of England, 1891-1944* (Cambridge, 1986), p. 121.

23. Ibid.

24. F.P. Walters, *A History of the League of Nations* (Oxford, 1952), p. 134. Walters was a former League official, and this book, published under the auspices of the Royal Institute for International Affairs, is often recriminating in tone.

25. Ibid., p. 378. Before the days of "Briandism," French delegates had attacked the League's budget in 1923 (p. 259).

26. Ibid., pp. 515-516.

27. D. Birn, *League of Nations Union*, p. 73.

28. PRO 30/69/750/408, Murray to MacDonald, Oxford, October 24, 1928. By contrast, MacDonald was quite comfortable in Conservative circles.

29. PRO 30/69/750/441, MacDonald to Murray, October 29, 1928.

30. Leventhal, pp. 144-148. D. Carlton describes the running feud between the Prime Minister and the Foreign Secretary in *MacDonald versus Henderson: the Foreign Policy of the Second Labour Government* (London, 1971).

31. Carlton, pp. 218-223.

32. Leventhal, pp. 127-130.

33. Even if the League ever reached this point, however, the French would want to see the entire system in place before giving up reliance on her own military forces. Henderson believed that nations had to reduce their armed forces to the level needed to make their contributions to the international force.

34. The Optional Clause was article 36 of the Statute of the Permanent Court of International Justice at the Hague, in which states "declare that they recognize as compulsory ipso facto and without special agreement, in relation to any other Member or state accepting the same obligation, the jurisdiction of the Court in any or all of the classes of legal disputes concerning:

    a) the interpretation of a treaty

    b) any question of international law

    c) the existence of any fact which, if established, would   constitute a breach of an international obligation.

The declaration referred to above may be made unconditionally or on condition of reciprocity on the part of several or certain Members or States, or foe a certain time" (Cmd. 3452, misc. no. 12 (1929)). The Optional Clause gave Article 2 of Treaty for the Renunciation of War as an Instrument of National Policy (the Kellogg-Briand Pact) a machinery for implementation. PREM 1/72/177-190.

35. Britain had signed the Kellogg-Briand Pact with the same reservation.

36. Leventhal, pp 146-147; 159-162.

37. Leventhal, p. 165.

38. Birn, pp. 86-87.

39. Henderson despatched Lindsay as Ambassador to Washington when the opportunity presented itself early in 1930. Leventhal, pp. 149-150.

40. The newspaper spoke with conviction: its editor, Walter Layton, was director of the League's Economic and Financial Section, and may have written the article (traditionally unsigned) himself.

41. The *Economist*, October 11, 1930, p. 652.

42. Ibid.

43. Ibid.

44. Ibid., p. 653.

45. HR 38/68-71, Rumbold to O'Malley (Foreign Office), October 10, 1930.

46. Ibid.

47. Birn, pp. 95-96; Barnett, *Collapse of British Power*, p. 302.

48. See, for example, the *Écho de Paris* for the third week of March 1931.

49. JO, Chambre, November 30, 1927, p. 554.

50. Ibid.

51. Ibid.

52. W.R. Sharp, *Government of the French Republic*, p. 292.

53. JO, Chambre, November 30, 1927, p. 569.

54. Ibid.

55. Ibid., p. 570. Briand's praise of the prevalent British attitude towards the League seems somewhat disingenuous to today's reader, given the differences of opinion that existed. Perhaps his great oratorical skills created a different effect.

56. Perhaps the theory behind French imperialism made France's empire appear to be less of a rival organization to the League than did the British Empire. While the British sought to teach their subject peoples about British administration and so on, there was no expectation that these people could actually *become* British. The British Empire gave the appearance of a world organization. While there was about as much diversity within the smaller French Empire, the controlling idea was that these peoples would all become civilized, i.e., French, just as their lands had become part of France. In any case, empire loomed larger in Britain's political identity than it did in France's.

57. Quai d'Orsay documents reflect this concern both in discussions of this crisis and in discussion of the Four-Power Pact in 1933. These documents will be discussed below.

58. PA 89 (Herriot)/29/200, MacDonald to Herriot, London, September 9, 1932.

59. Fischer-Galati, ed., p. 39. The wording of the article reflected beliefs that were common in the interwar period. The main point of the article was that the "maintenance of peace requires the reduction of national armaments to the lowest point consistent with national safety." More striking were the strong words reserved for private arms manufacturers: "manufacture by private enterprise of munitions and implements of war is open to grave objections"; the Council was to "advise how the evil effects attendant upon such manufacture can be prevented."

60. Ibid; and G. Scott, *The Rise and Fall of the League of Nations* (New York, 1973), pp. 175-6.

61. BL MS 51107/1-9, Noel-Baker to Cecil, April 2, 1928.

62. "The *Times* Review of the Year 1930," January 1, 1931, p. iv.

63. "The *Times* Review of the Year 1931," January 1, 1932, p. iii.

64. Ibid.

65. Baldwin papers, 118/164-169, Londonderry to Baldwin, February 22, 1932.
66. *Le Temps*, February 3, 1932, p. 1.
67. From Paul-Boncour's memoirs, quoted in Binion, *Defeated Leaders*, p. 312.
68. Quoted from Tardieu's *Devant le pays* in Binion, p. 312.
69. Binion, p. 313.
70. LKEN 12, Geneva, February 8, 1932.
71. LKEN 12, Paris, February 14, 1932. Kennedy apparently had few qualms about seeking to influence the Foreign Secretary.
72. On June 24, 1932, he wrote in his diary (LKEN 13): "a 'Times' leader is not always meant to be an expression of public opinion, but should more often be an instrument of policy."
73. LKEN 12, entries for February 14, March 27, April 17.
74. Binion, p. 315.
75. Baldwin papers 118/191-195, MacDonald to Baldwin, June 15, 1932.
76. Thorne, p. 109.
77. FO 800/687/338-344, Londonderry to Simon, July 11, 1932; on the influence of Douhet, see D. MacIsaac, "Voices from the Central Blue: the Air Power Theorists," in P. Paret, ed., *Makers of Modern Strategy* (Princeton, 1986), pp. 629-635.
78. House of Commons debates, November 10, 1932, 630-638.
79. LKEN 13, London, September 13, 1932.
80. BL MS 51143/4, Cot to Cecil, April 9, 1932. Cot later became Daladier's Air Minister.
81. Ibid; Binion, pp. 313-314.
82. BL MS 51143/5, Cot to Cecil, October 27, 1932.
83. LKEN 13, Boulogne, October 14, 1932.
84. Ibid., and FO 425/405/20, Tyrrell to Henderson, Paris, April 14, 1930.
85. PA 89 (Herriot)/26 (Journal)/110, June 14, 1932.
86. This lump sum was never paid. By 1933, Germany had paid one-eighth of the original bill, even though it had received loans totalling one-fifth of the amount demanded. D. Weigall, *Britain and the World, 1815-1986* (Oxford, 1987), pp. 167-8.
87. HNKY 4/24/3-7, Hankey to J.D.B. Fergusson (H.M. Treasury), March 10, 1932.
88. PRO 30/69/1442/137-138, MacDonald to Cecil, September 13, 1932.
89. Ibid.
90. Bennett, pp. 202-207.
91. Ibid. Graf Albrecht von Bernstorff was Counsellor at the German Embassy in London.
92. Ibid.
93. Barros, *Office Without Power*, pp. 14-15.
94. M. Gilbert, *Sir Horace Rumbold, Portrait of a Diplomat, 1869-1941* (London, 1973), p. 231. Marshall-Cornwall had changed his name from Cornwall in 1929 (p. 329).
95. Gilbert, p. 322. Rumbold enclosed Cornwall's report in a despatch to the Foreign Office on September 28(FO 371/ 12889).
96. Gilbert, p. 322.
97. LKEN 13, London, September 13, 1932.
98. Ibid.
99. LKEN 13, Calais, October 15, 1932.
100. This idea gave rise to discussions about an "Eastern Locarno" in 1934, while Louis Barthou was France's foreign minister.

101. Ibid.

102. Quoted in Roskill, *Hankey*, volume 3, p. 65.

103. See especially C. Thorne, *The Limits of Foreign Policy: the West, the League and the Far Eastern Crisis of 1931-1933* (London, 1972).

104. Britain still accounted for 36.7% of all foreign investment in China (including Manchuria and Hong Kong); this share was down only slightly from 1914 (37.7%). Japan, however, now accounted for 35.1% (up from 13.6%); Russia accounted for 8.4% (down from 16.7%), the U.S. for 6.1% (up from 3.1%), France for 5.9% (down from 10.7%), and Germany for 2.7% (down from 16.4%). Meanwhile, the United States had replaced Britain as Japan's main trading partner. Between 1925 and 1929, 37.1% of Japan's exports went to the United States, and 20.7% went to China. Of Japan's imports, 23.2% came from the U.S., 13.4% from China, 6.1% from Britain and 12.7% from India. W.G. Beasley, *Japanese Imperialism, 1894-1945* (Oxford, 1987), p. 127, 133, 211. France ranked eleventh among Japan's trading partners, behind Soviet Russia. DDF, series I, vol. 2, no. 198.

105. For Mussolini's views of the League and its capacity to thwart his ambitions, see G. Baer, *The Coming of the Italo-Ethiopian War* (Cambridge, Mass., 1967), pp. 25-26.

106. R.P. Shay, *British Rearmament in the Thirties: Politics and Profits* (Princeton, 1977), p. 20.

107. Barnett, p. 298.

108. Quoted in Shay, p. 23.

109. Birn, pp. 95-6.

110. Birn, p. 107.

111. P. Kennedy, *The Realities behind Diplomacy*, p. 244.

112. Thorne, p. 137.

113. Barnett, p. 302.

114. Thorne, p. 174. Japanese expansionism was not perceived widely as a potential threat to Indochina until 1935.

115. Thorne, p. 147.

116. Thorne, pp. 147, 175, 296. Thorne convincingly demonstrates that the rumors to this effect were false, since the Japanese made overtures along these lines to French ambassador de Martel in Tokyo and to Massigli in Geneva in the summer of 1932 (such an approach would not be necessary, Thorne reasons, if an agreement already existed). The ambassador in Tokyo was interested, but Massigli, one of the few strong French supporters of the League at this point, was glad to receive instructions from the Quai d'Orsay not to respond to such advances.

117. DDF, series I, vol. 2, nos. 198 and 375, both "Notes de la Sous-direction Asie-Océanie," dated January 15 and March 6, 1933 respectively.

118. BL MS 51080/246, Baldwin to Cecil, March 12, 1933.

119. Two weeks of talks in 1934 finally brought the Disarmament Conference to an end.

120. "The *Times* Review of the Year 1933," January 1, 1934, p. iii.

121. BL MS 51108/37-44, Memorandum from Noel-Baker to Cecil, July 5, 1933.

122. LKEN 15, Geneva, December 15, 1933.

123. Ibid.

5

Visions of a
New Europe

Even Napoleon, at St. Helena, realised that a European war was in the nature of a civil war.
— Robert Cecil[1]

The League of Nations was created to preserve peace by enforcing international law. Only indirectly could it address the *sources* of conflict, among which nationalism appeared to be the main culprit. In the 1920s and 1930s a few individuals scattered throughout Europe dared to look beyond the narrow interests of their nations to examine whether or not, in the interest of peace, these interests could be more broadly defined. One great power — France, through its foreign minister Briand — put forth a vague proposal for a unified Europe; but the other major powers — Britain, Germany, Italy — rejected it outright.

Those who sought to remedy the evils of nationalism in European politics could take some comfort from history: nationalism had not always gripped the peoples of Europe as it had in the period before the Great War; in the Middle Ages, for example, the idea of Christendom had created a common bond (among Christians at least) and the Roman Catholic Church possessed the authority to set stringent conditions under which princes could resort to war. Princes suited these doctrines of just war to their own purposes, but the church nevertheless provided a strong element of cohesion in European society.[2] Divisions in the church and the emergence of nation-states fractured European society, which nevertheless retained many common characteristics, as diverse and fundamental as aesthetics, technology, and social structures. In a time of fierce nationalism, however, factors such as advancing technology exacerbated the competition between states.

After the Great War, some Europeans began to ask whether common values and aspirations might become the basis for cooperation rather than conflict. "Pan-European" organizations and publications appeared in many European countries; the headquarters of Count Richard Coudenhove-Kalergi's "Pan-European Union," founded in 1922, was in Vienna.[3] In official circles, however, the movement was strongest in France. As prime minister and foreign minister of the Cartel des Gauches government, Édouard Herriot had called for the formation of a "United States of Europe" in speeches at the Sorbonne (October 1924) and in the Chamber of Deputies (January 1925).[4]

Some scholars see the Geneva Economic Conference of 1927 as setting the stage for the Briand plan, even though the meeting yielded few concrete results. Louis Loucheur, the chairman of France's preparatory committee, a friend of Briand and a member of the Pan-European Union, had said in 1926 that "the long-term goal...is the constitution of a United States of Europe, the only economic formula capable of an effective struggle against the United States of America."[5] Though leaders denied any anti-American impulse in the pan-European movement, the desire to resist American economic hegemony certainly drove business interests towards the European idea. In Britain, business leaders took the idea of European union more seriously than did the Foreign Office.[6]

In calling for a United States of Europe in 1929, Aristide Briand became the first political leader to propose European union in the international arena. Briand realized that economic integration was probably the wisest first step to unity, but personally he had no passion for economics; in this regard he was an old-style, political diplomat. He wavered between calls for economic integration and greater political unity, failing to establish a clear relationship between the two within his plan. Those who viewed the plan with skepticism and suspicion attacked this and other apparent weaknesses. Some, inevitably, detected a plot against the Anglo-Saxon powers for French hegemony. Indeed, the Briand Plan was not a plan, but it was a noble sentiment. The response to it, therefore, was significant, for it demonstrated the poisonous state of European politics at the beginning of the new decade.

Growth of the European Idea in France

The idea of European federation was not new, as Briand acknowledged when he first brought it before the General Assembly of the League of Nations on September 5, 1929: "The idea, which was first conceived many years ago, which has haunted the imagination of philosophers and poets and has won from them a certain *succès d'estime* — this idea has now forged ahead in virtue of its own intrinsic worth and has been seen at last to supply the answer to a real need."[7] At issue in Briand's proposal was the principle of national sovereignty as the primary factor in the social, economic and political life of Europe. National rivalries had produced the conflagration of 1914-1918; Europeans, therefore, had to set aside their differences to pursue the common goal of peace.

Despite the utopian tone of the proposal, Briand's thoughts on European unity were the result of sober consideration of France's position in the postwar period. No one in France doubted Germany's economic and military potential. French opinion split, however, over how to face this ineluctable fact. The political right sought to maintain the order established by the Treaty of Versailles; Poincaré, therefore, ordered the occupation of the Ruhr in 1923 when Germany refused to pay reparations. On the left, the Socialists and Communists saw the solution to Europe's ills in the international solidarity of workers, not in treaty enforcement. To the outside world, the policies of the right seemed chauvinistic; the Ruhr occupation deepened the split between Britain and France. Though few among Britain's leaders championed the international solidarity of workers, most of them shared the left's disregard for the treaty.

Immediately after the war, Briand, himself a socialist, had shared the nationalist belief that Germany had to be held in check. By the time of the Ruhr occupation in 1923, however, he was certain of two important facts: the first was that France had to cooperate with Great Britain to preserve the peace; the second, which followed in part from the first, was that France would have to develop a new relationship with Germany. The Ruhr episode demonstrated Britain's opposition to the use of military power to enforce the treaty. Already in October 1921 Briand had spoken in the National Assembly of an "international formation" to guarantee French security; he used this phrase in a discussion on the recent Wiesbaden accords, in which Louis Loucheur and Walter Rathenau had agreed to increase the amount of reparations which Germany could pay in kind. Such agreements, Briand believed, contributed to an "atmosphere of peace."[8]

Of course, Briand was talking about relations between victor and vanquished powers, but he also believed that Germany could play a leading role in the solution of Europe's problems. Locarno became for him an important symbol of a new German orientation. Germany's entrance into the League of Nations also marked an important transition, both for Germany and the League: looking outward from Geneva, Briand could imagine a rehabilitated Germany prepared to play a constructive role in Europe; and, with Germany as a member, the League would lose the aspect of a domineering winners' circle.[9]

The goal of Franco-German reconciliation was ambitious enough for this period, but Briand hoped to make it the basis for a new European organization which would complement rather than supplant the League of Nations. The League, ostensibly a world organization, would benefit from a subsidiary that would bring peace and stability to its most unruly continent. Briand believed such a federation to be essential, as he told the Chamber of Deputies in July 1929: "I believe that it is necessary to organize Europe, not against any country or any group of countries, but to strengthen the conditions of peace, to put an end to the state of anarchy that will give rise to conflicts as long as actions are not sufficiently coordinated to organize the vital interests of the peoples of the continent."[10]

Briand described his vision to the League's Tenth Assembly in vague, broad terms: "I think that among peoples constituting geographical groups, like the peoples of Europe, there should be some kind of federal bond; it should be possible for them to get in touch at any time, to confer about their interests, to agree on joint resolutions and to establish among themselves a bond of solidarity which will enable them, if need be, to meet any grave emergency that may arise. That is the link I want to forge."[11] He did not wish to undermine the League, but "the European states may feel the need of a special, more immediate and more direct action" to deal with questions of specific concern to them, questions with which they were "specially competent to deal, because of their racial affinities and their common ideals of civilisation."[12] Briand did not deal in specifics; his was a creative intellect, not given to sorting out details.[13] He urged representatives to discuss the idea unofficially and submit it to their governments. In the absence of a clear proposal, each nation was left to imagine its own version of such a union, with greater or lesser degrees of enthusiasm.

In light of subsequent events, Briand's proposal might appear specious: high-minded, internationalist, pacific, while at the same time calling upon the disgruntled powers of Europe either to join the chorus or demonstrate to the world their evil intentions. At the time, some saw this as a French attempt to preserve her fragile hegemony in Europe, or even to create a new Continental System. Yet few could attribute such motives to Briand himself; whatever the prejudices the French and British reserved for each other, Briand escaped the stereotyping of French politicians as duplicitous, narrow-minded and self-serving.

The foundation of European federation had to be Franco-German reconciliation. British observers, while aware of steps that had been taken in this direction, were perhaps more aware than their French counterparts of the apparent incongruities in this scheme, most notably the fact that Germany refused to recognize her current borders with her eastern neighbors — France's allies — as final. Some in France were willing to consider revision as an acceptable price for reconciliation with Germany: for example Jean Montigny, a leading Radical voice in the Chamber on foreign affairs, did not regard maintenance of the Polish Corridor as a vital interest.[14] Yet most chose simply not to focus on these problems, hoping that time would work to rehabilitate and pacify Germany, and render such issues as the eastern frontier less volatile.

Briand announced his vision of a federalized Europe during a period of détente; for some years already he and others had been working to foster ties between France and Germany, beginning on the economic level with the steel and potash cartels. In August 1927 France and Germany signed a trade agreement, mutually granting most favored nation status; the German government, writes Peter Krüger, had taken a "firm decision in favor of international cooperation and an open, liberal world market," even though not all Germans supported this policy.[15]

On the German side, one of the driving forces behind this policy was Arnold Rechberg. A sculptor in Paris before the war, and now a wealthy businessman with large potash interests, he believed that the intertwining of French and German industries would render war between the two nations impossible.[16] Franco-German conciliation ought not to be left to the parties of the left, he thought; cooperation would form a barrier against Bolshevism and allow Germany to distance herself from the Soviet Union.[17] He also advocated a Franco-German military alliance, which would guarantee France's eastern alliances once the corridor had been returned to Germany in return for free Polish navigation of the Vistula.[18]

Of course, Rechberg was neither the German government nor even a member of it; he "represented only himself." Yet Poincaré, during their first meeting in December 1923, had reminded him that German foreign policy was the province of the German Foreign Office. Undaunted, Rechberg had met with Marshal Foch shortly thereafter to discuss the military question. In 1926 he met with Briand, and Jules Sauerwein published the substance of Rechberg's idea in *Le Matin*; the Quai d'Orsay, however, asserted that it did not approve of the scheme.[19] At a meeting with Poincaré early in 1929, the prime minister had said that France would not press Poland on the corridor question, though by Rechberg's account he seemed interested in the idea of a military accord. Rechberg justified his diplomatic activities:

Mr. Stresemann...has been...morbidly jealous of me because I initiated the Franco-German industrial alliance....Therefore Mr. Stresemann did not wish to leave to me the crowning of the industrial alliance...with a political alliance between the two great neighbors, even though I several times offered to leave to Mr. Stresemann all the public acclaim and to retreat to the shadows once the great work had been accomplished.[20]

A Franco-German political and military alliance would establish the foundation of a lasting peace in Western Europe, and a sure defense against both the Bolshevik menace and the "rapidly growing financial and industrial hegemony of the United States."[21]

Rechberg's chief French contact was the politician Paul Reynaud, who since 1923 had made several trips to Berlin, meeting Rechberg's friends in the Reichstag and in the *Stahlhelm* paramilitary organization. A member of the conservative nationalist *union républicaine démocratique*, Reynaud was no pawn for German interests, though he was more flexible (cautiously so) than Poincaré had been on the question of pressing Poland on the Corridor.[22] In December 1929 he spoke on the subject of security in the Chamber of Deputies. France, he said, could no longer rely upon her allies from the Great War. Among the other former allies, Italy made no secret of the fact that her policy was guided by "sacred self-interest," and the United States had neither ratified the Treaty of Versailles nor joined the League of Nations.

Britain, meanwhile, had curtailed its commitments to France. At Cannes in 1922 Lloyd George had offered Briand nothing better than a ten-year alliance, without a military convention. With a Labour government in power now, the prospects were even worse:

Do you believe that today Labour would be more disposed to accord us an alliance? They are much more insular than the Conservatives. I don't reproach them for it; it's in the nature of things. Why? Because the miner from Wales, or from Yorkshire, isn't as involved in international life as the wholesaler from the City of London. If today England were allied with France by a *bona fide* treaty, we would run the danger of seeing the Labour Cabinet...denounce the treaty.[23]

In the present circumstances, France could expect little more from Britain:

...I figure that Locarno gives us the maximum of commitment that England wants to make — that she can make. Why? Because to the extent that her Dominions recover their independence, England loses her own, because England has become the presiding member of a federation of nations spread throughout the world, because the citizen of Australia, preoccupied with keeping for a few million whites the unheard-of privilege of an entire continent, interests himself much more with the question of how he will be defended — and little matter whether this be by British-flagged or by American-flagged battleships — than with the question of whether Czechoslovakia, which he has barely heard of, will be guaranteed against an attack from Germany.[24]

With Britain thus distracted, France had become the sole guarantor of the peace of Europe. The problem called for bold and imaginative solutions. "The more you tell me that Locarno is incomplete, that the Geneva Protocol will not be ratified, the more I will tell you that these facts push you forward by both shoulders towards new paths in search of security," he said. "We must make incursions into recently enemy terrain... and...since we cannot have security in adding up our common interests, we must see if we cannot achieve it through our opposite interests. That... means rapprochement with Germany."[25]

Henry Franklin Bouillon reminded the Chamber that France's relations with Germany had consequences for France's eastern allies. In response, Reynaud quoted Prince Radziwill, president of the Polish *sejm*'s foreign affairs commission (whom Franklin-Bouillon also had quoted to support the opposite point of view), as saying that the Poles had no right to prescribe how France should regulate her relations with Germany, but that they had the right to express one reservation: "that this regulation not be realized at our expense."[26] The foreign minister himself, August Zaleski, had said more than once during the past two years that he did not fear Franco-German rapprochement. In any case, Reynaud argued, financial agreements between Poland and Germany suggested that the two countries also were moving toward normal relations.

However, Reynaud knew that Germany and Poland would never enjoy completely normal relations as long as the Polish corridor existed. Intended to give Poland use of the Vistula and access to the Baltic at Danzig, the corridor separated East Prussia from the rest of Germany. Every German schoolchild learned about the injustices of the Treaty of Versailles, and the corridor provided literally graphic evidence of Allied treachery; even to the dull and the distracted, this "wound" stared from every wall map. German leaders could negotiate reparations and occupation, but they could never accept the eastern frontier as permanent.[27]

Most Germans did not disagree. Danzig, with a large German population and a proud history as a member of the Hanseatic League, had fallen under international control; tensions there between Poles and Germans ran high, particularly after the Poles — with less than complete faith in the powers of the League — built their own new port at Gdynia, with French and Italian financial help.[28] Activity at Gdynia increased greatly after the

Poles captured coal markets in Scandinavia during Britain's strike in 1926; in 1928 Gdynia handled almost two million tons of traffic, compared to Danzig's 8.6 million tons. Danzig's figures for the following years show a decline in the amount of shipping, while Gdynia's figures continued to grow rapidly. Gdynia was not on the Vistula, so freight arrived there by rail; Germans complained that the Poles were allowing the Vistula to deteriorate.[29] Observers on the scene quickly recognized the intractability of the situation.

Reynaud also discussed the disposition of Poland's southern neighbor Czechoslovakia. If anything, this country was in greater danger than Poland, often represented in newsreels as a nut between the two arms of the nutcracker, Germany and Austria; yet foreign minister Eduard Beneš did not appear to be worried about Franco-German rapprochement. On October 19, 1929 Beneš had said that Czechoslovakia's participation at Locarno and in the Kellogg-Briand Pact had guaranteed peace and collaboration with her large neighbor: "We are justified in saying today that we can consider peace assured for our country for many tens of years, and that we can now use this time to build our state definitively, to shore it up internally and thereby establish its permanent security."[30]

World opinion, Reynaud continued, now called upon France to resume her role as "guide at the head of the European nations." During the war, France had called on the world for aid; now the world was calling on France, and France had responded with its proposal for a "United States of Europe" at Geneva. To compete with the United States of America on the world market, Europe had to form a large interior market of her own. France and Germany could now work together. In order for nations to lower their tariff barriers, they needed security; the key to European security, both politically and economically, was the rapprochement of France and Germany. Reynaud did not advocate French disarmament or attempts to transform Germany; many spoke of a "good" and a "bad" Germany, he said, but France had to work with Germany as she was.[31]

Could France establish a normal relationship with Germany "as she was," without ultimately compromising France's commitments to Germany's neighbors? Even without an evolving relationship with Germany as a complicating factor, France's relations with and commitments to Poland and Czechoslovakia were troubled and ambiguous.[32] By contrast, Germany's position on the Polish Corridor was clear, but that issue was not forced until 1939. The question of Germany's relations with Austria, which produced a crisis in 1931, interfered more directly with Briand's plans.

Germany, Austria and the New Europe

For all the hatred Germans felt for the Treaty of Versailles, the Austrians had lost far more by the Treaty of St. Germain. Once a vast empire, Austria was now a small, landlocked republic of about 80,000 square kilometers, less than one-third the size of Italy. The Habsburgs, monarchs since the eleventh century, were barred from the throne. The strange new reality was tangible in Vienna, which still looked like the grand imperial city it had been, but now merely served as the capital and industrial center of a country of 6.5 million people. Vienna's working class provided the base for Austria's left-wing parties, while most people living outside the capital were devoutly Catholic and far more conservative in outlook.

The breakup of the Habsburg Empire seriously disrupted the economy of the whole region. Austria needed to reestablish trade relations disrupted by the war, imperial collapse, and protectionism.[33] Earlier, Austria's food supply had come largely from the agricultural regions of Bohemia and Hungary, now outside her borders; now food was in short supply. Conversely, Austria's industries tripped over each other in meeting Austrian demand for manufactured goods, and unemployment rose. In 1922, Austria declared bankruptcy. The League provided loans, which managed to stabilize the country, more or less, by the middle of the decade.[34] Serious doubts remained, however, about Austria's long-term viability.

Political tensions persisted. In July 1927 riots in Vienna killed 80 people and injured 400. The riots reinforced Austrians' perceptions of Vienna as a city teeming with revolutionaries, and discredited the republican regime as unable to shield Austria from the communist contagion. Right-wing groups profited at the expense of the Social Democrats, so that already before economic disaster struck in 1929, and before National Socialism became an important political movement, Austria's republican institutions were threatened by such paramilitary organizations as the *Heimwehr* (the equivalent of Germany's *Stahlhelm*), which had a membership of 350,000, of whom 120,000 were armed. This group was controlled by aristocrats and ex-officers of the Imperial Army. But republicans defended themselves as well; the Republican Defence League had a membership of 300,000, of which 90,000 were armed.[35] Many feared civil war.

To those who viewed Austria's political and economic problems as insurmountable, two possible solutions presented themselves: union with Germany, or some sort of federation with other Danubean states, possibly led by relatively stable Czechoslovakia. Though there were no polls to measure public opinion, *Anschluss* appeared to be the more popular solution among Austrians, and justifiable by the principle of national self-determination. However, Article 88 of the Treaty of St. Germain forbade *Anschluss*, and Austria had had to reaffirm its pledge not to seek union with Germany when it received financial assistance from the League in 1922.[36]

In 1927, the Austrian press began to discuss *Anschluss* openly, despite the reaction it drew from France. "*L'Anschluss, c'est la guerre,*" Briand declared in 1928.[37] The Quai d'Orsay vigilantly monitored Austria and kept in close contact with Beneš. Beneš could not and did not ignore the question, but he occasionally seemed less worried about the question than his interlocutors expected him to be. Speaking with the French minister Charles-Roux in Prague in December 1927, Beneš had said that *Anschluss* was little more than a bogey and a means of blackmailing those who feared it. Charles-Roux replied that he was less optimistic; true, the idea seemed to be a little less popular in Austria at the moment, but work towards unification continued in both Berlin and Vienna. The question, he believed, would have to be dealt with in the same manner that Europe had handled the question of French union with Belgium in 1830. At that time a group of nations opposed the union, and it never took place. To prevent *Anschluss*, opposing nations would have to prevail in a contest of wills against Austria and Germany.[38]

British officials typically worried less about Austrian politics than did their French counterparts. In July 1928, the British ambassador, Sir Eric Phipps, wrote that his French colleague Clauzel was "suffering from a somewhat acute attack of 'Anschluss' fever" because of a number of recent incidents; such incidents included a warming of relations between Germany and Austria's chancellors, and Austria's refusal to become involved in any kind of economic arrangement with the Little Entente as long as it excluded Germany. Phipps believed that the French press, especially *Le Temps* and the *Journal des Débats*, overreacted to such incidents. The most recent cause for concern was "the approaching invasion of Vienna by a quarter of a million lusty Teutons" to celebrate the Schubert centenary; looking at the program, the French ambassador had been alarmed to see an announcement for an "*Anschlusskundgebung.*"[39] Clauzel had demanded an explanation from officials, who told him that the event was not official and would not be attended by Austrian or German ministers. Phipps proposed giving this solace to his colleague, that Austria could yearn for *Anschluss* as much as she wanted to, but that as long as Germany realized that the "game was not worth the candle," it would not happen.[40]

Phipps' regarded the whole question of Austria's future with a sense of detached contempt:

> I met [Anatole de Monzie] at dinner last night at the French Legation and afterwards had some conversation with him and some prominent Austrians. When the latter remarked that the 'Anschluss' would eventually be inevitable, M. de Monzie's face and manners changed and in harsh tones he declared this to be an impossibility: moreover he asked, what had Austria to offer France in return? He seemed to take it for granted that Great Britain would get nothing. Later on in the evening one of the Austrians in question remarked to me with a twinkle in his eye that in his opinion the more Austrians spoke to Frenchmen about the 'Anschluss' the better, for the more they would be likely to extract from France. This amiable blackmailing attitude is typical of the Austrian mentality, and I continue to think...that silence is the most effective method of dealing with it so far as the ex-allied press is concerned.[41]

Britons were not the only ones to criticize nervous French reactions to talk of *Anschluss*. Léon Blum wrote in *Le Populaire* that right to self-determination, inscribed in Wilson's Fourteen Points and proclaimed by international socialism, applied to Austrians as to all other peoples. True, the treaties made an exception in the case of Austria, but they also had provided for their own revision; indeed they had made revision necessary by creating an inviable nation, cut off from its Hungarian and Czechoslovak markets, unable to feed itself, and dependent on the great powers for financial support. *Anschluss* was a natural solution for Austria: " *Anschluss*, they tell us, once again creates the risk of a "Greater Germany," fearful to all of Europe. The worst hypocrisy of our press on this matter is that it evokes the Austria of before the war, the Austria of Mitteleuropa, and not the minuscule and weak Austria which the Treaty of Versailles forgot on the map."[42]   Germany's birth rate, he argued, would produce the same population increase in about fifteen years; would anyone move to stop that?

Given French preoccupation with the question, both British and French observers were surprised at Beneš' assurance that *Anschluss* would never happen. Leo Kennedy of the *Times* met with "that extraordinarily interesting little man" in Geneva in September 1928:

> what struck me most was the sureness and confidence with which he predicted...*Anschluss* — actual definite union between Germany and Austria [—] he ruled out as impossible. A cultural, social and almost administrative (i.e., postal services, etc.) union, yes. But political, no. And he outlined how it could be prevented, through the Council of the League, with the threat of warlike action behind it. The neighbours of Germany would, he thought, be ready to fight, but it would not be necessary.[43]

The moment Austria proposed economic union with Germany, Beneš would offer Austria economic union with Czechoslovakia. Austria's ultimate destiny, he believed, was to become neutral, like Switzerland.

The events of 1928, however, showed that pro-*Anschluss* sentiment was not waning. The summer Schubert celebrations had furnished the occasion for the mayor of Vienna to declare, with Germany's President of the Reichstag and the Minister of the Interior present, that Austria and Germany were "one people, one nation." Soon after a former Justice Minister had asserted Austria's right to join the mother country before the German Reichstag. Most worrisome, however, were the comments of the chancellor himself, Monsignor Seipel, who in an interview had said that Austria, in making economic arrangements with her neighbors, would have to maintain her freedom of action; but union with Germany would be preferable. French, Italian, Czech and even Hungarian newspapers commented on these incidents, and the French Government made it clear that such incidents could only slow the "regulation of outstanding questions with France."[44]

The danger of *Anschluss* fostered unlikely alliances. François Charles-Roux, the French minister in Prague, reported that his Italian counterpart made several visits to Kamil Krofta, secretary general at the Czechoslovak Foreign Ministry, to discuss the common danger that *Anschluss* represented for their countries. Hearing similar lines from several different Italian officials, the Czechs had concluded that the line had been prescribed by Rome. At the same time, however, Mussolini's government also encouraged revisionism in Hungary, which threatened Czechoslovakia.[45]

Again, *Anschluss* was not the only possible solution to Austria's problems. Headquartered in Vienna itself was the Pan-European Union, dedicated to the cause of European integration. In September 1928 Briand received a despatch from his chargé d'affaires in Vienna, A. Barois, summarizing an article written by the Union's founder, Count Richard Coudenhove-Kalergi.[46] The article helped to illuminate the *Anschluss* question, Barois wrote; it was unusual, after all, for a country to seek to forfeit its independence in an age of nationalism. The explanation, Coudenhove-Kalergi thought, lay not in any particular affinity between Austrians and Germans (even Bavarians and Prussians were in many ways different), but in an Austrian sense of weakness. This lack of confidence lay embedded in Austria's history and in the character of its people. In no other country was patriotism so lacking.[47]

For Germany, the article continued, the motives were different and varied. First and foremost, the annexation of Austria would help to offset the losses resulting from the war. Beyond this, the attraction to the idea was widespread: right-wing parties stressed a common national ideology; federalists and democrats saw in Austria a counterweight to northern Germany (especially Prussia) and its centralizing impulse; Catholics favored the addition of a mainly Catholic population; business leaders saw potential markets and a springboard for economic domination of what had been Austria's empire.

Anschluss was not, however, simply an Austrian or German problem, argued Coudenhove-Kalergi. The matter had to be considered from a European point of view; here one could find arguments both for and against such a union. The principle of national self-determination would seem to give Austrians freedom to determine their own political organization; furthermore, *Anschluss* would help to reconcile Germany with Europe. On the other hand, it would upset the European equilibrium (such as it was) and exacerbate fears of Germany. Austria's geographical position further complicated matters. According to Coudenhove-Kalergi, European equilibrium meant a balance of power among the powers France, Italy and Germany.[48] The Italians would not be enthusiastic about Germans positioned at the Brenner Pass; furthermore, Austria would give Germany better access to the Balkans, a region where the Italians had their own ambitions. And no country would be so threatened as Czechoslovakia, which would find itself enclosed on three sides. The solution to this problem lay in a "pan-European" arrangement: Austrians needed an idea to replace that of *Anschluss*; and Vienna, given its central location, might regain some of its former importance.

The Pan-European Union remained primarily an intellectual movement, however. In Austria and Germany it had little influence among leaders or the population at large. Nor did the cause impress the top official at the League, Sir Eric Drummond, who urged restraint: "Please, don't go too fast," he told Coudenhove-Kalergi. Conversely, Briand, who received Coudenhove-Kalergi at the Quai d'Orsay in 1926 and 1927, encouraged him to move quickly.[49]

The German and Austrian governments pursued a different goal, however. In 1929 and 1930 German foreign minister Julius Curtius, having convinced himself that the League had not prohibited a customs union specifically, met several times with the Austrian Chancellor Johann Schober to discuss the question. The consensus among scholars has been that the

German government sought a foreign policy "success" to calm the restive domestic political scene.[50] Curtius was the main advocate, but Chancellor Brüning supported the idea after the National Socialist electoral victories in September 1930. Though he knew that the reaction in Europe might be strong, Curtius believed that "however great the shock might be here and there, the customs union must still be our goal."[51] When the announcement came, it not only diminished the dream of a "Paneuropa"; it also renewed fears of Mitteleuropa. In the meantime, Germany had to respond to Briand's proposal.

Britain's Response to the Briand Plan

Some of the strongest opposition to Briand's plan from within France came from those who worried about its possible repercussions in Britain.[52] Already in July 1929 a senator, Maurice Ordinaire, had written to Poincaré that Briand's talk of a United States of Europe caused "bitter anxiety" among many of his colleagues:

> 'If England does not lend herself to the economic accord being prepared,' says in effect M. Sauerwein, whose ties with the Quai d'Orsay we know, 'too bad for her!' If even, according to many indications, the 'United States of Europe' — that is to say a Franco-German alliance, given the certainty of England's refusal to join, because of her wish to remain on good terms with the United States — take a long time to become a reality, what effect would be produced by this quasi-rupture with the Anglo-Saxon world?[53]

Ordinaire, deeply concerned that France, in reaching for an elusive goal, might do serious damage to her relations with Britain and the United States, wrote that a majority in the Senate might oppose the idea. The potential for alienating the United States was great; though Britain would be welcome to join the union, the primacy of her overseas concerns would clearly militate against such intimacy with the Continent.

Indeed, *Le Temps*, the semi-official newspaper, seemed to reach the same conclusion just days after Briand's speech in Geneva. The British ambassador in Paris, William Tyrrell, quoted the issue of 10 September 1929 as saying that "the English press receives the scheme in a most discouraging manner if not with hostility."[54] *Le Temps*, characterizing Britain's dilemma from a French point of view, erroneously assumed the primacy of Europe in British foreign policy. Yet the result was the same: if England, given her inescapable ties to Europe, were to join such a federation, she would remove herself further from the Dominions and colonies.

Tyrrell could only wonder, therefore, what Briand expected: did he also underestimate the importance of the Empire to Britain?

Relations with the Dominions and Colonies being complicated enough, Britain could hardly be expected to countenance a new and closer political relationship with Europe. But would rejection of the plan on that basis jeopardize Britain's economic ties with the Continent? Advocates of a system of imperial preference might point to a declining European market for British manufactured goods to make a case for turning away from the Continent, but over one-third of Britain's exports still went there.[55] Closer economic ties between France and Germany, perhaps even to the exclusion of Britain, threatened its European markets further.[56] Signs of economic rapprochement had appeared already: Orme Sargent wrote in February 1930 that, though it was difficult to know "how much fire there [was] behind all this smoke," steel and potash cartels had been established, and upcoming negotiations over the return of the Saarland to Germany might result in a similar arrangement for the coal and iron industries.[57]

Tyrrell suspected that Louis Loucheur was "once again actively engaged in working on some further Franco-German economic agreement, to the exclusion of this country":

> Tyrrell notices that the Germans in Paris seem to be hand in glove with the French at the moment, and the intimacy of their relations constantly surprises him and would probably very considerably startle people in London. The explanation, no doubt, lies in the fact that now that the 'liquidation' of the war…is about to be completed, there will be infinitely less occasion for friction between France and Germany, and if Germany proves herself amenable, the French Government are out to do all they can to bring her into the Europe which France has set herself to organize and the basis of which…can only be Franco-German reconciliation and co-operation — with a French eye on Italy. No doubt, however, many Frenchmen would welcome British participation merely because they dread German preponderance.[58]

Whether or not British industries would participate in such arrangements was the Board of Trade's concern, but the prospect of Britain being excluded was disturbing. After hearing how French and German negotiators had maneuvered at the Hague to work out arrangements for the evacuation of the Rhineland, Tyrrell had written: "we should realize how close the cooperation is between French and German officials even in political questions, if they mean to reach an agreement."[59] He need not have worried, for many obstacles still blocked the path to Franco-German friendship. However, in a time of "liquidation" of past disputes, the future was uncertain; Tyrrell's misperception arose from the fear that Britain might find herself excluded from a new European order.

In addition, the fact that the proposal came from a French leader did not help; though Briand enjoyed a great deal of respect, Tyrrell's opinion of many of Briand's colleagues was low. Particularly during this time, from the British point of view, the French displayed a maddening tendency to use their relative prosperity and financial strength as a diplomatic club:

> The situation is not made any easier by the conviction prevailing here that the country is much more solid and secure than it was a few years ago. All the information I gather in commercial and financial circles is to the effect that never was France so economically sound as she is today. She has built up huge gold reserves both in America and in England which she imagines to give her great strength and means of pressure. They are taking a short view of the future but that is their unfortunate habit. The only man among public men here who takes a long and broad view of the future of Europe is Briand.[60]

Though the priority of the Empire was sufficient to explain Britain's lack of enthusiasm for the plan, suspicion of French attempts to dominate Europe economically, militarily and politically might explain the "hostility" which *Le Temps* had detected.

Tyrrell did recognize that the trend toward cooperation could improve the political situation in Europe, and that political stability might in turn further strengthen economic prosperity: "It is only necessary to consider the effect on the vital national industries of a political decision which would render further European war impossible." Outright rejection, then, might not be the wisest course: "by a wise diplomacy we might keep this movement on lines from which we may benefit and need not suffer." Two factors could profoundly affect the political and economic situation in Europe: the first was the "liquidation of the war," which could produce major changes in Franco-German relations; the second was the growing recognition in France that, without closer European political and economic organization, the future was too uncertain and dangerous. Tyrrell expressed ambivalence (either his own or that which he anticipated of his colleagues) about the possible outcome: "We should not forget that, whatever may be our views as to the desirability of such a result, 'France, by working for general peace, works for herself and assures her supremacy.'"[61]

Britain's attitude toward the plan also would affect the attitudes of other powers. German leaders eagerly awaited the response of the British government, if only because they expected it to be negative. Briand's vision assumed a neighborly, republican Germany, but Horace Rumbold believed that the predominant German vision of Europe was incompatible with any arrangement that would perpetuate the territorial status quo in Eastern Europe. Responding to Tyrrell's opinions about the plan, which had been circulated to the British embassies on the Continent, he wrote:

> [Germany] would be hostile for the simple reason that such a federalisation would be flatly opposed to the Europe of which Germany dreams. In that Europe Germany would be reunited with the Province of East Prussia and with the Free City of Danzig and possibly with some German-speaking areas which are said to exist in Upper Silesia and along the eastern frontier generally. Germany will not readily resign the right to secure the modification of the existing settlement by peaceful means.[62]

A Europe unified under French auspices would be stabilized at first by a system of alliances, Rumbold continued, and then by a general federalization "more in accord with the spirit of the age." This plan, he concluded, "cannot be otherwise than profoundly obnoxious to the country against which it is principally directed."[63]

Curiously, Rumbold did not pause to consider whether or not the plan indeed was directed against Germany. It may have been a thinly concealed plan to secure the status quo, but the proposal also contained an important element of conciliation. True, France would not agree to territorial concessions to dissatisfied powers, but the principle aim of the plan was greater European prosperity and harmony, which, was in the interest of all. Briand may have underestimated the primacy of German and Italian revisionism, but he hardly could be blamed for failing to go out of his way to accommodate their aggressive ambitions. Rumbold's words suggested that Germany's grievances were legitimate, and that France was using this scheme to pursue its oppression of Germany. He thought the French deceived themselves as to the state of their relations with Germany; while they believed that "questions which have hitherto rendered Franco-German relations difficult are approaching a settlement....[T]he question of the eastern frontier is not included."[64]

On the economic side, Rumbold wrote that the Germans could greatly benefit from reduced trade barriers in Europe. They had "a natural predilection for all kinds of combines, syndicates and cartels," and were involved in a number of such arrangements on an international level, including an agreement between French and German chemical and potash industries. France and Germany also had an extensive commercial treaty. As for an economic federation of Europe, Rumbold was unsure what the

German attitude would be. While Germany would be opposed to "any association prompted by direct economic hostility either to England and America," she would have "a great deal to gain by some sort of economic federation of Europe."[65] Her industrial strength and geographical position put her in a good strategic position to dominate that market.

Rumbold's conclusions about Tyrrell's despatch addressed the difficult issue of reconciling political and economic agenda:

> It is tempting to translate Lord Tyrrell's political maxims into the economic sphere and to write that France is ambitious of taking the lead in economic Europe and containing the British Empire and America by linking to herself the other European powers which she in turn contains through their fear of America and the Empire. But I believe it to be a mistake to attempt such a reconciliation of French ideas in the two spheres of politics and economics. Indeed, just as arbitration may be destined to supersede alliances, so eventually may economics supersede politics. The eventual ends which are being pursued are thus different in kind and the means differ accordingly.[66]

Rumbold assumed that France intended to dominate Europe politically. Rumbold's hesitance to draw similar conclusions about French economic motives reveals a mind caught between two different conceptions of international relations, one dominated by political imperatives, the other by more mysterious economic forces. Rumbold could conceive of the possibility of a Europe united economically, but the vision vanished upon introduction of the political dimension; too much evidence remained of the "old nature" of fractious nationalistic politics.

Like Germany, Italy would reject the proposal. Britain's ambassador in Rome, Sir Ronald Graham, wrote that the bad state of relations between France and Italy made the scheme virtually impossible. In fact, Italy might well be making other arrangements: "The absence of any improvement in Franco-Italian relations, the failure to eliminate the points of friction which have made these relations difficult, have necessarily turned my attention to the prospects of an Italo-German rapprochement, which might eventually be supplemented by closer relations with Russia, though at the moment this seems far off."[67]

Graham believed that Europe was a blank slate: "We must take our stand on the fact that...that the war has now, practically speaking, been liquidated." Old antagonisms might now be replaced by new ones, and ties formed which formerly were considered impossible. But the Europe France was trying to organize, by leaving Italy without a definite place, "vitiates the scheme outlined, and would appear to indicate a flaw in French policy." At the end of May 1930, Graham reported that the "Minister for Foreign Affairs [Grandi] told me he has not yet had time to examine M. Briand's scheme in detail but that Italy would certainly not accept it and he had already been authorised by Signor Mussolini to reject it." Out of "consideration for M. Briand's feelings," he would delay the announcement.[68]

On May 9, 1930 Henderson and Briand discussed the plan in Paris, Henderson having promised his government's full consideration once Briand set forth some concrete ideas. Briand hastened to assure the foreign secretary that "there would be nothing in the scheme which would give it even the semblance of being directed against the United States of America."[69] Naval competition, different philosophies of trade and the growing U.S. corporate presence in Britain during the 1920s had created tensions between the two powers, but nothing worried British leaders more than the prospect of conflict.

On May 17 the Ambassador Fleuriau delivered a copy of Briand's memorandum further explaining the idea of European federation to the British government. All other European members of the League of Nations received the same communication. Striking to today's reader for its use of the terms "common market" and "European Community" twenty-seven years before the Treaty of Rome, Briand's memorandum once again emphasized the political dimensions of federation over the economic.[70]

On May 30 the Foreign Office produced a sharply critical internal memorandum, written by Reginald Leeper.[71] The opening words conveyed a note of irritation: "The Memorandum, for which M. Briand has kept Europe waiting all these months, is, at least from first sight, a surprising and disappointing work. It is permeated by a vague and puzzling idealism expressed in such phrases as 'collective responsibility in the face of the danger which threatens the peace of Europe', 'need for a permanent regime of solidarity', and much else which may mean a great deal or may mean nothing at all."[72] Leeper considered the possible French motives for making such a proposal, as well as the likely responses of other European governments. Briand's substitution of political for economic problems as the chief focus of the proposed association might well undermine the authority of the League; the motives for this switch of priorities were unclear, but one possibility was that by formulating a proposal that Germany and Italy would have to reject (because it insisted on the maintenance of the territorial status quo), France might appear to be the only major power in Europe truly interested in the continent's salvation. Briand, however, came closest of all Frenchmen to being beyond reproach in the eyes of the British; perhaps a more likely motive, therefore, was the belief that political stability was a prerequisite for economic cooperation.

In the end, however, Leeper's memorandum called for no reply to be given before the plan was explained more clearly and before "the countries primarily concerned have spoken their minds."[73] After all, this proposal concerned Continental Europe more directly than it did Great Britain; the relationship of these proposals to British imperial and world interests would have to be carefully examined.   Nevertheless, while remaining non-committal on the proposals, Britain ought to endorse the principles which Briand invoked. Not surprisingly, the Foreign Office mustered little enthusiasm for the Briand plan. Britain could hardly be expected to embrace the idea of closer association with the Continent; after the Great War, the predominant impulse was to get out and tend to imperial matters. Yet the idea of a Continental association rationalizing the European market without her could also be seen as potentially harmful to British interests. However, Britain's failure to join would probably "wreck the scheme" in any case.[74]

Among Henderson's closest associates at the Foreign Office — Dalton, Cecil, and Noel-Baker — opinions on the proposal had a common theme: the potential damage to the League of Nations. Philip Noel-Baker's note dealt with little else. He applauded the impulse to stress the common interests among nations, but few governments would accept the political implications of "federal Union"; as for the "practical economic and technical activities which he proposed for his European Union there is none on which work has not already been begun by the various organs of the League of Nations."[75]

Robert Cecil's thoughts ranged more widely, incorporating the imperial concerns which many Britons would raise. There was, he believed, "no need to seek recondite motives in M. Briand's action"; he simply wanted peace for France and the world, and saw Europe as "the chief probable storm centre of war." As if to address the suspicions expressed by some at the Foreign Office, he wrote that Briand might "wish to restore the economic balance between Europe and America," but he doubted (correctly) whether Briand took "much personal interest in economic questions."[76]

So far as motives were concerned, therefore, Britain had nothing to fear from the Briand plan. Yet Cecil saw "grave danger" in the plan, "to the League on our side and the British Empire on the other." If economic cooperation were not pursued through the League, a successful federation of Europe would encourage similar organization on other continents. The proper response in the face of these possible changes in the world order would not be formation of an "empire group":

> I know that some people like Mr. Amery have a dream of a British empire group which could be independent of the rest of the world. I see no prospect of such a result. He and others seem to think that Great Britain could divorce herself from Europe. Why? She has been culturally, economically and politically part of Europe for many centuries and still is. Indeed the obstacle of the channel has become far less than it was.[77]

Even if Britain could remain independent of a European organization, other parts of the Empire, for example Canada or India, might find it more difficult to remain aloof from the regional associations that would subsequently appear in America and Asia. Without the coordinating influence of the League, this regionalization would be "a seriously disintegrating influence on the Empire."[78]

In July 1930 a Cabinet Committee on the proposed federal union met for the first time. In a memorandum obviously influenced by Cecil, Henderson wrote that Briand's chief motivation was a desire for peace, stability and prosperity. The French foreign minister wanted Europeans to drop their traditional antagonisms and focus on their common interests. This was consistent with his policy of the past ten years:

> He believes in peace, both for his country and for the world, and he sees that Europe is still the chief probable storm centre of war. He therefore wishes to strengthen international safeguards against European war, and for that purpose to increase European co-operation. Some of his colleagues are, no doubt, also actuated by the desire to restore the economic balance between Europe and America.[79]

This "main purpose" of Briand's plan, he concluded, had to receive full British support: "More than ever before peace is the first of British interests, and especially peace in Europe."[80]

Henderson insisted that the plan be discussed within the context of the League of Nations, against the will of both Briand and Secretary-General Drummond. Hugh Dalton wrote that Briand wished to keep the matter to the states directly involved and "presumably, to have it handled by Quai d'Orsay officials." Drummond's objections were of a different sort, according to Dalton; the League had had a bad run of luck lately, and did not need another failure on its record:

> There is a good deal of defeatism and demoralisation in the Secretariat at present. Several recent International Conferences have been complete or substantial failures

(Tariff Truce, Export Prohibition, coal and cooperation of International Law). We have undoubtedly struck a bad patch....On Disarmament Uncle [Henderson] made a good and strong speech (I put in the strongest passages), and made a marked impression. But the German Election, with Nazi and Communist successes, came just afterward, and upset the French more than ever, and the Franco-Italian Naval Discussions are still sticking pretty badly. So the atmosphere is not good, even for the Preparatory Commission..."[81]

Dalton held out little hope for the plan; the recent failure of more modest schemes reinforced his pessimistic outlook.

Henderson's July 16 reply to the French government echoed the affirmative tone of his July 3 memorandum, but postponed the definite reply requested, pleading a need to consult with the Dominions. Henderson also reiterated his deep concern over the relationship of Briand's proposed federation to the League of Nations. He believed that Briand could attain his ends by working through the machinery of the League, and that not doing so might cause suspicion and fear among non-European League members. He proposed that the matter be put on the agenda of the next League assembly.[82] He prevailed: in September the discussion moved to the League of Nations, where it remained.

As responses to the proposal arrived at the Quai d'Orsay, the *Economist* stressed the merits of Briand's proposal. The responses of the various governments in July were necessary statements of their positions; the objections made clearer the "practical limits of common action." Briand now could "assuage unfounded fears" and seek cooperative solutions to European problems within the context of the League.[83] Whether or not (and probably not) a European Confederation emerged from all this, cooperation, at least on the economic level, was now a live option.

The Demise of the Plan

From the revisionist powers, the response also was negative. The Germans sent their response on July 11. The note was not as blunt as Hungary's, which flatly rejected a proposal which perpetuated the current territorial and minority problems, but it echoed the sentiment. The German government "appreciated" the French government's interpretation of Europe's problems, the document stated, suggesting that Germany had a different perspective on these problems. One major concern the German government cited was the danger of damaging relations with other countries and continents. To form a genuine European confederation, furthermore, Russia and Turkey would have to be invited to join.[84]

The German response affirmed Briand's emphasis on the political side of the question, but said that "it is hopeless to want to build a new Europe on a foundation that would not be able to withstand the brisk development of events." Some economic cooperation might be possible, but political integration depended on "full equality of rights" and the "peaceful adjustment of the natural necessities of life."[85] Of course, Germany stood to gain from closer economic cooperation, and the note acknowledged that improved economic relations might improve the political atmosphere. But Germany would not join an organization whose goal was to guarantee the status quo.

The Italian reply to Briand's memorandum reflected the Fascist government's general hostility to France.[86] Though Italy had not disrupted European politics in recent years, the behavior of her representatives at Geneva underscored the fact that Italy was dissatisfied with her current status in Europe. Sir Hughe Knatchbull-Hugessen's private assessment of the Italian situation in February 1931 reflected discussions he had had with colleagues in the Foreign Office. Italy, like Germany, had contributed greatly to the sense of unease in Europe. Franco-Italian relations had not improved; some progress had been made in naval questions, but Italy's current disposition did not enhance the prospects of either Briand's plan or the upcoming disarmament conference:

> But I am sceptical even of this and altogether sceptical of Italy's desire to improve matters. She has let her bad relations with Yugoslavia drag on for years now. I fear she will find it convenient to do the same with France. Meanwhile she gathers round her all the discontented elements in Europe and draws closer to Russia. I regard Italy with great anxiety as to future developments. Her attitude to Briand's scheme requires interpretation. Many evidently think that she has pressed for the invitation to Russia and Turkey as a means of killing the scheme (possibly of discrediting the League). Then there is the disarmament question and the Conference fixed for next February. If the fate of Briand's scheme is not very cheerful, I do not see how the fate of the Disarmament Conference can be better. It is open to attack from the same form of disease.[87]

Knatchbull-Hugessen felt that the League of Nations was headed for a "supreme test," and that the Disarmament Conference might well be it.

The reasons for Italy's hostility toward France became clear to Leo Kennedy of the *Times*, who met Mussolini in Rome in March 1931. Having completed the trek across the enormous room which served as the *duce*'s office, Kennedy was pelted with questions about Britain and Europe. He later wrote in his diary that he was not terribly impressed by Mussolini, whose opinions on international affairs seemed outmoded: "he is a tremendous conservative. This may seem rather trite, but I did not realize before how blind he is to the progress really being made by Communist ideas in various parts of the world, or how sincerely he believes in the probability of war. His mind in that way is absolutely pre-War."[88] Kennedy also saw little of the vigor for which Mussolini was known. Gone was the "mesmeric influence"; what remained was "the hulk of a man, whose exuberance is spent."[89]

Mussolini believed that France was using her power — a large army and navy, gold reserves and satellite states — to secure hegemony in Europe. When he said that France could conquer Europe, Kennedy disagreed, "and gave as reasons that in the first place France itself would not dream of following any leader who was foolish enough to suggest any such adventure. There was too much communism in France."[90] When Mussolini said there was no communism in France, Kennedy replied that there was at least an extreme form of socialism which was anti-militarist, and therefore likely to bring down any war effort.

The subject of French hegemony remained with Kennedy, and a few weeks later, in Briand's special coach en route from Geneva to Paris, he asked Alexis Léger, Briand's right-hand man, about it. Léger explained France's situation:

> France has got a position of hegemony. But she (i.e.) Briand does not use it selfishly. She is trying to reconstruct Europe. She is trying to help other countries. She has no aggressive designs whatever. She wants others to trust her. Moreover she considers Great Britain an equal partner, and always welcomes her co-operation — would in fact like more of it. Those two countries are the two pillars of new Europe. And in time there should be four pillars — Italy and Germany as well as France and Great Britain. At present the other two are very jealous. Briand is doing all he can to win them over.[91]

Kennedy found that Léger shared his impressions of Mussolini:

> Italy under Mussolini's guidance has done all she can to oppose France (this is most true) — Locarno was at first opposed by Italy, so was the Briand-Kellogg Pact. In both cases Italy came around. But Mussolini remains stubbornly aloof from European collaboration. Grandi is doing what he can. But Mussolini is obsessed by his idées démodées (most true). He is by nature adaptable and forward-looking. But he is hemmed in. He cannot leave Italy. He does not come into contact with the new forces that are moving in Europe (just what I noticed). La collectivité, la [sic] communisme — they are nothing to him.[92]

Kennedy said that Mussolini had told him: "France can conquer Europe." "Typical," Léger had replied. "We know that is nonsense. We don't fear a war; we fear a civil war."[93]

Briand had failed to convince the leader of Europe's other major powers, however. The governments of Britain, Germany, and Italy all were hostile to his plan. Yet the sentiment that called for European cooperation was a good one, and no major power could therefore condemn Briand's efforts outright and bring the discussion to an end. At the Eleventh Assembly of the League of Nations in September 1930, a Commission of Inquiry for European Union was formed.

The story from this point became one of procedural maneuvering by opponents of the idea to evade serious discussion. The unfortunate effect was to make the whole idea seem unthinkable, if not occasionally ridiculous. As Briand himself later asked before the Chamber of Deputies, "What kind of sarcasms did this initiative not receive?"[94] Refusing to contemplate that such a European federation might in fact complement the League's work, Arthur Henderson insisted on full League of Nations participation in the discussion. He proved himself to be more amenable to Curtius and Grandi, the German and Italian foreign ministers, than to his friend Briand. At the second session of the Commission in January, Henderson suggested that *all* nations be invited to participate in these discussions, whether they were members of the League or not. Grandi and Curtius quickly agreed.[95] Under these circumstances, obviously, Briand's plan could make no headway.

In March 1931, the first conference of yet another Committee dealing with the question of European union, the Committee on Constitution, Organization and Procedure, met in Paris. Besides Briand, three foreign ministers attended the three-day conference: Zaleski of Poland, Munch of Denmark and Britain's Arthur Henderson. Germany and Italy sent lower-ranking officials. A Soviet representative also attended.

As the conferees gathered, news broke of the Austro-German customs union proposal. "The German and Austrian governments profess to regard the agreement as a first step toward giving effect to the idea of European union advocated by M. Briand," the *Times* reported. But the article expressed skepticism: "Formally and immediately the procedure outlined may be purely economic, but in perspective it takes on a certain political hue."[96] Any German leader with the smallest sense of external politics had to know that the proposal would cause great alarm in France, as it did, though not across the whole political spectrum. The Radical-Socialist paper *La République* said too much was being made of the matter, while Blum's

Le Populaire said that those who revived fears of *Mitteleuropa* were the victims of their prewar memories. Yet in London the *Times* wrote that "those who have been most active in promoting a Franco-German *rapprochement* are much disturbed and disappointed."[97]

Meanwhile the hapless conference concluded in a "somewhat disconcerting atmosphere," having discussed the question of European federation almost solely from the economic angle. Briand himself cautiously avoided discussion of the political dimension. The conference succeeded in charting a course for European federation, but in the process transformed Briand's poetic vision into a more prosaic committee of the League of Nations.[98] A date in May was set for the next meeting, to be held in Geneva. The *Times* seemed pleased with the results, reasoning that the "present organization probably contains more durable elements than if there were a strong political component."[99]

Yet the fragile foundation of European unity — Franco-German cooperation — was eroding. At the Quai d'Orsay, Alexis Léger told Leo Kennedy that he believed an Austro-German customs union would ultimately lead to political union, and that nations like Hungary and Yugoslavia would be drawn into the German sphere of influence, eventually creating two opposing camps in Europe and another arms race. Briand therefore was doing all he could to incorporate the idea into a larger scheme.[100] Yet his policy of rapprochement with Germany faced increasing criticism at home, and French officials were not compassionate during the Austrian and German financial crises of the spring and summer.[101]

Efforts did continue: Briand and Laval received an unexpectedly warm welcome upon their arrival in Berlin in September 1931, but the results of their visit were insubstantial.[102] The new French Ambassador in Berlin, André François-Poncet, had established an economic commission to discuss matters of foreign exchange, commerce, transportation and industry. Twenty French and twenty German civil servants and business leaders met "without incident and without warmth" in Berlin at the time of the Briand-Laval visit.[103] Of course, some in France would carry hopes for Franco-German cooperation beyond the Nazi victories of 1933, but at that time collaboration acquired a wholly new meaning.

The End?

Speaking with Leo Kennedy in June 1931, Count Coudenhove-Kalergi related a conversation he had had at a luncheon with Kennedy's boss at the

Times, Geoffrey Dawson. Leo Amery, Austen Chamberlain and Arthur Henderson had also been present:

> They had a tremendous argument, it seems, about Europe and the part that England ought to play. Amery is so imperialist that his instinct is to keep clear of Europe; AC and Henderson both argued that our influence was great and could and should be usefully employed; that if it wasn't the European countries would fall out much more quickly than they do anyway, and we should become involved; that our proper function is mediatorial.[104]

Kennedy's sympathies tended in both directions, reflecting the classic British dilemma between Europe and Empire.

Fear of Bolshevism appeared to fuel Coudenhove-Kalergi's efforts for European unity. A Communist Germany would "join hands territorially" with Russia, of course at Poland's expense; to unify on the Briand basis was the only alternative to unity on a Communist basis. Yet Coudenhove-Kalergi "criticized Briand a little as not understanding Germany. He does not know Germany or the Germans. Tardieu understands the Germans much better; and may possibly bring about Briand's dream more effectively than he, the dreamer, could. Tardieu of course is an absolute opportunist."[105] Coudenhove-Kalergi also believed that good economic relations between countries formed the basis of sound political relations. Kennedy wondered, therefore, about Britain's system of imperial preference: "As C.-K. said, you cannot have two preferences."[106]

Discussion of the idea of European Union did not end, despite the ever-increasing gulf between the vision and the reality. In July 1933 — with Hitler in power, the League failing in its disarmament efforts, and much of the world economy in depression — an article in the *Economist* suggested that "the idea of the United States of Europe has perhaps been brought nearer to realisation within the last few days than ever before."[107] It had been assumed that such proposals would come at a time of political and economic stability, and that they would begin with proposals for economic integration.

Now, however, the article continued, the idea seemed to be gaining new currency, despite all the economic and political turmoil: "the very extremity of chaos into which the world has plunged has at last stimulated the even the most parochially-minded Governments and peoples to make substantial sacrifices of cherished sacrifices and policies on the altar of reconstruction." The writer had in mind two small-minded governments, those of Italy and France, which were now finding common ground on two fronts. Both sought to prevent *Anschluss* between Germany and Austria, and both hoped to prevent inflation by remaining on the gold standard, even though the United States had just abandoned it:

> A war on two fronts against Germany and the United States to prevent the *Anschluss* and to prevent inflation! This is a unifying force which the two Latin Powers could hardly withstand with the worst will in the world. And if these two powers hold together, and bring their respective East European satellites into line, their battle in the political sphere is as good as won; for Germany will have virtually no alternative but to come into the Franco-Italian camp on Franco-Italian terms — the more so in as much as, in the economic sphere, Germany with her memories of her own inflation of the mark of the mark is bound to be at least a tacit member of the gold group, however sharply this economic alignment may clash with her political aspirations.[108]

Now, at last, the article suggested, leading governments in Europe were heeding warnings preached since the war, that if Europe did not pull together it would be subject to domination by the American giant to the West, and the Russian giant to the East. Britain, of course, would remain detached from the Continental group, as leader of the sterling bloc, and could mediate between America and Europe because of its special ties with both. However, the formation of regional groups such as a United States of Europe could not substitute for the "world-wide collective system of security which we have been striving to build up on the basis of the League Covenant and the Kellogg Pact. For that system, indeed, there can be no substitute whatever."[109] The article sounds like a flight of fancy in light of current and subsequent events, but the *Economist* had its own version of the vision.

From hindsight, Briand's vision of a new Europe seems both utopian and prophetic, the attempt to realize it both futile and heroic. In its own day, it was greeted with incredulity and even suspicion; few nations were prepared to make the leap of faith required to cast their lot in with other nations, least of all nations whose territory they wanted. Yet the proposal attempted to address a glaring problem: the instability of Europe in the wake of a conflict in which the traditional balance of power had been upset.

The Briand plan marked the high point of France's efforts to regulate European politics in the interwar period. This was an internationalist solution to European problems which happened to coincide largely with France's national interests. Unfortunately, Briand's vision could not be imposed on reality. The circumstances in which such a union might be possible — if indeed they had ever existed — were rapidly disappearing in 1930. Carl Pegg recalled that there was much talk of European union in the cafés of Paris in the spring of 1930.[110] By late summer — almost incredibly, since France still dwarfed Germany militarily and the French people had no desire to rekindle the conflict — talk turned to the fear of war.

Notes

1. FO 800/281/239-240, Cecil to Henderson, June 1, 1930. More recently, D.C. Watt has described the wars of 1914-1918 and 1939-1945 as European civil wars. See *Too Serious a Business* (London, 1975), pp. 10-31; *How War Came* (New York, 1989), chapters 1 and 2.
2. J. Lukacs, *Decline and Rise of Europe* (New York, 1965), pp. 108-111.
3. Oudin, *Aristide Briand*, p. 524.
4. C. Pegg, *The Evolution of the European Idea* (Chapel Hill, 1983), pp. 34-40.
5. Orde, *British Policy and European Reconstruction*, p. 317; R. Boyce, "Britain's First 'No' to Europe: Britain and the Briand Plan, 1929-1930," *European Studies Review* 10:1 (January 1980), p. 26.
6. Boyce in P.Stirk, ed., *European Unity in Context: the Interwar Period* (London, 1989), pp. 68-69.
7. Quoted in the introductory note to a section on British attitudes towards the Briand Plan in DBFP, series II, volume 1, p. 312.
8. J. Hermans, *L'évolution de la pensée européenne d'Aristide Briand* (Nancy, 1965), pp. 10-12; C. Maier, *Recasting Bourgeois Europe* (Princeton, 1975), pp. 253, 262-263.
9. Hermans, p. 20.
10. Quoted in C. Pegg, p. 112.
11. DBFP, series II, volume 1, pp. 312-313.
12. Today's readers will be struck by the note of racism in Briand's proposal, which drew no comment at the time. League of Nations Documents A/46/1930/VII, Documents Relating to the Organisation of a System of European Federal Union, Geneva, September 15, 1930, p. 9.
13. Oudin, pp. 11-17.
14. Wandycz, *Twilight of French Eastern Alliances*, p. 124.
15. Peter Krüger, in his article in Stirk, pp. 87-96.
16. This belief reflected the influence of the British journalist and internationalist Norman Angell. In his widely read book *The Great Illusion* (London, 1910), he argued that an invader, by attempting to destroy the trade of an enemy, merely destroyed his own actual or potential market, an act which was "commercially suicidal" (p. 32).
17. The support of industrialists Robert Bosch (German), Emile Mayrisch (Luxembourger), Ernest Mercier and René Duchemin (both French) suggest that the "politics of Locarno" had support on the political right. Oudin, p. 524.
18. C. Paillat, *Dossiers secrets de la France contemporaine*, volume 3, *La guerre à l'horizon* (Paris, 1981), pp. 33-34.
19. Wandycz, pp. 60-61. *Le Matin* had become a pro-German paper and remained so into the Nazi era.
20. Poincaré XXIII, n.a.fr. 16014/169-171, Rechberg to Poincaré, Berlin, October 16, 1929.
21. 74 AP 11 (Reynaud papers), Rechberg to Reynaud, October 15, 1929.

22. Wandycz, p. 139.
23. JO, Chambre, December 24, 1929, p. 1598.
24. Ibid., pp. 1598-1599.
25. Ibid. The Geneva Protocol called for signature of the Optional Clause, by which nations would submit disputes to the Permanent Court at the Hague.
26. Ibid.
27. Stresemann himself never suggested that Germany would be willing to make concessions on these claims. H. Gatzke, *Stresemann and the Rearmament of Germany*, p. 113.
28. N.Pease, *Poland, the United States, and the Stabilization of Europe, 1919-1933* (New York, 1986), pp. 24, 75, 127, 152. A Franco-Polish consortium built the port. Pease suggests that, in the early years of the alliance, French financial interest in Poland was "tepid," due in part to France's own financial weakness. After 1926, however, French investors played a somewhat greater role in the development of Poland's infrastructure; in 1930, for example, a Franco-Polish company was formed to electrify southwest Poland, and in 1931 a French firm began construction on the Silesian-Baltic railroad.
29. Gdynia continued to gain on Danzig; in 1931, for example, Gdynia handled 5 million tons, compared to Danzig's 8.1 million tons. FO 408/61/21, Memorandum by Hankey, February 1, 1933.
30. JO, Chambre, December 24, 1929, p. 1599.
31. Ibid.
32. See Wandycz's appraisal in *Twilight*, pp. 448-478.
33. Between 1920 and 1937, Austria never achieved a positive trade balance (one might add that Austria-Hungary's last positive balance had been in 1906). In the 1920s the best year was 1925, when imports were only 43% greater than exports. Mitchell, *European Historical Statistics*, p. 513.
34. F.L. Carsten, *The First Austrian Republic, 1918-1938* (London, 1986), p. 97.
35. Carsten, p. 137.
36. Bennett, p. 40.
37. Quoted in F. Knipping, *Deutschland, Frankreich und das Ende der Locarno-Ära, 1928-1931* (Munich, 1987), p. 214.
38. MAE, series Z (1918-1929), Austria 80/9-11, F. Charles-Roux to Briand, Prague, December 17, 1927.
39. *Anschluss* rally.
40. PHPP 1/8/5-6, Phipps to Chamberlain, July 5, 1928.
41. PHPP 1/8/7-8, Phipps to Chamberlain, December 6, 1928. It should be added that Phipps disliked Anatole de Monzie personally: his financial diplomacy entailed use of methods which were "too much even for the Quai d'Orsay to stomach." The Foreign Office, in its list of leading French personalities, characterized him as a man of "low financial integrity." PHPP 2/15/64-66, Phipps to Tyrrell, Paris, February 1, 1928; FO 425/405/20, Tyrrell to Henderson, Paris, April 14, 1930.
42. Blum papers, 1 BL 15/4/a, *Le Populaire*, July 27, 1928.
43. LKEN 6 (Diary), September 13, 1928.
44. MAE, series Z (1918-1929), Austria 81/72-73, Note on *Anschluss*, August 30, 1928.
45. MAE, series Z (1918-1929), Austria 81/123, Charles-Roux to Briand, Prague, September 24, 1928.
46. Coudenhove-Kalergi, the founder of the "Paneuropa" movement, was an aristocrat of diverse ethnic origin. Already in the Middle Ages, the Coudenhoves had left Brabant

to serve the Habsburgs in Austria; the Kalergis were Greek. Coudenhove-Kalergi's mother was Japanese. He moved in the highest diplomatic circles. LKEN 11, June 10, 1931.

47. MAE, series Z (1918-1929), Austria 81/124-126, M.A. Barois to Briand, Vienna, September 25, 1928.

48. Apparently Britain and the Soviet Union did not figure in this system.

49. Oudin, p. 525.

50. P. Krüger, *Die Außenpolitik der Republik von Weimar*, p. 533; Knipping, pp. 205-214; Bennett, pp. 40-52.

51. Bennett, p. 44.

52. German leaders shared this concern. Krüger, p. 533.

53. Poincaré XX, n.a.fr. 16011/216-217, M. Ordinaire to Poincaré, Paris, July 17, 1929. Sauerwein, attached to "Le Matin", was, according to Tyrrell, one of the best interviewers and reporters in the French press. An ardent supporter of the cause of peace, he was frequently in Geneva and attended most international conferences. Though "personally fond of England," he was a great admirer of the United States, and would take "their side against ours" (Tyrrell to Henderson, April 14, 1933. FO 425/405/20).

54. FO 408/55/17, Tyrrell to Henderson, Paris, February 17, 1930.

55. 34.7% of Britain's exports went to Europe in 1929, the same proportion as in 1913; by comparison, exports to the Dominions and Colonies had increased from 37.2% to 41.5% during the same period. Mowat, p. 266.

56. D.C. Watt suggests that French and German economic cooperation was in itself a reaction to the increase of American economic and financial activity on the Continent. Failure to negotiate entry into these agreements pushed Britain toward imperial preference, which in turn drew a hostile American response. *Succeeding John Bull* (Cambridge, 1984), p. 56.

57. FO 800/275/85-89, O. Sargent to E. Grigg, Foreign Office, February 3, 1930.

58. Ibid.

59. FO 800/281/45-46, Tyrrell to Henderson, Paris, February 1, 1930.

60. FO 800/281/177-179, Tyrrell to Henderson, Paris, March 28, 1930.

61. Ibid.

62. FO 408/55/29, Rumbold to Henderson, Berlin, March 14, 1930.

63. Ibid.

64. Ibid.

65. Ibid.

66. Ibid.

67. FO 408/55/31, Graham to Henderson, Rome, March 14, 1930.

68. DBFP, series II, volume 1, no. 190, pp. 333-334.

69. DBFP, series II, volume 2, no. 185, p. 313.

70. Oudin, pp. 531-532.

71. Boyce, "Britain's First 'No' to Europe," p. 35.

72. DBFP, series II, volume 1, no. 189, p. 326.

73. Ibid., p. 326.

74. Ibid., pp. 331-332.

75. FO 800/281/237-238, note on M. Briand's Memorandum, June 7, 1930.

76. FO 800/281/239-240, "M. Briand's proposals," June 1, 1930.

77. Ibid.

78. Ibid.

79. CAB 27/424/7, memorandum by Henderson, July 14, 1930.

80. Ibid.

81. Dalton I/13/167-168 (Diary), September 7-October 1, 1930.

82. DBFP, series II, volume 1, nos. 193-194, pp. 336-347.

83. The *Economist*, July 26, 1930, p. 165.

84. The Italian reply, almost mocking in tone, also demanded that Russia and Turkey be invited to join. Pegg, pp. 151-152.

85. ADAP 1918-1945, series B (1925-1933), volume 15, no. 6, Berlin, July 11, 1930.

86. For English translations of the replies of the Italian and other European governments, see League of Nations Documents A/46/1930/VII.

87. KNAT 1/7/3-8, February 5, 1931.

88. LKEN 10 (Diary), March 25, 1931.

89. Ibid.

90. Ibid. Kennedy assumed that the prospect of communist revolution restrained French leaders from using war as an instrument of policy.

91. LKEN 11 (Diary), Paris, May 23, 1931.

92. Ibid.

93. Ibid.

94. Speech printed in J. Wheeler-Bennett, ed., *Documents on International Affairs 1930* (London, 1931), p. 89.

95. Pegg, pp. 160.

96. The *Times*, March 23, 1931, p. 11.

97. The *Times*, March 25, 1931, p. 14.

98. The *Times*, March 24, 1931, p. 15; March 25, 1931, p. 13.

99. March 26, 1931, p. 13.

100. LKEN 11 (Diary), Paris, May 23, 1931.

101. Kindleberger, pp. 142-158.

102. *New York Times*, September 27, 1931, p. 18.

103. Ibid.; R. Solo, "André François-Poncet: Ambassador of France" (Ph.D. dissertation, Michigan State University, 1978), pp. 83-84.

104. LKEN 11 (Diary), June 10, 1931.

105. Ibid.

106. Ibid.

107. The *Economist*, July 15, 1933.

108. Ibid.

109. Ibid.

110. Pegg, p. ix.

6

Life with Nazi Germany

I reflect upon the responsibility of France for all this....Its mishandling of its relations with Germany and of its own satellite states could not have been worse, and its treatment of Italy has been shortsighted....We must not trust France unduly.
— Ramsay MacDonald, March 1933[1]

The whole world knows our peaceful intentions....We seek neither to menace nor humiliate any people, no matter what kind of regime it gives itself or supports.
— Édouard Daladier, October 1933[2]

By the time Hitler became chancellor of Germany at the end of January 1933, rumors and fears of war had circulated throughout Europe for a few years already. Revisionism and racism had catapulted the National Socialists into power, but the conduct of British and French policy hardly changed. By instinctive impulse, Ramsay MacDonald blamed France for the turn of events in Germany; French leaders like Daladier behaved as though they were at fault. D.C. Watt has written that "those responsible for ultimate decisions could not be convinced of the unavoidable nature of the coming conflict. They could see a threat but not its certainty."[3] Anxious to avoid conflict at all costs, they also failed to address the threat of conflict, adopting a reactive stance to whatever initiatives Germany might undertake.

The Economy, Domestic Politics and the Military

The economic and political realities facing French and British leaders provide the context for the events of 1933. With the world economy in depression, Britain and France, with their financial structures intact, were better off than the United States and Germany. The French economy had been the last to slide into depression; within a relatively self-contained economy, small- and medium-sized businesses produced goods mostly for the domestic market.[4] An undervalued franc made exports competitive on the world market before the crises of 1931, but now French prices, which had been about 20% below the world average, were about 20% higher than average. Industrial production fell; with an index of 100 for 1928, overall production stood at 108 in 1930, 96 in 1931, 83 in 1932 and 90 in 1933. Worst hit were sectors on which many depended for their livelihood: in 1932 coal, iron and steel production was 58% of what it had been in 1928, textiles 74%. The newer industries, however, managed to hold their own: these included electricity, oil refining, and chemicals.[5] Automobile production (private cars and commercial vehicles) stood at 164,000 units in 1932 and 189,000 in 1933, compared to 223,000 in 1928.

For much of Europe, including France, 1933, though certainly not a prosperous year, at least was better than 1932. For Britain some statistics even show an improvement over 1928: the British automobile industry produced 232,000 units in 1932 and 287,000 in 1933 compared to 212,000 in 1928. In Germany, meanwhile, production had fallen from 123,000 in 1928 to 51,000 in 1932, rising again to 105,000 in 1933. Italy was also affected by the slump: in 1928, 57,700 motor vehicles were produced; production bottomed out at 28,600 units in 1931, improving slightly in 1932 to 30,100 and in 1933 to 41,500 vehicles. In the Soviet Union, Stalin's first Five-Year Plan resulted in that country's first substantial production of motor vehicles (mostly for commercial use) in 1932, and in the following year output exceeded Italy's.[6]

German crude steel production in 1932 had been only 35.4% of what it had been in 1927, but in 1933, all the major European producers increased output over the previous year. The figures for total production in four of them were remarkably close: Germany produced 7,617,000 tons, Britain 7,138,000 tons, the Soviet Union 6,889,000, and France 6,577,000 tons. However, for Germany production was 53.1% less than it had been in 1929, for Britain 27.1% less, and for France 32.4% less; the Soviet Union's figure was 41.9% higher. The Italian steel industry produced 1,771,000 tons (16.5% less than in 1929), ranking behind both Belgium and Luxembourg.[7]

In 1933, unemployment was up slightly in France (305,000, up 4,000 from the previous year) and in Italy (1,019,000, up 13,000).[8] In Germany, where the depression had struck hardest, some 700,000 fewer people were unemployed than in 1932; still, about 26.3% of the labor force was out of work — about 4.8 million people. In Britain the worst also seemed to have passed, with unemployment at 2,521,000 (21.3%), down from 2,745,000 (22.5%).[9]

Despite improvements in production figures over the previous year, trade among the major industrial nations declined. In most cases the value of trade any two countries fell both in 1933 and 1934.[10] In 1927, twenty-seven nations had agreed in principle to a tariff truce (to last until April 1931) at the World Economic Conference in Geneva. Since then the United States had raised tariffs to an average of 59% with the Smoot-Hawley Tariff Act; many nations retaliated, in some cases without waiting for news of Smoot-Hawley's final enactment on June 17, 1930. Only seven nations, including Britain, ratified the 1927 agreement by the November 1930 deadline, but Britain subsequently took steps toward the establishment of an imperial trading bloc with the 1932 Ottawa Agreements.[11] As Charles Kindleberger has written, "the world economy lost its cohesion."[12] The failure of liberalism in world trade did not bode well for collective solutions to the world's political problems.

Nor did politics within Britain and France suggest any emergence from the foreign-policy torpor of the previous years. The crises had left political structures in Britain and France intact, though in Britain, the all-party, Conservative-dominated National Government remained in power. Sir John Simon, despite regular interference from Ramsay MacDonald, remained foreign secretary. France had no National Government; cabinets came and went as before, and with Briand's retirement in January 1932, the foreign minister's portfolio became part of the regular shuffling. Though with varying degrees of conviction his successors carried on his policies, they did not have his personality, on which so much had depended.

By the beginning of 1933, the postwar dream of a new international order, with the League of Nations as the keystone, had faded. The German delegation had walked out of the Disarmament Conference the previous September 16, and on December 11 the Conference lamely had conceded "equality of rights within a system that guarantees the security of all nations."[13] But after its failure in the Manchurian crisis, the League could hardly claim to represent collective security. The war had been "liquidated" in the sense that all the troops had gone home and reparations had been cancelled, but five months of disarmament talks in 1932 had produced only acrimony.

The Manchurian crisis had forced British officials to abandon the Ten Year Rule and to assess the state of the Empire's defenses. As the Disarmament Conference struggled on, the Chiefs of Staff Subcommittee debated what to do about the atrophied services: an army unprepared for a major European conflict; an air force which had fallen from one of the world's best to fifth place; and a navy with only 56 cruisers (of 70 thought necessary), 34 of which would become obsolete in the next ten years.[14] The Treasury nevertheless maintained tight controls on defense expenditures, which would remain in the 12-15% range of total government spending until 1936.[15]   Assessments of the German military danger during that time remained relatively optimistic.[16]   In the early 1930s, dealing with the economic crisis and alleviating its effects remained the top priorities.

In 1933, military spending accounted for 3% of Britain's national income, but 5.2% of France's.[17]   The French armed services were not as formidable as many in Britain believed they were, however. The slump was having an effect; while the amounts appropriated for the 1933 Labor, Health and Education budgets increased slightly, the government cut the War and Marine ministries' budgets significantly.[18] Hitler had received 13,420,000 votes in the second round of Germany's presidential election in April 1932, but the Radical Socialists, ruling with the support of the Socialists, faced the more immediate peril of a five billion franc budgetary shortfall.[19]   The army's budget for 1933 was 5.5 billion francs, down from 7.6 billion for 1932; the navy's budget was reduced from 3.3 billion francs to 2.8 billion.[20] Nevertheless, the national defense sector still accounted for 21.3% of government expenditures for 1933, as compared to 21.9% for 1929-1930, and 24.2% for 1931-1932.[21]

France in 1933 still had the largest army in Europe, with a standing force of 340,000 men; various special forces brought the total strength to about 450,000 men, plus reserves (formed by the three most recent classes of conscripts) of another 720,000 men. Germany's army, by contrast, was limited to 100,000 soldiers.[22] Despite its size, however, the French army was a deeply troubled organization.   Its purpose being to defend the republic, its strategy for defending France was purely defensive, designed to avoid a repetition of 1914-1918. Yet such a strategy made it impossible for the army to come to the assistance of any French ally (other than Belgium) that came under attack.   The Maginot Line effectively sealed France's border with Germany. It had been built in part to address France's demographic problem with respect to Germany; ironically, it also fostered the illusion that manpower had become less important to the nation's defense.[23] Military leaders came under pressure from the civilian leaders to make cuts in personnel. Politicians also knew that reducing the length of military service for recruits was popular.[24]

French strategists planned for a long, defensive war; to that end the *Conseil Supérieur de la Défense Nationale* (CSDN) placed strong emphasis on the role of the navy in ultimately defeating Germany. In 1932 thirty vessels were finished, including nineteen submarines, and construction began on thirteen new ships.[25] Nevertheless, because of the growth of the air force, the navy's share of the armed services budget between 1929 and 1933 shrank slightly, from 26% of the total in 1929-1930 to 23.8% in 1933.[26]

Despite the fact that there had been an independent air ministry since 1928, the air force in effect remained subservient to the army; French strategy called for aircraft to support activity on the ground in wartime. In 1933 the Air Ministry struggled against the Army for a strategic bombing arm. Deputies criticized the air ministry for its heavy emphasis on the development of many costly prototypes, very few of which went into production.[27] British observers, however, were much impressed by the French aviation industry's technological prowess.[28] While spending on the army and navy decreased in 1933, the Air Ministry's budget increased from 2 billion to 3.4 billion francs.[29] The three branches remained largely independent of one another, despite Tardieu's creation of Ministry of National Defense and CSDN's attempts to coordinate strategy. The Ministry did not begin to integrate the armed services successfully until 1936, during the time of the Popular Front.[30]

Britain: Taking on Public Opinion

With the Nazi revolution sweeping Germany, those responsible for Britain's defense began to count war as a future possibility, though estimates of German armed strength, which remained optimistic until 1936, forestalled any immediate sense of danger.[31] British leaders wondered whether public opinion, faced with this prospect, would be able to manage an about-face which the government itself found difficult to make. Such a reorientation, after all, required Britons to countenance the possible destruction of civilization: as Stanley Baldwin had said in his famous Commons speech of November 10, 1932, "the bomber will always get through."[32] In the following months, the Oxford Union and other groups of university students pledged to refuse to go to war for "King or country."[33]

The press was reluctant to present Nazi Germany as evil or menacing. Franklin Gannon has written that "[b]oth financially and intellectually it was unwise for the British Press to adopt a strongly critical line towards Nazi Germany: the readers did not want to read it, and the intellectuals did not want to write it." Though only the *Daily Mail* was actually pro-Nazi, much of the popular press chose to focus on the entertainment value of National Socialist pageantry rather than the brutal actions of the new regime.[34]

The government, technically speaking, did not exercise censorship over the press. Yet there was a curious relationship between the two,

which, given the developments of the later 1930s, later cast the press in a
bad light. Humbert Wolfe had described it succinctly in 1930:

> You cannot hope to bribe or twist
> Thank God! the British journalist.
>
> But, seeing what the man will do
> Unbribed, there's no occasion to.[35]

Particularly in the realm of foreign affairs, newspaper readers received far
less information than correspondents and editors possessed. As Stephen
Koss wrote of editors during this era: "Their circumspection, increasingly
in defiance rather than in ignorance of the facts, was a misguided response
to the growing threat of war and the dread of national defeat. Resolved to
avoid — or, at least, not to hasten — the inevitable, they took it upon
themselves to calm prevailing fears. In this way, they variously qualified
as appeasers or the de facto accomplices of the statesmen who practiced
appeasement."[36] He adds that the *Times* was undoubtedly the greatest
offender in this regard.

Not all papers withheld information to the extent that the *Times* did,
however. In May and June 1933, Basil Liddell Hart wrote detailed articles
on German rearmament and military expansion in the *Daily Telegraph*.[37]
The *Manchester Guardian* and the *Observer*, which in 1919 had warned
readers that the Allied victors "had sown dragon's teeth," now "took the
lead in warning that the dragon was alive, powerful, malevolent — but their
earlier success made the task harder, and the news from Germany was in
any case outrageous, hard to believe."[38] Already during the week that Hitler
became chancellor, Garvin wrote that, "whatever the result of an election,
Hitler would never surrender power. It was no longer possible to be
optimistic about Germany."[39] Nevertheless, it was difficult for the British
public, until now asked to recognize the injustice of the treaties, to give up
its quiet sympathy for Germany and its hostility towards France.[40]

Maurice Hankey meanwhile argued against what he perceived to be
a dangerous pacifism on the part of spiritual leaders. A devout man
himself, Hankey was concerned about the influence of the clergy on public
opinion. He wrote a lengthy letter to Edward Woods, the Bishop of
Croydon, in response to the bishop's recent book, *A Faith that Works*,
which contained a section entitled "Force and Faith." Though he found
much of the book compelling, Hankey took issue with the bishop's stand on

war, armaments and the League of Nations, and reminded him that the church had supported Britain's war effort in 1914:

> War, no doubt, is a terrible evil. I doubt if modern war, however, is as terrible as ancient war, when whole populations were destroyed or carried off captive. Poison gas is much exaggerated in your chapters, and the radius action of aircraft and the damage they can do is restricted, though of course it is serious. Still, as I began saying, war is a great evil.

> Sometimes, however, not to go to war is an even greater evil! Personally I think that if we had stood aside and acted on pacific principles in 1914 and allowed to Germany the hegemony of Europe, the soul of our people would have been destroyed. That, I believe, was the general view of the Churches at the time. Early in the war I got to know the late Archbishop of Canterbury and formed a friendship with him which lasted until his death. I don't believe he ever thought we were wrong in 1914.[41]

Hankey argued that war had liberated people, and that wars had been fought for just causes: "How many peoples have fought that they might worship God as they believed right? Would you not fight for this yourself in the last resort?"[42]

War, of course, was a last resort. The League of Nations was "by far the most hopeful instrument for peace that the world has seen," but the Covenant itself provided for the use of force if all else failed. Hankey cited the Manchurian and South American conflicts as instances where it was "difficult to say who [was] the aggressor" — in other words, instances in which the League had been unable to act effectively.

Similarly, the disarmament question could contribute to tensions rather than alleviate them:

> ...I am convinced that disarmament, though useful, is over-rated as an element of peace....[T]hese Conferences do, unfortunately, arouse the most bitter suspicions and animosities. France and Italy, for example, have hardly been on speaking terms since the Washington Conference ten years ago, though they have every reason to be good friends. And the present Disarmament Conference is unfortunately responsible for much of the shocking unrest in Europe today. The moment you talk disarmament, nations turn to their security and find it precarious and become suspicious. I always thought it a mistake for the Churches, stimulated by the League of Nations Union, to arouse so much expectation from the Conference. It is like the press shouting that we are bound to win the Test Match! It leads to disillusionment, and in the long run it is bad.[43]

Furthermore, other nations were cynical about British and American pressure for disarmament: "Of course they want the status quo and disarmament to preserve it." They had no Polish corridors, no Bessarabias, no Tyrols to defend or to try to win back.

In view of the present situation, Hankey argued, Britain ought not to outdistance the rest of the world in its crusade for peace:

> ...so long as war is a possibility, however remote (and I only wish I thought it more remote in the state of the world today) we ought to prepare for it, whether the war is with the League or despite the League. Otherwise, however just be our cause, we may bring the most frightful suffering to an innocent people, and even be destroyed as a nation and an Empire — an Empire which is by far the greatest influence for right and justice and peace today.[44]

An acceptable level of preparedness was difficult to maintain in these days when "the schools and universities are turning out nothing but pacifists under the influence of the League of Nations Union," but was nevertheless necessary, given the prevalent mentality on the Continent. Britain, he wrote, must not allow herself to get too far ahead of other nations in this respect. On the continent nations appeared to be preparing for war, or at least to defend themselves.

Hankey thus affirmed the beliefs which motivated the League of Nations Union, but warned against the dangers of disarming while such a mentality was far from the norm in Europe:

> Believing, as I do, that the principles you seek to promote are right, and that only by our leadership can they be accomplished; believing that they will take long to establish universally, with many slips by the way, believing all this, I ask for perspective, and that we shall not lead our people so far ahead of the rest of the nations that, like Rome of old, they shall lose their aptitude for arms and succumb, like Rome did, to a hardier, if lower civilisation, plunging the world into a new Dark Ages.[45]

Hankey pleaded with the bishop not to place too much faith in the League; just as belief in public morality did not justify abolition of the police, so too belief in the League should not demand disarmament, particularly if that demand was one-sided.

France: the Worst Confirmed

For many in France, belief in a peaceful future had always been difficult; now faith was failing completely. Conservatives believed the worst of Hitler from the very beginning of his chancellorship. Jacques Bardoux, a shipping executive influential in the *Fédération républicaine* (and later a senator), wrote to Tardieu on 2 February 1933 that he had learned from an informer that Mussolini had lent 40 million lire to Hitler when the latter had run out of money. Following this loan (not yet repaid), an accord was reached on foreign policy. Mussolini agreed to give Hitler a free hand in the Corridor in return for a free hand to provoke difficulties between Hungary and Yugoslavia and to pursue his plans for Albania. Bardoux also had learned that the German Foreign Office would raise the question of eastern frontier revision at the next session of the Disarmament Conference.[46]

The foreign minister (and now former Socialist), Joseph Paul-Boncour, wrote to the ambassador in London, Aimé de Fleuriau, that he believed the British underestimated the threat posed by Hitler:

> It seems to me that the English do not weigh sufficiently the dangers of Hitler's activities and of the military preparations being made; they seem to believe that a first disarmament convention (which would necessarily be very limited) will be able to remedy the situation. I do not believe it. Certainly we have to apply ourselves to all these efforts, but at the same time we will have to act energetically. We must make every effort to prepare their minds for that.[47]

This judgment was not entirely fair: to British observers, the brutality of the regime and the dangers it posed were clear. For example, Hugh Dalton, the former parliamentary undersecretary at the Foreign Office, wrote after a four-day trip to Berlin: "I leave tonight by the night train....I wake up in Holland with a sense of freedom. Germany is horrible.... War must be counted now among the probabilities of the next ten years. We were right not to go on breeding!"[48] Yet for the British leaders with whom Paul-Boncour had to work — especially MacDonald and Simon — a meeting of the minds on the subject of Germany was still a distant prospect.

German mistreatment of Jewish citizens did not escape the attention of the French Minister in Munich, who wrote to the Quai d'Orsay that the persecution of the Jews was "developing systematically," with the exclusion of Jews from the legal profession. Nor did the irony of this situation escape him: such legislation amounted to "the outlaw of a category of Germans who are being treated, in their own country, as a minority by those who never cease to pose as defenders of minorities."[49]

The brutality of the National Socialists was plain to see. Less clear was what France was willing or able to do about the growing menace. Military leaders might discuss the possibility of a preventive war, but their own strategy made no provision for it. As in Britain, the politicians faced developments in Germany with dismay. As the French economy sank further into depression, the elections of 1932 had given the Radical Socialists, somewhat rejuvenated by a "Young Turk" movement within the party, control of the government; they had been firm supporters of Briand's foreign policy. Herriot had bargained in good faith at the disarmament talks in 1932, hoping to bolster the collapsing Weimar Republic in the wake of the Nazi Reichstag victories in May. In 1933, with Hitler in power, French foreign policy did not change significantly. At the Quai d'Orsay, the new secretary-general, Alexis Léger, carried the torch of Briandism. The government, with Daladier as prime minister and Paul-Boncour as foreign minister, quietly set about efforts to shore up France's security without provoking Germany. The Radicals focused on improving relations with Britain.

Meanwhile, the major diplomatic initiative of 1933 came from neither Britain nor France, but from Italy. In March, Mussolini proposed to Germany, France and Britain a four-power pact that would recognize Germany's rights to equality in arms and approve the principle of treaty revision.[50] He could claim that there was nothing new in these proposals, but in fact he was singling these issues out for resolution by an old-fashioned Concert of Europe. Mussolini had no qualms about openly insulting the League of Nations, as well as the leaders of Europe's smaller powers. MacDonald had welcomed the proposal, but French leaders were concerned for their allies.

The debate in the Chamber of Deputies on April 6, 1933 illustrated the range of opinion in France on the four-power proposal and the European situation in general. The ruling Radicals seemed to combine defense of French rights with conciliation towards Germany in a way that displeased their colleagues both to the left and the right. Léo Lagrange, a left-wing deputy, took exception to this sentence in the report of the Foreign Affairs Commission which denounced pacifism: "Pacifism, which consists of always yielding to the unreasonable demands of strong foreign governments, is called, in good French, cowardice." Though events later in the decade would demonstrate that pacifism was not the exclusive province of the left, this definition was greeted by exclamations on the left and applause on the right. Lagrange said: "I am surprised that the reporter of the foreign affairs budget [M. Dariac]... dares to write that a pacifist policy is a cowardly policy. For the honor of the whole Assembly, whose desire for peace and peaceful action I imagine to be unanimous, it is dangerous and regrettable to include such a sentence in an official report, which could justify the most abominable propaganda against our country."[51]

Louis Marin, leader of the *Union républicaine démocratique*, a right-wing parliamentary group that had backed Tardieu, replied sharply: "Then ask the German Socialists, now that their eyes have been opened, if they do not share the opinions of M. Dariac...try not to believe in them, as you did in 1914, and yield to their representations in favor of the new government." Dariac defended himself by saying that he desired peace as much as Lagrange did; he wanted peace with dignity, however. He also criticized "pactomania," which involved the sacrifice of vital interests for nothing in return: "to that I oppose a policy of character and of simple courage in the affirmation of our essential rights."[52]

During this debate, Daladier reiterated the government's policy on disarmament: France would "reduce progressively our armaments on the condition that no one rearms." Armaments would be closely monitored, and the private manufacture of arms would be banned or strictly regulated. Such a policy was "of a nature to render impossible a return to that arms race which again would cover Europe with blood and would provoke its definitive ruin." That was why the French government was considering seriously the latest British disarmament proposal, and also the four-power pact. The tone of Daladier's speech was conciliatory, but firm: "There is no task higher or nobler than to give or to restore order, confidence and security to Europe. France, I repeat, knows neither hate nor fear. She believes that international collaboration can be based only on justice."[53] He admitted that no treaty was eternal, but that principles of international justice would prevail.

Gaston Bergery, a Deputy from the left wing of the Radical party but who had just left the party, saw the solution to the problems of security and disarmament as a two-step process: the first would be a limited disarmament along with the establishment of some apparatus of control (the recent proposal made by MacDonald to save the Disarmament Conference would achieve this end); the second step would be possible once the first had achieved a measure of calm, and would consist of recognizing equality and creating organs of security and revision. The four-power proposal might be the basis for such a body; these were, after all, the four permanent members left on the League of Nations Council since the departure of Japan. If, however, these four powers planned to use their "alliance" to force unjust decisions on smaller powers, or to act in concert against the Soviet Union,

Bergery said he would oppose it. Later that year he gave up his seat, disillusioned with the Radical party's failings.

Léon Blum opposed the four-power pact because granting equality of rights to Germany would doom the Disarmament Conference to failure. As for the revision of treaties, Blum, quoting fellow socialist Marcel Déat, said that the Socialist solution lay in the "progressive devaluation of frontiers," to be achieved through disarmament and economic cooperation. He urged his compatriots not to respond to the threats posed by Hitler with their own dangerous actions:

> I entreat you, gentlemen, in the name of peace: do not respond to one danger with another danger that multiplies it.   Do not respond to nationalist campaigns of provocation with a similar campaign; these only reflect and exacerbate one another. At the moment when the greatest danger to the peace of Europe is indeed the rearmament of Germany and all [its]...consequences, convince yourselves...that today, more than ever, in spite of appearances... security lies in peace, the will for peace, the peace organizations, and the Disarmament Conference, which serves to nourish this desire...[54]

Blum was calling upon his colleagues to place their faith in this spirit of internationalism because forces of extreme nationalism, chauvinism and racism threatened to set the tone for the way not only Germany, but also other European nations, conducted themselves. To respond in kind to the brutality of Germany only legitimized the behavior of the National Socialists.

Further to the left, communism offered a third alternative, opposed to the liberal internationalism of the League of Nations and the traditional power politics of Mussolini's four-power pact. Speaking for the Communists, Gabriel Péri said that the Versailles system was cracking, and that it carried with it the "germs of armed conflagration."   However, the Communists rejected "imperialist revisions" of the system. Their model was the Soviet system: "The Soviet example has demonstrated how the proletariat, in charge of power, knows how to substitute for national hatred the fraternal community of a hundred peoples of different language and culture. The peace pact is neither a five-power pact nor the pact of Geneva; it is the alliance of the world's revolutionary proletariat."[55]

Henry Franklin-Bouillon, another former radical, denounced the four-power pact as a betrayal of France's allies. He saw it as "the expression of the will of three powers, which are resolved against us to organize, as Mr. MacDonald has said, first and foremost, the revision of the treaties."   The government seemed to be equivocating on a policy that envisioned nothing less than the "destruction of the frontiers of our allies." A tone of unreality had crept into the debate, he said, particularly in Blum's speech: "We have...heard some admirable discourse on the meaning of disarmament, the revision of treaties, and European peace. We have simply forgotten the psychology of the people with whom we hope to deal, and the facts that dominate the debate." Acceptance of the pact would sow among the allies feelings "not...of distrust, but of anxiety and discouragement." The policy was bound to fail anyway, and France would "find herself facing great powers more hostile to us than ever, and the smaller ones more anxious every day, more weakened and more divided."

The current state of affairs, he continued, resulted from a failure to resist efforts by other countries to impose measures such as equality of rights, disarmament and treaty revision: "this failure is the result of our mistakes, the mistakes of leaders who had neither the intelligence nor the courage necessary to confront the events." France's chief mistake had been to trust Germany. In a leap of faith France had made many concessions, receiving in return only more demands. The latest of these, equality of rights, would give Germany the right to rearm and prepare for war: "the misfortune of our country in light of this new and outrageous claim is to not have admitted courageously that we had been mistaken in our belief in a pacific Germany, a republican Germany that did not exist." Now, however, France was yielding to British pressure to accord Germany equality of rights in arms — another mistake. Once Germany was allowed to rearm, she would never accept limits.

Franklin-Bouillon suggested an alternative. He said that there should be no conferences on questions of revision before the countries concerned stated specifically what they wanted: "This no longer has to do with a dogmatic discussion of theories and possibilities; each of these countries will have to specify both its definition of the word 'revision' and the modifications it intends to make to the map of Europe.... [E]very square centimeter to be 'revised' will have to be specified by the country that has the audacity to demand it." France had to pursue a simple policy of courage and clarity. He concluded with the following words: "France...has the right to direct the evolution of Europe, because she is the only absolutely disinterested power and the one which has bled the most for liberty. Show the way and the world will follow you."[56] His speech was enthusiastically applauded on the right and from various benches in the center of the Chamber. Franklin-Bouillon recognized the German menace and the mistakes the other powers were making in attempting to deal with it, but, even in France, he found little support for a resolute policy.

Édouard Herriot described Franklin-Bouillon's idea as "obviously very vigorous, but perhaps also very aggressive." Rather than singling out one article for emphasis, Herriot believed that the whole Covenant of the League ought to be followed. Such proposals as the four-power pact seemed to mark the return of an oligarchic or hierarchical international system, which stood in opposition to the new order:

> We are having trouble making [this new order] prevail, because we are running up against the old tradition of the politics of the old regime; in particular, to the tradition...of the nineteenth century, which never ceased to increase its efforts to create this kind of triple or quadruple alliance. These doctrines have generated wars wherever they were applied, wherever they were allowed. The League of Nations is founded on a new principle, on the principle of equality; and as it happens that, on this point, our engagements, our declarations are in agreement with the traditional policy of France, which already defended at the Congress of Vienna, by the voice of Talleyrand, the policy of small nations, I intend to remain faithful to this doctrine.

Under the present circumstances, France had three choices as to which "doctrine" of foreign policy to follow: the theory of isolation, under which a power would rely on her own strength; a theory of alliances, which "history has condemned" and which an analysis of the present situation showed to be unadvisable; and lastly the policy of the League of Nations, "which consists of staying on the road which France helped to open and from which she has never distanced herself."[57] For Herriot, the only choice was the third. Enthusiastic applause from the extreme left, left and center of the Chamber, and even from some benches on the right — demonstrated strong support for a pro-League policy. The League's basic principles, which France had done more to nurture than any other great power, were now being threatened by Germany, Italy and Japan. The nature of these principles was such that their rejection would signify a change of heart, a loss of faith, a mood of cynical pessimism. Now more than ever France had to keep the faith.

Paul-Boncour, the foreign minister, defended his government's decision to participate in the four-power pact, insisting that it did not undermine the League. The world, he said, was "evolving" towards the principles on which the League was founded, but the old ways lingered. Competition, rivalries and suspicions would continue, but they would take a legal form instead of the form of force and war. Recent events in Germany did not fundamentally challenge these conceptions: "What makes for the somewhat tragic paradox of the situation is that at the same time that these ideas are making progress... events and attitudes arise in some countries which contradict and sometimes obviously violate everything that is happening."[58] These attitudes and events only made the work of Geneva more important. The policies of Germany, Italy, Bulgaria, Hungary and Austria, for example, had complicated efforts towards disarmament. Two blocs had arisen, "which, if they continue... will create for the future a Europe of war."[59] Rejecting the idea of a great-power directory to rule Europe, Paul-Boncour defended the four-power pact as a much-needed action to address this split; without this minimal agreement, nothing could be accomplished at Geneva.

Like the politicians, the press greeted the changes in Germany with a wide range of responses. By and large, the popular press in France sheltered the public from brutal realities. The four largest Paris papers of the 1920s all faced declining sales in the 1930s. Three moved to the far right politically: *Le Matin* became pro-Hitler; *Le Journal* became pro-Mussolini; *Le Petit Journal* supported French movements of the extreme right (such as the Croix de Feu and Parti Social Français). *Le Petit Parisien* remained mainstream, but all four papers lost readers to *Paris-Soir*, a new paper which by 1939 had a circulation of 1.75 million.[60] Conservative papers, which tended to concentrate on the perils of socialism and communism, blunted the edges of right-wing ideological excesses.

Le Temps harbored no illusions, however, describing "Hitlerism" as the greatest danger facing freedom-loving people and nations. After the book-burnings in many German cities and towns on May 10, a correspondent wrote that this was "new proof...that what is dangerous about Germany is not that a dictator impresses his outlook on an entire country, but that the politics and morals of the dictator are already those of the German people....He only had to appear and appeal to this ancient German spirit in order for all of Germany to find itself in him."[61] Journalists like Geneviève Tabouis, André Géraud (Pertinax) and Emile Buré would keep French readers informed of the latest Nazi treachery throughout the decade.

Understanding Hitler and National Socialism

In May 1933 Sir John Simon received a detailed assessment of the situation in Germany from Malcolm Robertson, whose "semi-German origin and life-long knowledge of the German people" enabled him to view Germany somewhat differently from the "pure-bred native of these islands."[62] Robertson had retired from a diplomatic career in 1930, having served as first secretary in Washington during the war and as deputy high commissioner and high commissioner in the Rhineland from 1919-1921. From conversations with the German Ambassador and the Nazi propagandist Rosenberg, Robertson decided that this was not the Germany of 1914, but "the Germany of 1813, the Germany of the War of Liberation," and that was far more dangerous:

> The whole of this Hitler movement and the wide response, almost religious in its intensity, that it has called forth, is based upon that pride of race....Pride of race, passionate belief in the Prussian spirit, the Prussian capacity for work, Prussian discipline, Prussian solidity and stolidity....[I]t is the re-awakening of faith in these things that has gripped the German people and that makes them yet more formidable than they were before the war.[63]

What was truly foreign to the British mind, however, was the spiritual quality of this extreme nationalism:

> There is an element, a strong element of mysticism about it which we simply must endeavour to understand. Strictly, the Prussians are not European. They are the Westernmost of the Eastern peoples. Hence the necessity for them to have a *ruler*, hence, also, their savagery, hence also that mysticism which can be almost fanatical. [Alfred] Rosenberg comes from the Baltic Provinces. He is probably yet more Slav than the Prussian. Hence the fanaticism which leaps from his eyes.[64]

The ultimate intention of a people that felt humiliated by the Treaty ending the last war, betrayed by "pacifist" socialists and cheated by Jews who had been allowed to dominate them, was clear: "That they ultimately mean to go to war with the immediate object of re-establishing their former frontiers and their fame as a warlike people, I have no shadow of a doubt." Robertson requested a meeting with Simon to discuss Germany; he considered it a bad sign that Hitler should have sent someone like Rosenberg to see him, for "Rosenberg is stupid and a fanatic." He found the whole situation frightening, and he stressed the need for intelligent government and press representatives in Berlin to monitor the situation.[65]

Yet many prominent figures in Britain did not regard Germany with such deep concern. Press magnate Lord Rothermere corresponded with Hitler in December 1933. An 'Anglo-German Group' counted among its members Lord Allen of Hurtwood, Lord Noel-Buxton, Philip Noel-Baker, John Wheeler-Bennett of the Royal Institute of International Affairs, the historian G.P. Gooch and Sir Walter Layton, publisher of the *Economist*.

Philip Conwell-Evans, who had been Noel-Buxton's private secretary during the second Labour government and was now a lecturer at the University of Königsberg, served as a liaison between these figures and influential people in Germany, and was among those who would help to lay the groundwork for visits by Lord Allen in 1934 and Philip Kerr (Lord Lothian), an 'alumnus' of Alfred Milner's pro-imperial 'Kindergarten' and founder of the *Round Table*, in 1935. For these people the threat of a rift in Anglo-German relations called for closer cooperation, their motives ranging from pacifism to opportunism.[66] Conwell-Evans wrote that the papers exaggerated their accounts of the persecution of the Jews; he was "convinced of the underlying pacific aims of the new Germany. We can win her confidence and ready co-operation if we treat her as a trusted equal."[67]

Though they were treading on dangerous ground, advocates of closer Anglo-German understanding were not necessarily anti-democratic or pro-Nazi. In a letter to Colonel Edward M. House in April 1933, Lord Lothian described his concern about the situation facing the democracies. He wrote that, after the war, President Wilson had tried to establish a world order based on justice and reason; the League of Nations was the manifestation of that effort. Today, however, among the Great Powers, only France, Britain and the United States adhered to this world view. Although he believed liberalism would return eventually to Germany, Italy and Japan, "I cannot say that the prospects at this moment look very bright." Now war loomed, though he feared that the immediate danger came, not from these powers, but from the Little Entente, with French right-wing support. What could the League of Nations do in a world dominated by powers that did not believe in the principles on which it was founded?

> If we can bring off through the active influence of the United States a European settlement...based on the League, so much the better, but we have...to recognise that it may not be possible either because the United States cannot play a sufficiently active part or because the forces of reaction, mainly Germany and Italy, succeed in recreating a balance of power in Europe with a possible preponderance on their own side, which will make the League nugatory. In that event it is obvious that the United States, France and the British Empire must stand together as the defenders of a civilisation based on individual rights, democracy, and the reign of reason and justice in both domestic and international affairs so far as they can be attained, as opposed to nations who base their Governments on the suppression of individual opinion, on autocracy and the belief that might makes right in international affairs.[68]

Consistent with his belief that liberalism would return to the dictatorships, Lothian advocated contacts with these powers to establish goodwill. Condemning Germany would only push her further towards the extremes.[69]

MacDonald appeared to be of the same mind as he responded to a letter from Lily Montagu, who had called for a British protest against the persecutions and militarism in Germany:

> Regarding these German outrages — we have to be exceedingly careful as a Government that we do not make things worse, and nothing is more likely to rouse bitter feeling and to make it more difficult for the German Government to draw out from its present policy than a debate in the House of Commons, where irresponsible people will indulge in uncontrolled language. You may rest assured that every pressure we can bring to bear, either privately or officially, is being used.[70]

In that spirit, MacDonald had gone to Geneva the previous month with a proposal intended to save the faltering Disarmament Conference. Over a five-year period, Germany would be given the "equality of rights" she so noisily had demanded in storming out the previous year. Limits would be set on the armaments of all powers; inspection rights and vague provisions for "consultation" were thrown in to placate the French.[71]

In light of MacDonald's recent efforts, Montagu was not reassured. In her reply, she restated her displeasure with the state of affairs in Germany:

> I wish it were possible to interfere with the militaristic education which is going on in [German] schools....I see how such interference is out of our sphere, but I do think it is in harmony with English tradition to protest against the ghastly cruelty which is being perpetrated. As an English woman I am jealous of the honour of England at this moment. If it is not a little more active in its efforts to evoke a better spirit in Germany, it will deservedly incur the anathema of future generations.[72]

Of course, MacDonald shared the goal of "evoking a better spirit in Germany," but he chose to cling to the sinking ship of disarmament. Japan had left the League of Nations on February 24; by May rumors circulated of Hitler's contempt for the discussions in Geneva.

The prime minister was clearly unwilling to disturb relations with Germany. Robert Vansittart's dire prognoses about Germany led MacDonald to suggest a convalescent holiday: "I have reason to believe that he is a bit over-strained, and complete rest away from papers is much required from him."[73] MacDonald himself felt that the situation was dire, but he could not contemplate bold action to improve it, as is evident in a letter to

Robert Cecil: "I cannot hide from you the fact that I am greatly disturbed by the general outlook. It is peace itself that is now in jeopardy , not only disarmament; but of course a failure of the Disarmament Conference would add greatly to that jeopardy. I am hoping, however, that we may save something that would be any rate fairly substantial, and then go on quietly to build upon it."[74] Events would have to take their course. When Hitler became chancellor, MacDonald had told his son Malcolm: "I shall not see peace again in my lifetime; I hope you will see it in yours."[75] According to David Marquand, these were years of "physical decline and political disappointment" for MacDonald. He was not so much deceived by Hitler as unable to decide what to do about him.[76] Consequently, meddlesome though he was in the realm of foreign affairs, he gave no direction to policy; once a champion of the League's liberal internationalism, he now championed Mussolini's idea of a four-power directory. Faced now with two dictators, MacDonald still could not recognize France as Britain's natural ally on the continent.

For all the difficulties in shaping policy toward Germany, opinion in Britain about the Nazi government was remarkably unanimous, according to the *Economist* of May 6. Giving expression to this opinion was the venerable Lord Grey, speaking before the Liberal Council: "The whole trend of her policy and of her mentality has been to shock British opinion which after the war was in many ways sympathetic with Germany....Do we not feel by what has happened in Germany recently [that] peace is threatened, and that the great security of peace is that Germany is not armed and not in a position to go to war?" Lord Grey, along with another former foreign secretary, Austen Chamberlain, recommended that Britain make no concessions to such a regime, founded, in the words of the *Times*, on an "abominable philosophy of force."[77]

However, the *Economist*, which the previous December had suggested political concessions while German economic recovery was still in its early stages, saw matters differently:

> If we make concessions to the Nazis the diplomatic triumphs which they will then be able to claim may, as in the case of Bismarck, maintain and prolong the power of their régime; than which there could be no greater disaster either for Germany or for Europe. But if we are going to embrace the alternative, and live up to Lord Grey's brave words, we should do so with open eyes. To refuse all concessions to Hitler will almost certainly be to force on him the dilemma of either admitting failure or embarking on some reckless foreign adventure. Are we really ready to contemplate this alternative?[78]

Britain's failure to act before the Nazis took power left leaders with a choice between evils. Given these unpleasant alternatives, however, MacDonald had even more reason now not to act.

MacDonald's lack of initiative drew a critical letter from the First Commissioner of Works (and a Conservative Member of Parliament), William Ormsby-Gore, who called for a reversal of the policy "we have played so consistently since 1919 of tempering the French wind to the shorn lamb, Germany." Now Germany, and not Bolshevik Russia, was the "great danger to the peace and progress of Western civilisation." Disagreeable as it might be, this situation called upon Britain to cooperate with Germany's neighbors, especially France, "and make it clear to our own people and to the world that we are doing so," in order to avoid the ambiguity of Britain's position in 1914. Italy was a difficult case, but Britain could not "afford to throw Mussolini into the arms of Hitler. I don't think he will be so thrown if Britain shows herself strong, definite and determined."[79]

Austen Chamberlain, who always had preferred France to Germany, echoed Ormsby-Gore's views. Though still a member of Parliament, Chamberlain had not been asked to return to the Foreign Office when the National Government was formed. Greatly disappointed, he became highly critical of the government's handling of European problems. He was aware, however, of the freedom afforded by his retirement, as he wrote to Hilda in August: "you sit between two brothers, one in [his half-brother Neville] and one out of office. I always think that ministers in office (self included) are apt to be too complacent and that men out of office are apt to think that nothing is being done or at least nothing done right — so between the two of us you ought to be near the truth."[80]

From the sidelines Austen Chamberlain followed the changes from the perspective of a diplomat. Struck by the change of tone in the British press after Hitler became chancellor, he wrote to Ida in May about the chancellor's upcoming speech before the Reichstag: "Will he say anything really reassuring? I doubt it. I hope our people will not be duped by mere words." Chamberlain noted how Hitler had inflamed British opinion: "The Times, Telegraph, Observer, Sunday Times and Manchester Guardian, all sing the same tune. Herr Rosenberg with his swastika on the Cenotaph has roused even Garvin to fury and they all unite to proclaim: To a Germany much, to *this* Germany nothing! And a very good thing, too."[81]

Yet the government, and Simon in particular, took no action, he wrote in August:

I read the Times and listen to the wireless. Events in Germany fill me with disgust at the domestic brutality of the regime and with deepening anxiety about its external consequences. What is our Government doing? Is it going to swallow the insolence of the official announcements about our representations and the continued broadcasts against the Austrian Government and recurring frontier incidents? Is Germany to be allowed to rearm and are we to continue to press others to disarm[?] Have we in fact a policy and is the Cabinet behind it and do our representatives abroad know what it is if it even exists?

From a reliable source Chamberlain had heard that since Simon took office, if not earlier, "no Ambassador has received a private letter from the Secretary of State or even seen his signature!"[82] Ormsby-Gore, Walter Elliot and Maurice Hankey shared the view that Simon "was a very bad Foreign Secretary."[83]

The press meanwhile wavered in its opinions; Chamberlain was dismayed by an apparent shift of public opinion back toward Germany in November, and he blamed the *Times*: "I am furious with that paper. Even the *Express* is steadfast compared to its wobbling. It doesn't seem to know where it stands, or what it wants. I think our prospects are bad, at present."[84] Yet Chamberlain himself could not help hoping that Hitler would "settle down into something more reasonable and statesmanlike than his first manifestation," a common hope among newspaper editors, not to mention politicians.[85] However, even if this hope were still plausible in 1933, it rested on the belief that the best situation was one in which Britain would not need to act.

Neville Chamberlain always had deferred to Austen on matters of foreign affairs. As Chancellor of the Exchequer, however, Neville Chamberlain played as important a role in shaping Britain's response to European developments as Austen ever had; under his leadership, the Treasury sought to keep expenditures for defense to a minimum, despite the clearly perceived threats which Japan and Germany posed to Britain's imperial interests. In any case, in 1933 he probably felt more hostile towards the United States than towards Germany, given the difficulties he encountered at the Economic Conference.

At a Cabinet meeting on February 27 he disagreed with Maurice Hankey's gloomy assessment of the state of Britain's armaments industry, especially the extent of its dependence on foreign orders. Hankey wrote to him afterwards:

The points of fact I want to make are the following:
I.   It is a very serious matter.

II. The armament industry does depend on other people.

III. The armament industry is a dying one in Great Britain — but not elsewhere.[86]

Whereas in 1914 twelve firms were capable of carrying out large orders, now only one could. Leftover stock from the war and the two Naval disarmament conventions partially explained the decline in production, but so did the "highly dangerous assumption that there could be no war for 10 years from any given date." In the present circumstances, "with the situation in the Far East and in Europe crumbling before our eyes," the government needed to reassess the state of its services:

> Today the conditions are beginning to change; war stocks are becoming obsolete or used up; new patterns are coming into existence; the 10 years assumption has been abolished. The international situation is so grave that I for one find it impossible to believe that the greatly needed rehabilitation of our services can much longer be delayed. I doubt, therefore, if the industry will be allowed to die. Unless, however, action is taken fairly soon to place more Government orders[,] foreign orders would seem indispensable to its survival.[87]

For Neville Chamberlain, however, more a businessman than a strategist, balanced books were the greater concern.

In September, Maurice Hankey and the Chiefs of Staff Subcommittee prevailed upon the Cabinet to form a Defence Requirements Committee; beginning with the assumption that Germany would pose a profound threat to British security within three to five years, the Committee would assess the Empire's military needs, leaving questions of economics and politics to the Cabinet. Yet the civilians, especially the Treasury's representative, Warren Fisher, dominated the committee.[88] Indeed, Britain's leaders had to make difficult decisions, given the financial constraints under which they were forced to operate. The Committee carried out its work on the assumption that France, the United States and Italy were friendly; in the end it recommended that "every effort be made to resume cordial relations with Japan."[89] In other words, Britain had little choice but to appease certain powers if it hoped to face the challenges of others. Even such "anti-appeasers" as Churchill, Eden and the Labour opposition offered the National Government no real alternative, advocating accommodation of Italy and Japan.[90]

While no one could predict the future, leaders could learn about Hitler and National Socialism by reading *Mein Kampf*, though for the complete text they still had to read the two volumes in German.[91] The message of the book itself was "extremely simple," as Horace Rumbold wrote in April

1933; "man is a fighting animal; therefore the nation is...a fighting unit....A country or a race which ceases to fight is...doomed."[92] Rumbold did not draw much attention to the anti-Semitism of *Mein Kampf.*[93] The appearance in the *Times* in July of excerpts from Edgar Dugdale's forthcoming abridged translation drew the same criticism from Zionist leader Chaim Weizmann. He wrote to Geoffrey Dawson, demonstrating with his own translations of key passages how Dugdale had diluted the venom of Hitler's anti-Semitism.[94]

Rumbold and Dugdale also failed to relate or translate the most vehemently anti-French passages of *Mein Kampf.* In October 1933, the new French ambassador in London, Charles Corbin, wrote to Paul-Boncour about the recent publication of *Mein Kampf* in English.[95] He summarized the content of a letter by Sir Phillip Hartog, a well-known academic scientist, which appeared in the *Times* on 23 October:

> Sir Phillip attracts the attention of 'Times' readers to the contrast that appears between the brutal militarism preached by Hitler in his work and the more peaceful tendencies of his recent declarations. However, 'Mein Kampf' is very widely distributed in Germany. More than a million copies of this publication have been distributed since the advent of the current government. The importance of the work in German schools and the Reich surpasses that of speeches specially prepared for foreign consumption. Sir Phillip was astonished at the omission in the English edition of a certain declaration of foreign policy to which Hitler attaches such importance that he qualifies it as a 'political testament'. In this document Hitler beseeches the Germans never to tolerate the development on their frontiers of a military power which could one day equal their own and constitute an eventual menace to the Reich. The power of the German people must be established not over dispersed colonies, but over the soil of their own fatherland in Europe.[96]

Corbin mentioned also Hartog's analysis of chapter 14, which essentially called for an alliance with Britain and Italy against France, to facilitate German expansion on the eastern frontier. Hartog did not mention it, leading Corbin to wonder whether it perhaps had not appeared in the English edition. The Dugdale translation did mention the alliance, but it omitted this passage: "Since we need strength for this [eastward expansion] but the mortal enemy of our nation, France, relentlessly throttles us and robs our strength, we must undertake every sacrifice which may help bring about a nullification of the French drive for European hegemony."[97]

Maurice Hankey read *Mein Kampf* in both German and English, and set out his views in a paper. Simon wanted to incorporate Hankey's work into a paper on disarmament, but Hankey demurred, as "I did not really feel competent to deal with the subject officially and the Foreign Office had not seen my effort."[98] He felt, nevertheless, that the government needed to deal with the matter of Hitler's ambitions: "Strictly between you and me, some people here are rather inclined to forget past deeds or misdeeds and to take the speeches of public men abroad at their face value. My suspicious temperament makes me hesitate. I remember so well in the War that nations which were contemplating anything particularly dastardly invariably covered their actions with smooth words."[99] The new ambassador to Germany, Sir Eric Phipps, agreed, and wrote that he was glad Hankey's views had been circulated, "for it is essential, in my humble opinion, that German peace bellowings should not be taken strictly at their face value."[100]

Hankey had been to Germany himself recently, and had been struck by the air of prosperity he encountered, in marked contrast to conditions in Belgium. The Nazis, he wrote to Phipps, did not seem to be armed yet, but the large numbers of German youth enlisted in Nazi organizations indicated to him that an important first step had been taken; given all he knew about Germany's capacity for industrial mobilization, Hankey could "understand French anxiety."[101] He wondered at the reasons for German exaltation, and believed it possible that "the real cause of confidence [was] the removal of the intense fear of Communism." People seemed willing to put up with restrictions on smoking in public and the use of cosmetics; women also did not seem to mind giving up their jobs so that men could be employed.

While travelling, Hankey was careful not to speak his mind too candidly on the subject of Hitler, but he did tell Germans he met how people in England regarded the persecution of Jews and pacifists: "They were rather taken aback when I told them that people of the type of [Albert] Einstein or [the chemist Fritz] Haber had always been regarded in England as representatives of the famous German culture, and that it had come as a surprise to many people to know that in reality they were Jews and repudiated by the Germans themselves. It lowered German prestige in the eyes of the world."[102] The people he met also belittled English concerns about German militarism: "No nation could possibly be more pacifist than Germany! The risk of war simply did not exist!" Hankey thought perhaps they were sincere, but he noted that none of them were Prussian. Both he and his wife felt considerably relieved to leave Germany: "In spite of the kindness and hospitality that we received and the extraordinary interest of our trip, on arriving in the quietness of Spa, my wife and I both had an astonishing sense of having come back to civilisation. All the shouting and singing of the Nazis; all the excitement and stimulation vanished....[N]ever have I felt so much the steady solidity of England as since my return from Germany."[103] Though Hitler's ultimate intentions remained uncertain, in little more than half a year the Nazi revolution had transformed Germany.

The changes in Germany not only reassured Britons that there was no place like home; William Tyrrell, recognizing the ideological importance of France to Britain, found new appreciation for France. In August he presented a sketch of France, comparing it to a Germany which under Hitler was "becoming increasingly militarist and anti-democratic":

> France now shares with Great Britain the honour of being one of the only two great liberal States left in Europe. To Fascist Italy, Hitlerite Germany and Soviet Russia the forms of liberal democratic government to which Great Britain and France owe their power and influence are equally repugnant. Fifteen years after the war to make the world safe for democracy, France is the only great continental state left where that ideal can be reasonably assured.[104]

The government relied on persuasion rather than brute force to pass legislation, and remained subject to criticism through free speech and a free press. France also had become a haven for refugees.

The French attitude toward military service provided the greatest contrast to the rest of Europe. Military service had been reduced from three years to one, and there were no paramilitary forces to speak of. Even Tardieu's reform proposals, which did not go beyond empowering the executive to dissolve parliament (as in Britain), envisioned no role for such forces: "The idea of even the followers of M. Tardieu, who come nearest to the Hitlerites in their conception of politics, enregimenting themselves and being drilled and marched about is quite inconceivable."[105] Men who had been labelled National Socialists by their opponents, such as MM. Renaudel, Déat and Marquet, "are no more revolutionary than the English Labour Party" (this was not true, but Tyrrell was a man of Conservative leanings). In the past conscription had been falsely interpreted as a sign of French militarism, whereas in fact it demonstrated an aversion to Bonapartism — a professional army used by an ambitious soldier to seize control of the state.

Tyrrell did not believe that the French could be blamed for the demise of democracy in Germany. Since 1870, Germany had been a democracy for only 13 years. The French attitude toward Germany in the first years after the war, when they took the lead among the allies in heaping upon Germany "all the humiliations of the reparation settlement and the Rhineland occupation" was "no doubt deplorable"; but by 1933 the Rhineland had been evacuated for two and a half years and the reparations question had been settled in Germany's favor. In 1933, as in 1914, "the German Liberals and Socialists... melted away before the sharp commands of higher authority."[106]

Tyrrell persisted, however, in minimizing France's security concerns, despite the country's democratic affinity to Britain:

> It cannot be too often stated that modern France is definitively on the defensive. Her views of a defensive may be mistaken. She may be wrong not to have made friends with her enemy while he was in the ways with her. By still persisting in maintaining a superiority of arms when she can never have a superiority of men, she may be fatally compromising the future. But her motives are pacifist, not militarist, born of fear not of pride. The noisy patriotism of Fascist Italy is as unnatural to her as the stark discipline of Germany. The waving of flags, the adoption of strange archaic devices and salutes, the wearing of uniforms and labels to prove one's patriotism, is all ridiculous to a Frenchman, who however much he may be afraid of his country being overwhelmed by a more numerous and barbarous Germany, has at least no inferiority complex where his civilisation is concerned.[107]

Yet Briand had made genuine attempts at Franco-German conciliation over his long tenure at the Quai d'Orsay, and had done so with overwhelming parliamentary and public approval — even with the devastation of northern France in recent memory. Conciliation had failed with a democratic Germany; how could it work with a dictatorship?

Tyrrell described the French obsession with defense in patronizing terms:

> The over-anxious and mistrustful qualities of the French peasant when introduced into international politics require to be corrected if they are not to be as fatal in their results as a policy of adventure. The natural numerical superiority of Germany, which is the subconscious obsession of the French mind, can only be overcome by measures of solidarity and control which will prevent the German colossos [sic] from having free play in Europe. The French reluctance to disarm has been based hitherto on fear that no disarmament convention will ever be concluded, and that, even if such a convention is concluded, it will yet contain gaps as to time and conditions which may leave France exposed single-handed to a German onslaught for a considerable period before the international machinery comes into play.[108]

Tyrrell believed that a solution could be found in a disarmament agreement that met French requirements, but in the event it was Germany that left the negotiating table.

Cooperation with France still provoked opposition. In conversation with Leo Kennedy in November, Simon explained the government's "rather stiffer attitude" toward Germany since the summer. Public stirrings over the "excesses of Hitlerism" had prompted the change, which "had had a great effect in France."[109] The mention of France seemed to strike a nerve with Kennedy, who presented his own version of public opinion:

> I answered this by saying that it was quite true that the tone of the comment was very naturally strongly anti-Nazi when these excesses were going on, but that British public opinion had not really changed from the view which it held before and still holds -- that on the whole Germany had not had a square deal since the war. I said that the public was getting tired of seeing British diplomacy apparently waiting upon French diplomacy and playing second fiddle, and being able to do nothing independently. I said that, as he had probably noticed from our leaders, what we hoped for was a plain and strong statement of British policy in the circumstances of the moment. He said, 'I am going to make a strong statement....The difficulty is to see what to follow it up with.'[110]

Kennedy himself believed that the way to preserve peace in Europe was to avoid close identity with French interests. Even with Hitler in power, he did not think it was too late to address the injustices of the peace settlement. While he believed that France remained implacably opposed to treaty revision, in fact French leaders increasingly followed Britain's lead.

And Yet, Talk of Moral Disarmament

Despite the fact that the chiefs of staff had made clear the deficiencies of Britain's armed services, fear of a new and prohibitively expensive arms race pushed the government towards acts which would further undermine British defense. Towards the end of 1933 the British Government considered adoption of a Convention on Moral Disarmament, intended to educate the public in the ways of peace, in the belief that "[e]ach stage towards the realisation of the limitation of armaments implies a parallel effort in the domain of moral disarmament."[111]

Naturally Maurice Hankey had some observations to make about the proposal. First of all, the world was not comprised of pacific nations alone; several very important powers had recently rejected the Covenant of the League of Nations: "Germany has never really abandoned militarism, and since the advent of Hitler this cult has received a great impetus. Fascism and Bolshevism are also based on principles that have no relation to moral disarmament. Japan has left the League of Nations in order to put into execution principles that have no relation to moral disarmament."[112] Even if these countries signed a convention on "moral disarmament," who possibly could believe in their pacific intentions? A few days earlier, on

November 12, 93% of Germany's electorate had approved Germany's withdrawal from the League of Nations.[113]

In Britain, however, such a convention would empower pacifist organizations to such a degree that all efforts to maintain the nation's defenses at an acceptable level would be loudly denounced as warmongering. Already Britain had been brought to the "edge of risk":

> Moral disarmament in this country has gone beyond the lowest point consistent with national safety or the enforcement by common action of international obligations. Any British Government, however convinced of the need and however powerful, is compelled by political considerations to think twice before asking the House of Commons to vote the funds necessary to fulfil its elementary duty of providing for national safety. This is the result of the pendulum swinging too far one way. We cannot afford further to upset the balance of public opinion.[114]

The government had to retain the power to control "both taps of public opinion," to turn on the "hot air of idealism" or the "cold air of realism" as needed. The government alone had all the information needed to properly assess the international situation, thought Hankey; some of this information, if made public, actually could aggravate controversy and increase the risk of war. It was the government's task to guide public opinion: "In recent years our governments have all been at pains to quieten the passions aroused by the Great War. The time may come — it may even be nearer than we think — when the trend of public opinion has to be given a different tendency."[115]

The collapse of the Disarmament Conference led Hankey to conclude that Germany intended to rearm. British politicians were "beginning to see that the re-armament of Germany is not likely to be stopped except by the most drastic measures, for which I do not believe public opinion either here or in France would stand." If Germany intended to rearm she would. "The difficulty here, however, is that the Government have repeatedly proclaimed from the housetops that there must be no re-armament of Germany. That is the dilemma, but not an unescapable one for the adroit politician."[116]

He described two schools of thought about Germany's "ultimate intentions." One was highly suspicious:

> Some think it is a case of 'Trust her not; she's fooling thee': that Hitler's approaches to France are mere *schwärmerei* intended to lull the Western Powers to sleep while he re-arms: that the flirtation with Poland is also part of a carefully conceived scheme to gain time by more or less protracted negotiations over commercial difficulties, and the like, to be followed later by territorial boundary discussions which would take even

longer: that towards the end of these latter negotiations a re-armed Germany would be such a menace as perhaps to be able to get what she wants without war, or, if that was found impossible, to enable her to say that she had used every peaceful means and must now resort to force in defence of Germans on the other side of the boundary.[117]

Though Hankey did not mention names, clearly the Foreign Office subscribed to this view, though not without hesitation.

The other school called for a more tolerant stand, based on the belief that National Socialism was a movement of national regeneration. A letter from the Bishop of Gloucester appeared in the *Times* on November 24:

Germany has made and is making many mistakes. Many foolish things have been said. There are unpleasant elements in the dominant party. If we adopt a purely censorious attitude, we shall only increase these mistakes. If we are sympathetic towards the efforts they are making to restore their country, and if we take them at their best and not at their worst, we may help them in the task they have undertaken. Let us remember that a bull may be a very peaceful animal, but goaded into fury it becomes very dangerous, and the attitude of Germany in future years to the rest of Europe depends on our being willing to judge them fairly.[118]

The bishop insisted that the German people did not want war; the National Socialists used militaristic language only to pursue their struggle against communism, and "the whole movement at the present time is a movement for disciplining themselves and the people of the country." Earlier he had gone so far as to blame the Jews in part for Communist violence, first in Russia and now in Germany: "they are not altogether a pleasant element in German, and in particular in Berlin life."[119] Hankey himself felt torn between the two poles of opinion: "The spiritual revival is no doubt there, and is being subtly used for the internal regeneration of the people. But there is also that deeply engrained desire, by hook or by crook, to get rid of the Treaty of Versailles, which lies at the root of all the German policy. The former may easily be used to prepare the way for the latter."[120] Given the fact that Nazism was a relatively recent phenomenon, one could expect different interpretations of its significance; yet for a man presumably educated in ethics and morality to describe Nazism as a kind of spiritual revival — at a time when the brutality of the regime, including its persecution of the Jews, was already well publicized — did not bode well.

Neither French nor British leaders suffered for lack of information about Hitler and the National Socialist revolution in Germany. In France, the facts supported the uncompromising views of Franklin-Bouillon, Marin and Mandel. Yet Germany's choice of National Socialism and its corollary enmity with France did not produce any lasting change in French policy or leadership. Franklin-Bouillon, Marin and Mandel still were far to the right on the political spectrum. Most of the French electorate appeared to prefer men of more moderate convictions, men willing to compromise in order to avoid another disastrous war. In Britain, too, Churchill, Austen Chamberlain, Boothby, and Ormsby-Gore were Conservatives "in the wilderness" during the time of MacDonald's National Government. At the time, and certainly in retrospect, the leadership of men like MacDonald and Simon, Daladier and Paul-Boncour was weak or poor; yet they were their country's elected leaders, and to a degree they represented the views of the majority.

Britain and France were unprepared militarily and morally to face the dangers Germany posed. The events and personalities of 1933 failed to stop further deterioration. Could Britain and France at least find common cause, as the two great liberal democracies of Europe? By this time many French leaders were beginning to display signs of complete dependence on Britain. France no doubt would have welcomed an alliance with Britain at any time; for many reasons, British leaders, though they recognized the importance of cooperation with France, were not prepared to commit themselves. MacDonald, for one, could not set aside his prejudices against the French, even though his general gloominess suggests that he pursued alternatives without confidence. Yet a return to alignments reminiscent of 1914, combined with the fear of a war far more destructive than the last one had been, was also a dismal prospect. In 1933 both British and French leaders recognized the dangers Hitler posed to Europe, but they were not prepared to resign themselves to grim scenarios.

Notes

1. Quoted in D. Marquand, *Ramsay MacDonald*, p. 753.
2. Speech before the Radical-Socialist Congress at Vichy, October 4, 1933. J. Wheeler-Bennett, ed. *Documents on International Affairs 1933* (London, 1934), p. 401.
3. *Personalities and Policies* (London, 1965), pp. 118-119.
4. J. Jackson, *The Politics of Depression in France, 1932-1936* (Cambridge, 1985), pp. 23-27.
5. S. Berstein and P. Milza, *Histoire du vingtième siècle*, volume 1, *Un monde déstabilisé* (Paris, 1987), pp. 278-280.
6. Mitchell, *European Historical Statistics*, pp. 488-489.
7. Mitchell, pp. 421-422. British, French, and Italian totals for 1929 had been the highest since the war. The German total for 1929 was only 0.4% less than in 1927.
8. Again, both these countries had large agricultural sectors, where unemployment was more difficult to measure.

9. Mitchell, pp. 174-179.

10. Mitchell, pp. 545, 548, 559, 600.

11. Kindleberger, *The World in Depression*, pp. 123-127.

12. Kindleberger, p. 230.

13. J. Bariéty, "Les partisans français de l'entente franco-allemande et la «prise du pouvoir» par Hitler, Avril 1932 - Avril 1934," in Bariéty et al., *La France et l'Allemagne* (Nancy, 1987), p. 24.

14. Shay, *British Rearmament in the Thirties*, p. 20.

15. Ibid., p. 297.

16. W.K. Wark, "British Military and Economic Intelligence: Assessments of Nazi Germany Before the Second World War," in C. Andrew and D. Dilks, editors, *The Missing Dimension* (London, 1984), p. 83.

17. R. Frankenstein, *Le Prix du réarmement français 1935-1939* (Paris, 1982), p. 35.

18. By and large, however, serious attempts at social legislation had to wait until after the 1936 elections, when the Popular Front took power. By then, however, the budget of the Ministry of National Defense claimed an increasingly large share of total government expenditures, jumping between four and five percentage points annually between 1935 (20.8%) and 1938 (34.5%). A. Sauvy, *Histoire économique de la France entre les deux guerres*, volume 1 (Paris, 1984), p. 384.

19. Bariéty, pp. 21, 24.

20. Deflation made these figures look worse than they in fact were, but the army especially felt the pinch. Sauvy, p. 384.

21. Sauvy, p. 384.

22. R.J. Young, *In Command of France: French Foreign Policy and Military Planning, 1933-1940* (Cambridge, Mass., 1978), pp. 36-37; Bankwitz, *Maxime Weygand and Civil-Military Relations in Modern France*, p. 41.

23. Frankenstein, p. 47; J. Doise and M. Vaïsse, *Diplomatie et outil militaire*, pp. 278-279.

24. Bankwitz, pp. 83-95.

25. Young, p. 34.

26. Sauvy, p.384.

27. D. Boussard, *Un problème de défense nationale: l'aeronautique militaire au parlement 1928-1940* (Vincennes, 1983), p. 39.

28. Young, p. 35.

29. Sauvy, p. 384.

30. Doise and Vaïsse, pp. 280-281; 326-327.

31. As mentioned above, assessments of the strength of Germany's armed forces remained rather optimistic until 1936. See W.K. Wark, *The Ultimate Enemy: British Intelligence and Nazi Germany, 1933-1939* (Ithaca, 1985).

32. Sontag, *A Broken World*, p. 250.

33. Ibid, p. 251.

34. *The British Press and Germany, 1936-1939* (Oxford, 1971), p. 2.

35. S. Koss, *The Rise and Fall of the Political Press in Britain*, p. 542.

36. Ibid.

37. Barnett, p. 411.

38. David Ayerst, *Garvin of the Observer* (London, 1985), p. 243.

39. Ibid.

40. On the persistence of anti-French attitudes throughout the press, see Gannon, pp. 12-14.

41. CAB 63/46/3-11, Hankey to the Bishop of Croydon, January 6, 1933.
42. Ibid.
43. Ibid.
44. Ibid.
45. Ibid.
46. 0324 AP 3, J. Bardoux to A. Tardieu, Paris, February 2, 1933. Bardoux was the grandfather of Valéry Giscard d'Estaing.
47. PA Fleuriau 3/78, J. Paul-Boncour to A. de Fleuriau, Geneva, February 7, 1933.
48. Dalton I/15a (Diary), April 30, 1933.
49. PA Canet 36/54, André d'Ormesson to the Foreign Minister, Munich, April 7, 1933. See also C. Fink, "Defender of Minorities: Germany in the League of Nations," *Central European History* 5 (December 1972), pp. 332-357.
50. Young, p. 44.
51. J.O. Chambre, 1933, sessions ordinaires, tome 1, p. 1928.
52. Ibid.
53. Ibid., p. 1930.
54. JO, Chambre, April 6, 1933, pp. 1935-7.
55. Ibid, p. 1940.
56. Ibid., pp. 1940-1943.
57. Ibid., p. 1945-7.
58. Ibid., p. 1948.
59. Ibid., p. 1949.
60. Bellanger, pp. 513-522; Bernard and Dubief, p. 263.
61. *Le Temps*, May 15, 1933, p. 1.
62. JS 76/137-141, M. A. Robertson to J. Simon, May 10, 1933.
63. Ibid.
64. Ibid.
65. Ibid.
66. D.C. Watt, *Personalities and Policies: Studies in the Formation of British Foreign Policy in the Twentieth Century* (London, 1965), pp. 123-127.
67. PRO 30/69/1443/361-412, T.P. Conwell-Evans, [n.d.] March 1933. Conwell-Evans later became an active opponent of appeasement. C. Andrew, *Secret Service: The Making of the British Intelligence Community* (London, 1985), p. 416.
68. PRO 30/69/679/570-576, Lothian to House, April 11, 1933.
69. See R. Griffiths, *Fellow Travellers of the Right: British Enthusiasts for Nazi Germany 1933-1939* (Oxford, 1983), pp. 78-79.
70. PRO 30/69/755/778-783, MacDonald to Lily Montagu, April 10, 1933.
71. E.W. Bennett, *German Rearmament*, pp. 360-367.
72. Ibid.
73. PRO 30/69/679/772-773, MacDonald to Simon, August 26, 1933. Vansittart declined the offer of a September vacation.
74. PRO 30/69/679/260, MacDonald to Cecil, October 11, 1933.
75. From MacDonald's diary, quoted by David Marquand in *Ramsay MacDonald* (London, 1977), p. 748.
76. Marquand, pp. 747-751.
77. The *Economist*, May 6, 1933, p. 957.
78. Ibid.
79. PRO 30/69/679/640-647, Ormsby-Gore to MacDonald, July 25, 1933. Later in the 1930s Ormsby-Gore opposed John Simon's conduct of foreign policy and became an

enthusiastic supporter of Anthony Eden.

80. AC 5/1/629, Austen to Hilda Chamberlain, August 13, 1933.

81. AC 5/1/616 Austen to Ida Chamberlain, May 14, 1933.

82. AC 5/1/629 Austen to Hilda Chamberlain, August 13, 1933.

83. Roskill, *Hankey*, volume 3, p. 85. Elliot was Minister of Agriculture and Fisheries.

84. AC 5/1/640, Austen to Ida Chamberlain, November 18, 1933.

85. AC 5/1/639, Austen to Hilda Chamberlain, November 11, 1933; Gannon, p. 289.

86. PRO 30/69/679/476-489, Hankey to N. Chamberlain, March 2, 1933.

87. Ibid.

88. Shay, p. 27.

89. Gibbs, pp. 93-94.

90. G. Schmidt, *The Politics and Economics of Appeasement* (Leamington Spa, 1986), pp. 9-10.

91. An unabridged French translation was published in 1934, but the Germans sought its suppression in French courts. A. Adamthwaite, *France and the Coming of the Second World War* (London, 1977), p. 283.

92. DBFP, second series , volume 5, no. 36, Rumbold to Simon, Berlin, April 26, 1933, pp. 47-55.

93. Rumbold's own anti-Semitism is described in M. Gilbert, *Horace Rumbold*, pp. 318-319.

94. J. and P. Barnes, *Hitler's* Mein Kampf *in Britain and America* (Cambridge, 1980), pp. 23-26. Weizmann's correspondence with Dawson is in FO 371/16759/6871/2-7.

95. Barnes, pp. 7-10.

96. MAE, series Z, Great Britain 685/48-9, C. Corbin to J. Paul-Boncour, London, October 23, 1933.

97. From Helmut Ripperger's unabridged translation of *Mein Kampf* published by Reynal and Hitchcock (New York, 1940), p. 966.

98. PHPP 3/3/27-29, M. Hankey to E. Phipps, October 30, 1933.

99. Ibid.

100. Ibid.

101. PHPP 3/3/7-24, M. Hankey to E. Phipps, September 1933.

102. Ibid.

103. Ibid.

104. FO 425/411/22 Tyrrell to Simon, Paris, August 10, 1933.

105. Ibid.

106. Ibid.

107. Ibid.

108. Ibid.

109. LKEN 15, London, November 17, 1933.

110. Ibid. However — and certainly in the days before the Peace Ballot and Mass-Observation — genuine "public opinion" remained an elusive entity; from Kennedy's diaries, one can draw the conclusion that, "public opinion" was a projection of the opinions of the *Times*' editorial staff. The British Government also invoked the term, but at least it was responsible to a national electorate, and not just a sector of British society.

111. CAB 63/47/60-63, note by Hankey, November 17, 1933.

112. Ibid.

113. R. Ferrell, ed. *The Twentieth Century: An Almanac* (New York, 1985), p.176.

114. CAB 63/47/60-63, note by Hankey, November 17, 1933.

Democracies at the Turning Point

115. Ibid.
116. PHPP 3/3/31-35, M. Hankey to E. Phipps, November 24, 1933.
117. Ibid.
118. The *Times*, November 24, 1933.
119. From an article in the bishop's diocesan magazine, quoted in Griffiths, p. 76.
120. PHPP 3/3/31-35 (cited above).

Conclusion

We are led by timid, nerveless old men.   — Hugh Dalton[1]

The years 1928 to 1933 did not constitute an era; rather, the preceding chapters reveal a broad variety of opinions about European politics during a period of dramatic transition from relative peace and prosperity to upheaval and uncertainty. The foreign policy communities in Britain and France witnessed a deterioration which they felt powerless to stop. Of course, mere observers could do little, but what about the leaders of the two great European democracies, the victors of the Great War? Did a great tide of events sweep them along toward the inevitable? Or did their errors of omission and commission turn a difficult situation into a disastrous one? Might better leaders have steered their countries away from the abyss?

Whatever their abilities, the leaders of Britain and France faced an extraordinarily difficult set of problems in the early 1930s. Britain had never really prospered since the war, and few economists — let alone politicians — knew what to do about it. The financial crisis of 1931 dealt a severe blow, and leaders faced a major force they hardly understood. After holding out until 1931, the French economy sank into depression, and again few good ideas emerged from the political arena as to what to do. One cannot measure the extent to which a sense of helplessness or ignorance on matters of economics and finance contributed to perceptions about political developments. Almost as difficult to grasp was the extent to which, regardless of perceptions, economic conditions actually shaped the political circumstances.

However, given this tangled mess of circumstances, leaders nevertheless had to make some sense of them. Whatever they knew or did not know of economics, they were experienced politicians, and in Europe they faced a set of political problems on which the security of their countries depended. Here they committed some grave errors. From 1929 to 1935, Ramsay MacDonald led Great Britain, a country in which antipathy toward France was inherent in the culture; but in the past Britain's leaders had recognized when an alliance with France was in order. Long after Germany's revisionist agenda came to the fore, and even into the Nazi era, MacDonald continued to blame France for Germany's ills. Whatever regard he once may have shown for the League of Nations and the new order, in 1933 he pushed Mussolini's Four-Power Pact, which would have allowed Germany and Italy to make their demands while France was held in check.

French leaders such as Herriot and Briand earlier had hoped to "organize the peace." They knew that the Treaty of Versailles alone would not produce a lasting peace with Germany, but they also understood that true security required both the treaty and improved ties. Skeptical of German ambitions, Briand pursued both tracks.[2] One could fault the visionary leader for lacking the discipline to put forward more concrete proposals, or to put the civil service to work on them. Ultimately, however, Briand's vision of a new Europe did not captivate Europeans. Leaders of Britain, Germany and Italy suspected a French plot to dominate Europe and defeated the plan.

Britain's desire to free itself from European commitments was clear already in the 1920s. France remained engaged, loudly protesting moves towards *Anschluss*, for example, but it had no real plans to defend its European allies militarily. In a time of war-weariness and financial stringency, British and French leaders could curtail their military budgets with the force of public opinion behind them; but they also understood better than the general public the risks they were taking. Reduced budgets and poor planning did not mean, after all, that France or Britain would not go to war to punish an egregious violation of the treaties. They did mean, however, that these countries would be less able to deter such aggression, and that they stood a greater chance of losing a war. In the meantime, both powers lost influence.

At the time observers noted this loss of influence on both sides of the Channel, and they singled out the leaders for blame. Austen Chamberlain lamented Britain's decline at the end of Hitler's first year in power. After a meeting with William Tyrrell, French ambassador Charles Corbin and the League's secretary general, Joseph Avenol, Chamberlain wrote that

> All are very disturbed and very hopeless about [Britain's] shifts of policy. We go on talking about our influence and we *ought* to exercise great influence, but to me it seems that in fact we are losing influence all the time. France has lost confidence in us, Italy goes its own way and Germany snaps her fingers at us all. 'Whom would you make foreign secretary' I asked Tyrrell. 'You, of course.' 'But I'm out of it.'' Then Neville; he's the only one who understands.' Pity there aren't half-a-dozen Nevilles! And to think that in times like these we have no better men to lead the three parties than Ramsay, S[tanley] B[aldwin] and Lansbury. Oh for a *man*![3]

Robert Cecil had complained in a similar vein to Lord Irwin already in September 1930:

> Perhaps the most formidable feature of the present situation is the dearth of any outstanding personalities. The most ardent admirer of Baldwin could not pretend that he is a man of first-rate intellectual power. Nor do I see among his lieutenants here anyone who is, unless it be Winston, who for other reasons is not available. The Labour Party are even worse off. Ramsay does not improve on near acquaintance, and there really is no-one else. The Liberals on the other hand have a certain number of men in the first rank, but the disquieting feature even of their situation is that all their best men are at or over sixty.[4]

Again, these leaders faced extraordinary circumstances, and both Chamberlain and Cecil looked upon their colleagues with a certain measure of bitterness, but one hardly can dispute that Baldwin and MacDonald were uninspiring and uninspired leaders.[5]

The foreign secretaries Austen Chamberlain, Arthur Henderson and John Simon all eventually managed to grasp the central problems of European politics and what sort of role Britain *ought* to play; but none managed to develop an effective policy, or even to make much progress toward building a consensus. Leo Kennedy of the *Times* marvelled at how Henderson had come around to see Chamberlain's view of the necessity of cooperation with France, despite the strong anti-French bias of the Labour Party and most of Britain. Yet Henderson's influence was limited. Many bitterly criticized John Simon for his indecisiveness, though his intelligence was never in doubt; yet he lingered on as foreign secretary until 1935.

In France, particularly after Briand's decline, the situation was similarly bleak. In May 1933 Wladimir d'Ormesson complained about the dearth of leaders in a letter to his mentor, Marshall Lyautey. As a foreign policy editor for *Le Temps*, *Le Figaro* and the *Journal de Genève*, Ormesson had been a strong supporter of Briand; though conservative, his views on foreign policy estranged him from right-wing politicians. During a lunch with André Tardieu, Ormesson was dismayed to hear the former premier make fun of "everyone and everything":

> He didn't say a word about politics. He made no reference to a single current problem.... He told jokes, jokes, jokes and more jokes.... And this is the man who presents himself as the one who is going to get the nation in shape, the one who personifies the Right! It's enough to make one cry! Or rather, grind one's teeth! Why must this country go from the "Café de Paris" incomprehension of a Tardieu to the legalistic incomprehension of Poincaré or the romantic incomprehension of an Herriot? Such politicians![6]

In the early 1920s Ormesson had returned from east central Europe with the firm conviction that Germany remained as powerful as ever.[7] An advocate of Franco-German rapprochement in the 1920s, he watched with growing frustration during the 1930s as Germany steered away from cooperation, Briand faded away and French policy became mired in indecision.

In 1932, as Germany sank into political and economic chaos, France's foreign policy, which Briand's personality had driven since the days of Locarno, began to drift. The frequent changes of government that were so characteristic of the Third Republic accounted in part for a succession of short stays at the Quai d'Orsay, but Briand also had left no heir. Herriot was a kindred spirit, but his involvement in Radical party politics deprived him of the kind of neutral-figure status that a longer tenure as foreign minister required. Only in 1934 did Louis Barthou try to address the problem of living in Europe with Nazi Germany, and a Croatian terrorist put an end to his attempt. Certainly the foreign ministers of the 1930s faced huge challenges, both internally and externally, but, with the exception of Barthou, there were few inspiring attempts to meet them.

Was democracy in Britain and France unable to produce leaders who could guide their countries through these adverse conditions? Though at the time some portrayed the democracies as "effete" or "decadent," the problem lay not in the fact that people elected their leaders but in political cultures in which mediocrity flourished and vanity propelled men to positions of power. Indeed, had Britain and France's leaders been driven by greater ideas, or even a sense of democratic idealism, they might have been better equipped to recognize the evils of the Nazi regime and the need for solidarity among the remaining democracies — another possible route to renewal of the wartime alliance.

Meanwhile, the crisis grew: German revisionism imperiled the peace Britain and France had established; only together could they prevent its destruction. But British leaders, antipathetic towards the French and like the French reluctant to contemplate another major war, could not easily reverse the economies they had undertaken both in terms of armaments and commitments. Today one can understand that the horrors of the last war, restiveness within the empire and very real economic constraints put British leaders in a very difficult position. The fact remains, however, that in continuing to regard France as the hegemonic power of Europe, they allowed Nazism to metastasize freely on the continent, a profound error that would bring Britain itself to the brink of destruction in 1940.

Britain and France had emerged from the war of 1914-1918 victorious but profoundly shaken. Though they had won with some crucial assistance from the United States towards the end, and President Wilson had played a key role in shaping the peace treaties, they essentially had to maintain the peace on their own. Certainly they had the potential to do it; but the alliance which almost defeated Germany in wartime failed in peacetime. Of course the treaties remained; but in "liquidating" the war the former allies gave up much of their leverage against Germany. However bitter relations between France and Britain had become in the 1920s, occupation of German territory preserved the key element of their alliance. In evacuating the Rhineland, in putting an end to reparations, in allowing disarmament to assume a central position in European politics, the former allies allowed Germany to shed its status as a pariah state, which eventually had to happen; but at the same time they forfeited much of their insurance against German revisionism. One could argue that revision of the treaties also was inevitable; but Britain and France failed to ensure that revision would take place in a suitable context, one in which their interests and those of their allies would be preserved as much as possible.

In history, the avoidable and the inevitable do not sort themselves neatly; nor do the possible and the impossible. The perceptions surrounding the liquidation of the war, political developments in Germany, the workings of the League of Nations and proposals for European integration suggest that leaders had to make important decisions even as momentous events seemed to sweep them along. It was *possible* for Britain and France, cooperatively, to lead Europe peacefully through the challenges of the 1930s. Looking back, one can say confidently that it would have been in both nations' interest. Of course, not knowing the consequences of their policies and actions kept leaders from choosing the right course, but so did prejudices, resentments, and the lack of vision, courage and ideas. The role that mentalities play in the unfolding of events remains an elusive problem, but in the 1920s and 1930s they prevented British and French leaders from recognizing their common interests and the road to lasting peace.

Notes

1. Remark made about the Labour party's leadership after an election manifesto committee meeting in March 1929. Dalton I/10/103 (Diary), March 13, 1929.
2. Wladimir d'Ormesson, "Une tentative de rapprochement franco-allemand entre les deux guerres," *La Revue de Paris* 69 (February 1962): 18.

3. AC 5/1/643, letter to Hilda, December 17, 1933. Austen Chamberlain died in 1937, before his half-brother's attempts to keep the peace in 1938 and 1939.

4. BL MS 51084/73-76, Cecil to Lord Irwin (Edward), September 5, 1930.

5. In both Britain and France, writers cultivated the myth of a "lost generation," which held that an entire generation of their "best and brightest" had perished on the battlefields of Belgium and France. However, though many had died in the Great War, more had come back, and most of them were in any case too young to have risen to the top positions of leadership by this time. See R. Wohl, *The Generation of 1914*, chapters 1 and 3; Barnett, *The Collapse of British Power*, pp. 425-428.

6. 475 AP 301 (Lyautey Papers) Wladimir d'Ormesson to Marshal Lyautey, May 30, 1933.

7. He recorded his observations in a series of articles, "Ce que j'ai vu en Europe Centrale," in the *Revue hebdomadaire*, August-September 1922.

Select Bibliography

I. Unpublished Documents

I-A. United Kingdom

Public Record Office
Foreign Office archives (FO)
War Office archives (WO)
Cabinet papers (CAB)
Special collections: J. Ramsay MacDonald papers (PRO 30/69)

British Library of Political and Economic Science
Hugh Dalton papers

British Library
Robert Cecil papers

Birmingham University
Chamberlain Papers (Austen and Neville)
Eden papers

Churchill College, Cambridge
Papers of: Maurice Hankey, Robert Vansittart, Eric Phipps, Hughe Knatch-
                    bull-Hugessen, Leo Aubrey Kennedy, Philip Noel-Baker

Bodleian Library, Oxford University
Papers of: John Simon, Horace Rumbold

I-B. France

Archives du Ministère des Affaires Etrangères
Y Series: International
Z Series: Europe
Papiers d'Agents: Joseph Avenol, Philippe Berthelot, Aristide Briand, Joseph
                    Caillaux, Jules Cambon, Louis Canet, Emile Dard, Gaston
                    Doumergue, Aimé de Fleuriau, Edouard Herriot, Henri de
                    Jouvenel, Louis Marin, René Massigli, André d'Ormesson, Joseph
                    Paul-Boncour,
Papiers 1940:   Édouard Daladier, Alexis Léger

Archives Nationales
Archives privées: Jacques Dumesnil, Paul Painlevé, Joseph Paul-Boncour, Paul
                    Reynaud, André Tardieu

Fondation Nationale des Sciènces Politiques
Papers of: Léon Blum, Pierre Cot, Edouard Daladier, Emile-Roche-J.
Caillaux correspondence, André Siegfried.

Bibliothèque Nationale
Papers of: Pierre-Etienne Flandin, Henri de Jouvenel, Raymond Poincaré

II. Selected Published Works

II-A. Collections of Documents or Statistics

Elisha, A., ed. *Aristide Briand: discours et écrits de politique étrangère: la paix,
l'union européenne, la Société des Nations.* Paris: Plon, 1965

France. Commission de publication des documents relatifs aux origines de la guerre.
Documents diplomatiques français 1932-1939. Paris: Imprimerie Nationale,
1963-1986.

____. *Journal Officiel des débats parlementaires.* Paris: Imprimerie Nationale, 1927-
1933.

Germany. *Auswärtiges Amt. Documents on German Foreign Policy, 1918-1945, from
the Archives of the German Foreign Ministry.* Washington, D.C.: U.S.
Government Printing Office, 1949-<1983>.

Great Britain. Foreign Office. *Documents on British Foreign Policy, 1919-1939.*
Woodward, E.L. et al, editors. London: HMSO, 1946-<1985>.

____. *Parliamentary Debates: Commons.* London, 1928-1933.

____. *British Documents on Foreign Affairs: Reports and Papers from the Foreign Office
Confidential Print.* Frederick: University Publications of America, 1989-1991.

League of Nations. *Official Documents.* Microfilm.

Mitchell, B.R. *European Historical Statistics 1750-1975.* New York: Facts on File,
1975.

Wheeler-Bennett, J.W., editor. *Documents on International Affairs.* Annual volumes
for 1928-1933. London: Oxford University Press, 1929-1934.

II-B. Biographies, Autobiographies, Memoirs

Aron, R. *Mémoires: 50 ans de réflexion politique.* Paris: Julliard, 1983.

Auffray, B. *Pierre de Margerie et la vie diplomatique de son temps.* Paris: Klinck-
sieck, 1976.

Bibliography   219

Ayerst, D. *Garvin of the Observer*. London: Croom Helm, 1985.

Barros, J. *Betrayal from Within: Joseph Avenol, Secretary-General of the League of
    Nations, 1933-1940*. New Haven: Yale University Press, 1969.

___. *Office without Power: Secretary-General Sir Eric Drummond, 1919-1933*.
    Oxford: Oxford University Press, 1979.

Binion, R. *Defeated Leaders: The Fate of Caillaux, Jouvenel, and Tardieu*. New
    York: Columbia University Press, 1960.

Bloch, M. *Memoirs of War, 1914-1915*. tr. Carole Fink. Cambridge: Cambridge
    University Press, 1988.

Colton, J. *Léon Blum, Humanist in Politics*. Cambridge: The MIT Press, 1966.

Coudenhove-Kalergi, R. *Crusade for Pan-Europe: Autobiography of a Man and a
    Movement*. New York: G.B. Putnam's Sons, 1943.

Daladier, É. *Défense du pays*. Paris: Flammarion, 1939.

Dalton, H. *The Political Diary of Hugh Dalton, 1918-1940; 1945-1960*. Edited by B.
    Pimlott. London: Jonathan Cape, 1986.

Dutton, D. *Austen Chamberlain: Gentleman in Politics*. Bolton: Ross Anderson,
    1985.

Flandin, P.-É. *Politique française 1919-1940*. Paris: Les Éditions nouvelles.

François-Poncet, A. *The Fateful Years: Memoirs of a French Ambassador in Berlin,
    1931-1938*. Translated by J. LeClercq. New York: H. Fertig, 1972.

Gilbert, M. *Sir Horace Rumbold: Portrait of a Diplomat, 1869-1941*. London:
    Heinemann, 1973.

___. *Winston S. Churchill*. Volume 5: *1922-1939*. London: Heinemann, 1976.

Grant Duff, S. *The Parting of Ways: A Personal Account of the Thirties*. London:
    Peter Owen, 1982.

Herriot, É. *Jadis*. Volume 2. Paris: Flammarion, 1952.

Kupferman, F. *Laval 1883-1945*. Paris: Balland, 1987.

Jones, T. *Whitehall Diary*. Volume 2: *1926-1930*. Edited by K. Middlemas. London:
    Oxford University Press, 1969.

Leventhal, M.F. *Arthur Henderson*. Manchester: Manchester University Press, 1989.

Marquand, D. *Ramsay MacDonald*. London: Jonathan Cape, 1977.

Miquel, P. *Poincaré*. Paris: Fayard, 1984.

Ostrovsky, E. *Under the Sign of Ambiguity: Saint-John Perse/ Alexis Leger*. New York: New York University Press, 1985.

Oudin, B. *Aristide Briand. La Paix: Idée neuve en Europe*. Paris: Robert Laffont, 1988.

Paul-Boncour, P. *Entre deux guerres: souvenirs sur la IIIème République*. 3 volumes. Paris: Plon, 1945.

Pimlott, B. *Hugh Dalton*. London: Jonathan Cape, 1985.

Reynaud, P. *Mémoires*. Paris: Flammarion, 1963.

Rhodes James, Robert. *Anthony Eden: A Biography*. New York: McGraw-Hill, 1986.

Rose, N. *Vansittart: Study of a Diplomat*. London: Heinemann, 1978.

Roskill, S. *Hankey, Man of Secrets*. 3 vols., Annapolis: Naval Institute Press, 1972.

Sherwood, J.M. *Georges Mandel and the Third Republic*. Stanford: Stanford University Press, 1970.

Solo, R. *André François-Poncet*. PhD dissertation. Michigan State University, 1978.

Soulié, M. *La vie politique d'Édouard Herriot*. Paris, 1962.

Suarez, G. *Briand: sa vie, son oeuvre avec son journal et de nombreux documents inédits*. Volume 6: *L'Artisan de la paix, 1923-1932*. Paris: Plon, 1952.

Tardieu, A. *Paroles réalistes*. Paris, 1928.

____. *L'épreuve du pouvoir*. Paris, 1931.

____. *Devant le pays*. Paris, 1932.

____. *L'Heure de la décision*. Paris, 1934.

____. *France in Danger! A Great Statesman's Warning*. Translated by G. Griffin. London, 1935.

Vansittart, R. *The Mist Procession*. London: Hutchinson, 1958.

II-C. Secondary Sources: Books and Articles

Adamthwaite, A. *France and the Coming of the Second World War, 1936-1939.* London: Frank Cass, 1977.

Aldcroft, D. *The Inter-War Economy: Britain 1919-1939.* New York: Columbia University Press, 1970.

____. *From Versailles to Wall Street: The International Economy in the 1920s.* Berkeley: University of California Press, 1977.

Andrew, C. *Secret Service: The Making of the British Intelligence Community.* London: Heinemann, 1985.

____. "British Intelligence and the Breach with Russia in 1927." *Historical Journal* 25:4 (December 1982): 956-964.

____ and Kanya-Forstner, S. *France Overseas: The Great War and the Climax of French Imperial Expansion.* London: Thames and Hudson, 1981.

____ and Dilks, D., editors. *The Missing Dimension.* London: Macmillan, 1984.

Ball, S. *Baldwin and the Conservative Party: The Crisis of 1929-1931.* New Haven: Yale University Press, 1988.

Bankwitz, P. *Maxime Weygand and Civil-Military Relations in Modern France.* Cambridge: Harvard University Press, 1967.

Bariéty, J. "Idée européenne et relations franco-allemandes." *Bulletin de la Faculté des lettres de Strasbourg* 46 (1968):571-584.

____. *Les illusions 1918-1932.* Paris, 1980.

____. *Les relations franco-allemandes 1933-1939.* Paris: Centre National de la Recherche Scientifique, 1976.

____. "Les relations franco-allemandes de 1924 à 1933." *Annales de la Société d'Histoire de la IIIe République (1962-1963):* 57-68.

____ et Bloch, C. "Une tentative de réconciliation franco-allemande et son échec 1932-1933." *Revue d'Histoire Moderne et Contemporaine* 15 (1968): 433-465.

____, Guth, A. and Valentin, J.-M. *La France et l'Allemagne entre deux guerres mondiales: actes du colloque tenu en Sorbonne (Paris IV), 15 - 17 janvier 1987.* Nancy: Presses universitaires de Nancy, 1987.

Barnes, J.J. and Barnes, P.P. *Hitler's* Mein Kampf *in Britain and America: A Publishing History, 1930-1939.* Cambridge: Cambridge University Press, 1980.

222   *Democracies at the Turning Point*

Barnett, C. *The Collapse of British Power.* Atlantic Highlands, N.J.: Humanities Press International, 1986.

Becker, J. and Hildebrand, K. *Internationale Beziehungen in der Weltwirtschaftskrise 1929-1933.* Munich: Vögel, 1980.

Bellanger, C., Godechot, C., Guiral, J. and Terrou, F. *Histoire générale de la presse française.* Volume 3: *De 1871 à 1940.* Paris: Presses Universitaires de France, 1972.

Bennett, E.W. *Germany and the Diplomacy of the Financial Crisis 1931.* Cambridge: Harvard University Press, 1962.

___. *German Rearmament and the West, 1932-1933.* Princeton: Princeton University Press, 1979.

Berghahn, V. and Kitchen M., editors. *Germany in the Age of Total War.* London: Croom Helm, 1981.

Bernard, P. and Dubief, H. *The Decline of the Third Republic 1914-1938.* Translated by A. Forster. Cambridge: Cambridge University Press, 1985.

Birn, D.S. *The League of Nations Union 1918-1945.* Oxford: Oxford University Press, 1981.

Bisceglia, L. *Norman Angell and Liberal Internationalism in Britain, 1931-1935.* New York: Garland, 1982.

Blumenthal, H. *Illusion and Reality in Franco-American Diplomacy, 1914-1945.* Baton Rouge: Louisiana State University Press, 1986.

Bond, B. *British Military Policy between the Two World Wars.* Oxford: Clarendon Press, 1980.

Bonnefous, É. *Histoire politique de la Troisième République.* Volumes 4 and 5. Paris: Presses Universitaires de France, 1960, 1962.

Borne, D. and Dubief, H. *La crise des années 30: 1929-1938.* Paris: Seuil, 1989.

Boussard, D. *Un problème de défense nationale: l'aéronautique militaire au parlement, 1928-1940.* Vincennes: Service historique de l'armée de l'air, 1983.

Boyce, R.W.D. *British Capitalism at the Crossroads, 1919-1932: A Study in Politics, Economics and International Relations.* Cambridge: Cambridge University Press, 1987.

___. "Britain's First 'No' to Europe: Britain and the Briand Plan, 1929-1930." *European Studies Review* 10:1 (January, 1980): 17-45.

___ and Robertson, E.M., editors. *Paths to War: New Essays on the Origins of the Second World War*. London: Macmillan, 1989.

Braubach, M. "Hitlers Machtergreifung. Die Berichte des französischen Botschafters François-Poncet über der Vorgange in Deutschland von Juli 1932 bis Juli 1933." *Festschrift für L. Brandt*. Cologne, 1968: 443-64.

Cairns, J.C. *Contemporary France*. New York: New Viewpoints, 1978.

___. "A Nation of Shopkeepers in Search of a Suitable France." *American Historical Review* 79:3 (June 1974): 710-43.

Carlton, D. *MacDonald versus Henderson: The Foreign Policy of the Second Labour Government*. London: Macmillan, 1970.

Carsten, F.L. *Britain and the Weimar Republic: the British Documents*. New York: Schocken, 1984.

___. *The First Austrian Republic, 1918-1938: A Study Based on British and Austrian Documents*. Aldershot: Gower, 1986.

Carr, E.H. *The Twenty Years' Crisis, 1919-1939*. New York: Harper Torchbooks, 1964.

Castellan, G. *Le réarmement clandestin du Reich, 1930-1935*. Paris, 1954.

Ceadel, M. "The 'King and Country' Debate, 1933: Student Politics, Pacifism and the Dictators." *Historical Journal* 22:1 (March 1979): 397-422.

Clague, M. "Vision and Myopia in the New Politics of André Tardieu." *French Historical Studies* 8 (1973): 105-129.

Clayton, A. *The British Empire as a Superpower, 1919-1939*. Athens: University of Georgia Press, 1986.

Cockett, R. *Twilight of Truth: Chamberlain, Appeasement, and the Manipulation of the Press*. New York: St. Martin's, 1989.

___. "the Foreign Office News Department and the Struggle Against Appeasement." *Historical Research* 63 (February 1990): 73-85.

Costigliola, F. *Awkward Dominion: American Political, Economic and Cultural Relations with Europe 1919-1933*. Ithaca: Cornell University Press, 1984.

___. "Anglo-American Financial Rivalry in the 1920s." *Journal of Economic History* 37 (December, 1977): 911-934.

Cowling, M. *The Impact of Hitler: British Politics and British Policy 1933-1940.* Cambridge: Cambridge University Press, 1975.

Craig, G.A. and Gilbert, F. *The Diplomats.* Princeton: Princeton University Press, 1953.

Darwin, J. "Imperialism in Decline? Tendencies in British Imperial Policy Between the Wars." *Historical Journal* 23:3 (September 1980): 657-679.

Dilks, D., editor. *Retreat from Power.* Volume 1: *1906-1939.* London: Macmillan, 1981.

Doise, J. and Vaïsse, M. *Diplomatie et Outil Militaire, 1871-1969.* Paris: Imprimerie Nationale, 1987.

Douglas, R. *World Crisis and British Decline, 1929-1956.* New York: St. Martin's, 1986.

Duroselle, J-B. *France and the United States: From the Beginnings to the Present.* Translated by D. Coltman. Chicago: Chicago University Press, 1978.

___. *La Décadence 1932-1939.* Paris: Imprimerie Nationale, 1979.

Ferris, J. *Men, Money and Diplomacy: The Evolution of British Strategic Policy, 1919-1926.* Ithaca: Cornell University Press, 1989.

___. "Treasury Control, the Ten Year Rule and British Service Policies, 1919-1924." *Historical Journal* 30:4 (December 1987): 859-883.

Fink, C. "Defender of Minorities: Germany in the League of Nations, 1925-1933." *Central European History* 5 (December 1972): 330-357.

Frankenstein, R. *Le Prix du réarmement français, 1935-1939.* Paris: Publications de la Sorbonne, 1982.

Furnia, A.H. *The Diplomacy of Appeasement: Anglo-French Relations and the Prelude to World War II, 1931-1938.* Washington, D.C.: University Press of Washington, D.C., 1960.

Fussell, P. *The Great War and Modern Memory.* Oxford: Oxford University Press, 1975.

Gannon, F.R. *The British Press and Germany, 1936-1939.* Oxford: Clarendon Press, 1971.

Gatzke, H. *Stresemann and the Rearmament of Germany.* Baltimore: Johns Hopkins Press, 1954.

___, editor. *European Diplomacy Between the Wars*. Chicago: Quadrangle, 1972.

Geyer, M. *Aufrüstung oder Sicherheit: Die Reichswehr in der Krise der Machtpolitik, 1924-1936*. Wiesbaden, 1980.

Gibbs, N. *Grand Strategy*. Volume 1: *Rearmament Policy*. London: Her Majesty's Stationery Office, 1976.

Gilbert, M. *Britain and Germany Between the Wars*. London: Longmans, 1964.

___. *The Roots of Appeasement*. New York: Plume Books, 1966.

Gombin, R. *Les socialistes at la guerre: la SFIO et la politique étrangère française entre les deux guerres mondiales*. Paris: Mouton, 1970.

Griffiths, R. *Fellow Travellers of the Right: British Enthusiasts for Nazi Germany 1933-1939*. Oxford: Oxford University Press, 1983.

Helbich, W.J. "Between Stresemann and Hitler: The Foreign Policy of the Brüning Government." *World Politics* 1959.

Hermans, J. *L'évolution de la pensée européenne d'Aristide Briand*. Nancy, 1965.

Hoffmann, S. *Decline or Renewal? France since the 1930s*. New York: Viking, 1973.

___, Kindleberger, C., Wylie, L., Pitts, J., Duroselle, J.-B. and Goguel, F. *In Search of France: The Economy, Society and Political System in the Twentieth Century*. New York: Harper and Row, 1963.

Hogan, M. *Informal Entente: The Private Structure of Cooperation in Anglo-American Economic Diplomacy, 1918-1928*. Chicago: Imprint Publications, 1991.

Holder, F.B. "André Tardieu, Politician and Statesman of the Third Republic: A Study of his Ministries and Policies, 1929-1932." Ph.D. dissertation, Berkeley, 1962.

Howard, M. *The Continental Commitment: the Dilemma of British Defence Policy in the Era of the Two World Wars*. London: Maurice Temple Smith, 1972.

Hughes, J. *To the Maginot Line: The Politics of French Military Preparation in the 1920s*. Cambridge: Harvard University Press, 1971.

Hynes, S. *The Auden Generation: Literature and Politics in England in the 1930s*. Princeton: Princeton University Press, 1972.

Jackson, J. *The Politics of Depression in France 1932-1936*. Cambridge: Cambridge University Press, 1985.

Jacobson, J. "Is There a New International History of the 1920s?" *American Historical Review* 88:3 (June, 1983): 617-645.

___. *Locarno Diplomacy: Germany and the West, 1925-1929.* Princeton, 1972.

James, H. *The German Slump: Politics and Economics, 1924-1936.* Oxford: Clarendon Press, 1986.

Jervis, R. *Perception and Misperception in International Politics.* Princeton: Princeton University Press, 1976.

Jordan, N. *The Popular Front and Central Europe: the Dilemmas of French Impotence, 1918-1940.* Cambridge: Cambridge University Press, 1992.

Jordan, W.M. *Great Britain, France and the German Problem, 1919-1939.* London, 1943.

Kaiser, D. *Economic Diplomacy and the Origins of the Second World War.* Princeton: Princeton University Press, 1980.

___. *Politics and War: European Conflict from Philip II to Hitler.* Cambridge: Harvard University Press, 1990.

Keeton, E. *Briand's Locarno Policy: French Economics, Politics and Diplomacy 1925-1929.* New York: Garland, 1987.

Kennedy, P.M. *The Realities behind Diplomacy: Background Influences on British External Policy, 1865-1980.* London: Fontana, 1981.

___. *Strategy and Diplomacy, 1870-1945: Eight Studies.* London: Fontana, 1984.

___. *The Rise and Fall of the Great Powers: Economic Change and Military Conflict from 1500 to 2000.* New York: Random House, 1987.

Kershaw, I., editor. *Weimar: Why Did Democracy Fail?* New York: St. Martin's, 1990.

Kimmich, C. *Germany and the League of Nations.* Chicago: University of Chicago Press, 1976.

Kindleberger, C. *The World in Depression 1929-1939.* Harmondsworth, Middlesex: Pelican, 1987.

Kissinger, Henry. *Diplomacy.* New York: Simon and Schuster, 1994.

Kitchen, M. *Europe Between the Wars: A Political History.* London: Longman, 1988.

Knipping, F. *Deutschland, Frankreich und das Ende der Locarno-Ära: Studien zur internationalen Politik in der Anfangsphase der Weltwirtschaftskrise.* Munich: R. Oldenbourg, 1987.

Komjathy, A. *The Crises of France's East Central European Diplomacy, 1933-1938.* New York: Columbia University Press, 1976.

Koss, S. *The Rise and Fall of the Political Press in Britain.* Volume 2, *The Twentieth Century.* London: Hamish Hamilton, 1984.

Krüger, P. *Die Aussenpolitik der Republik von Weimar.* Darmstadt: Wissenschaftliche Buchgesellschaft, 1985.

____. "Friedenssicherheit und deutsche Revisionspolitik. Die deutsche Aussenpolitik und die verhandlungen über den Kellogg-Pakt." *Vierteljahreshefte für Zeitgeschichte* 22 (1974): 227-257.

Kunz, Diane B. *The Battle for Britain's Gold Standard in 1931.* London: Croom Helm, 1987.

Lamb, R. *The Drift to War, 1922-1939.* London: W.H. Allen, 1989.

Landes, D. *The Unbound Prometheus: Technological Change and Industrial Development in Western Europe from 1750 to the Present.* Cambridge: Cambridge University Press, 1969.

Larmour, P.J. *The French Radical Party in the 1930s.* Stanford: Stanford University Press, 1964.

Leffler, M.P. *The Elusive Quest: America's Pursuit of European Stability and French Security 1919-1933.* Chapel Hill: University of North Carolina Press, 1979.

Le Goyet, P. *France-Pologne, 1919-1939: de l'amitié romantique à la méfiance réciproque.* Paris: Editions France-Empire, 1991.

Lewis, T.L. *A Climate for Appeasement.* New York: P. Lang, 1991.

Liauzu, C. *Aux origines des tiers-mondismes: colonisés et anticolonialistes en France 1919-1939.* Paris: L'Harmattan, 1982.

Maier, C.S. *Recasting Bourgeois Europe: Stabilization in France, Germany and Italy in the Decade after World War I.* Princeton: Princeton University Press, 1975.

Marks, S. *The Illusion of Peace: International Relations in Europe, 1919-1933.* New York: St. Martin's, 1976.

____. "The Myths of Reparations." *Central European History* 11 (1978): 231-255.

Mayer, Karl J. *Die Weimarer Republik und das Problem der Sicherheit in den deutsch-französischen Beziehungen, 1918-1925.* New York: Peter Lang, 1990.

McKercher, B.J.C. *The Second Baldwin Government and the United States, 1924-1929: Attitudes and Diplomacy.* Cambridge: Cambridge University Press, 1984.

____, ed. *Anglo-American Relations in the 1920s: The Struggle for Supremacy.* Houndmills: Macmillan, 1991.

____ and Moss, D.J., editors. *Shadow and Substance in British Foreign Policy, 1895-1939.* Edmonton: University of Alberta Press, 1984.

McNeil, W. *American Money and the Weimar Republic: Economics and Politics on the Eve of the Great Depression.* New York: Columbia University Press, 1986.

Medlicott, W.N. *Britain and Germany: The Search for Agreement 1930-1937.* London: Athlone, 1969.

McIntyre, A., editor. *Aging and Political Leadership.* Albany: State University of New York Press, 1988.

Metcalfe, P. *1933.* New York: Harper and Row, 1988.

Middlemas, K. *The Diplomacy of Illusion.* London: Weidenfeld and Nicolson, 1972.

Miquel, P. *La paix de Versailles et l'opinion publique française.* Paris: Flammarion, 1972.

Morris, B. *The Roots of Appeasement: The British Weekly Press and Nazi Germany during the 1930s.* London: F. Cass, 1991.

Mowat, C.L. *Britain Between the Wars 1918-1940.* Chicago: University of Chicago Press, 1955.

Nadolny, S. *Abrüstungsdiplomatie 1932-1933. Deutschland auf der Genfer Konferenz in übergang von Weimar zu Hitler.* Munich: Tuduv-Verlagsgesellschaft, 1978.

Néré, J. *The Foreign Policy of France from 1914 to 1945.* London: Routledge and Kegan Paul, 1975.

Newman, K. *European Democracy Between the Wars.* Translated by K. Morgan. London: Allen and Unwin, 1970.

Northedge, F.S. *The Troubled Giant: Britain among the Great Powers, 1916-1939.* New York: Praeger, 1966.

____. *The League of Nations.* New York: Holmes and Meier, 1986.

Orde, A. *Great Britain and International Security, 1920-1926.* London: Royal Historical Society, 1978.

___. *British Policy and European Reconstruction after the First World War.* Cambridge: Cambridge University Press, 1990.

Paillat, C. *Dossiers secrets de la France contemporaine.* Volume 3: *La guerre à l'horizon 1930-1938.* Paris: Robert Laffont, 1981.

Parker, R.A.C. *Chamberlain and Appeasement: British Policy and the Coming of the Second World War.* New York: St. Martin's, 1993.

Payne, H.C. *As the Storm Clouds Gathered: European Perceptions of American Foreign Policy in the 1930s.* Durham, North Carolina: Moore, 1979.

Pease, N. *Poland, the United States, and the Stabilization of Europe, 1919-1923.* New York: Oxford University Press, 1986.

Peden, G.C. *British Rearmament and the Treasury, 1932-1939.* Edinburgh: Scottish Academic Press, 1979.

Peele, G. and Cook, C. *The Politics of Reappraisal, 1918-1939.* London: Macmillan, 1975.

Pegg, C. *Evolution of the European Idea 1919-1932.* Chapel Hill: University of North Carolina Press, 1983.

Pitts, V. *France and the German Problem: Politics and Economics in the Locarno era, 1924-1929.* New York: Garland, 1987.

Poidevin, R. and Bariéty, J. *Les Relations franco-allemandes, 1815-1975.* Paris: Armand Colin, 1977.

Post, G. *The Civil-Military Fabric of Weimar Foreign Policy.* Princeton: Princeton University Press, 1973.

___. *Dilemmas of Appeasement: British Deterrence and Defense, 1934-1937.* Ithaca: Cornell University Press, 1993.

Rock, W.R. *British Appeasement in the 1930s.* New York: Norton, 1977.

Rolo, P.J.V. *Britain and the Briand Plan: The Common Market that Never Was.* Keele: University of Keele, 1972.

Roskill, S. *Naval Policy Between the Wars.* Volume 1: *The Period of Anglo-American Antagonism.* New York: Walker and Company, 1968. Volume 2: *The Period of Reluctant Rearmament.* Annapolis: Naval Institute Press, 1976.

Rossler, H. *Locarno und die Weltpolitik, 1924-1932.* Göttingen, 1969.

Sauvy, A. *Histoire économique de la France entre les deux guerres.* 3 volumes. Paris: Economica, 1984.

Schmidt, G. *The Politic and Economics of Appeasement: British Foreign Policy in the 1930s.* Translated by J. Bennett-Ruete. Leamington Spa: Berg, 1986.

Schuker, S.A. *The End of French Predominance in Europe: the Financial Crisis of 1924 and the Adoption of the Dawes Plan.* Chapel Hill: University of North Carolina Press, 1976.

Schumacher, A. *La Politique de sécurité française face à l'Allemagne: les controverses de l'opinion française entre 1932 et 1935.* Frankfurt am Main: Lang, 1978.

Scott, G. *The Rise and Fall of the League of Nations.* New York: Macmillan, 1974.

Scott, W.E. *Alliance Against Hitler: The Origins of the Franco-Soviet Pact.* Durham, N.C.: Duke University Press, 1962.

Shamir, H. *Economic Crisis and French Foreign Policy 1930-1936.* Leiden: E.J. Brill, 1989.

___, ed. *France and Germany in an Age of Crisis: Studies in Memory of Charles Bloch.* Leiden: E.J. Brill, 1990.

Shay, R.P. *British Rearmament in the Thirties: Politics and Profits.* Princeton: Princeton University Press, 1977.

Shorrock, W.I. *From Ally to Enemy: The Enigma of Fascist Italy in French Diplomacy 1920-1940.* Kent, Ohio, 1988.

Skidelsky, R. *Politicians and the Slump: the Labour Government of 1929-1931.* London: Macmillan, 1967.

Soucy, R. *French Fascism: the First Wave, 1924-1933.* New Haven: Yale University Press, 1986.

Stirk, P.M.R., editor. *European Unity in Context: The Interwar Period.* London: Pinter, 1989.

Taylor, P.M. *The Projection of Britain: British Overseas Publicity and Propaganda, 1919-1939.* Cambridge: Cambridge University Press, 1981.

Thorne, C. *The Limits of Foreign Policy: the West, the League and the Far Eastern Crisis of 1931-1933.* London: Hamilton, 1972.

Thurlow, R. *Fascism in Britain, 1918-1985.* Oxford: Basil Blackwell, 1987.

Toynbee, A. *Survey of International Affairs*. London: Royal Institute of International Affairs, 1929-1934.

Tucker, W.R. *The Attitude of the British Labour Party towards European and Collective Security Problems, 1920-1939*. Geneva, 1950.

Vaïsse, M. *Sécurité d'abord: La politique française en matière de désarmement 9 décembre 1931 - 17 avril 1934*. Paris: Institut d'histoire des relations internationales contemporaines, 1981.

Waites, N.H. "British Foreign Policy towards France Regarding the German Problem from 1929 to 1934." Ph.D. dissertation, London, 1972.

___, ed. *Troubled Neighbours: Franco-British Relations in the Twentieth Century*. London: Weidenfeld, 1971.

Walters, F.P. *A History of the League of Nations*. London: Oxford University Press, 1952.

Wandycz, P.S. *France and her Eastern Allies, 1919-1925: French-Polish-Czechoslovak Relations from the Paris Peace Conference to Locarno*. Minneapolis: University of Minnesota Press, 1962.

___. *The Twilight of French Eastern Alliances, 1926-1936*. Princeton: Princeton University Press, 1988.

Ward, S. *The War Generation: Veterans of the First World War*. Port Washington, N.Y.: Kennikat Press, 1975.

Wark, W.K. *The Ultimate Enemy: British Intelligence and Nazi Germany, 1933-1939*. Ithaca: Cornell University Press, 1985.

Watt, D.C. *Personalities and Policies: Studies in the Formulation of British Foreign Policy in the Twentieth Century*. London, 1965.

___. *Too Serious a Business: European Armed Forces and the Approach to the Second World War*. London: Temple Smith, 1975.

___. *Succeeding John Bull: America in Britain's Place, 1900-1975*. New York: Cambridge University Press, 1984.

Weinberg, Gerhard. *The Foreign Policy of Hitler's Germany: Diplomatic Revolution in Europe, 1933-1936*. Chicago: University of Chicago Press, 1970.

Williams, A. *Labour and Russia: The Attitude of the Labour Party to the USSR, 1924-1934*. Manchester: Manchester University Press, 1989.

Williamson, P. "A 'Bankers' Ramp'? Financiers and the British Political Crisis of 1931." *English Historical Review* 99:4 (October 1984): 770-806.

Wohl, R. *The Generation of 1914*. Cambridge: Harvard University Press, 1979.

Wolfers, A. *Britain and France between Two Wars: Conflicting Strategies of Peace from Versailles to World War II*. New York: Harcourt, Brace and Company, 1940.

Young, R.J. *In Command of France: French Foreign Policy and Military Planning, 1933-1940*. Cambridge: Harvard University Press, 1978.

II-D. Newspapers

France: *Journal des Débats, Le Temps, L'Écho de Paris, Le Populaire, L'Humanité, Le Matin, Paris-Soir, Le Petit Journal*

Britain: *The Economist, The Times (London)*

United States: *New York Times*

Index

Algeria, 125

All Quiet on the Western Front, 48, 101

Allen of Hurtwood, Lord, 192-193

Amery, Leopold (First Lord of the Admiralty, Secretary of State for Colonies, Dominions), 165, 171

Angell, Norman (writer on international relations), 75, 149

Anschluss, 23, 26, 59, 66, 73, 84, 85, 90, 154-157, 172, 212

Army, French 14-15, 30-31, 180-181

Austria, 19, 48, 52, 59, 64, 65, 73, 74, 84, 103, 119, 130, 152-157, 172, 191

Avenol, Joseph (secretary general of the League of Nations), 125, 139, 212

Baldwin, Stanley (British prime minister), 10, 24, 29, 39, 71, 74, 98, 116, 131, 136, 139; on U.S. "money power," 27; on Mussolini, 37; on aerial bombing, 132, 181; Robert Cecil on, 213.

Balfour, Arthur (former Foreign Secretary, member of Committee of Imperial Defence), 29, 32, 95

Bardoux, Jacques (shipping executive, senator), 184-5

Barois, A. (French chargé d'affaires, Vienna), 156

Beaverbrook, Lord (newspaper magnate), 12

Beneš, Eduard (Czechoslovak foreign minister), 115, 135, 136, 152, 154, 156

Bérard, Victor (president, Senate Foreign Affairs Commission), 65

Bergery, Gaston (deputy), 187

Berthelot, Philippe (secretary general, French foreign ministry), 39, 51, 93

Blum, Léon (French socialist party leader, deputy), 14, 52, 60, 66, 155, 188

Borah, William (Idaho senator), 33

Bracke (deputy), 84

Briand, Aristide (French prime minister and foreign minister), 11, 13, 20, 23, 25, 51, 56, 73-75, 83, 99, 105, 125-127, 130, 145-150, 154, 202, 212-214; on "organization" of the peace, 2, 4, 15-16, 24, 32, 39; on prospects for lasting peace, 7; support for policies, 13, 19, 49, 53, 66-67, 88; leadership style, 16-17; intentions for pact with U.S., 17-32-33; on Stresemann, 53; at Hague Conference, 55-57; on war rumors, 61-62; position shaken, 64-69, 92-93; on *Anschluss*, 84, 154; on League of Nations, 126-127; on Manchurian crisis, 138; *see also* Briand Plan, Kellogg-Briand Pact

Briand Plan, 4, 146-152, 158-173, 212; British response, 158-166; German response, 160-162, 166-167; Italian response, 162-163, 167-9

Bridgeman, William S. (First Lord of the Admiralty), 29

Brüning, Heinrich (German chancellor), 91, 92, 100, 105, 134, 158

Bucard, Marcel (writer), 49

Cachin, Marcel (communist deputy), 126

Cambridge University, 25, 47

Cassel, Gustav (economist), 76

Cecil, Robert (cabinet member, League of Nations founder and activist), 68, 75, 115, 118-120, 129, 132-134, 145, 164, 165, 195; resignation from Baldwin cabinet (1927), 16, 119; on League of Nations, 23-24, 30-32, 122; on war, 30, 36, association with Henderson, 122, on Manchurian crisis, 138-139; on Briand Plan, 164-165; on leaders, 213

Chamberlain, Austen (foreign secretary), 48-52, 62, 75, 92, 99, 120, 127, 154, 155, 171, 206; post-Locarno inactivity, 10, 24-25, 36; on empire, 16, 119; on France, 24-25; style, 25; on likelihood of war, 29-30, 92; on Kellogg-Briand Pact, 33-36; on Mussolini, 37; on Germany 38-39, 53-54, 196-197; on Britain's decline 98, 212; on leaders, 196-197, 213; *see also Dawn* controversy

Chamberlain, Neville (Chancellor of the Exchequer), 137-138, 196, 197-198, 212

Charles, J.R.G. (British Major-General), 95-98

Charles-Roux, François (French diplomat), 154, 156

Chaumeix, André (journalist), 52

Chéron, Henri (finance minister), 56

Churchill, Winston (Chancellor of the Exchequer, member of parliament), 29-31, 37, 198, 206

Claudel, Paul (French ambassador to Washington, poet, dramatist), 33, 93

Clauzel (French diplomat), 154

Comert, Pierre (French socialist), 22, 23

Committee of Imperial Defence, 14, 29, 30, 39, 106, 138

Conservative Party (Britain), 10, 54

Conwell-Evans, Philip (professor) 109, 110, 193

Corbin, Charles (French ambassador to London), 199, 212

Cornwall, James Marshall (British military attaché, Berlin), 87, 135

Cot, Pierre (deputy, Air Minister), 94, 132

Coudenhove-Kalergi, Richard (Pan-European Union founder), 156, 157, 170, 171

Curtius, Julius (German foreign minister), 63, 88, 89, 91, 101, 105, 157, 158, 169

Customs Union, Austro-German proposal for, 64-66, 73, 88, 101, 105, 130, 157-158, 169, 170

Czechoslovakia, 24, 36, 53, 103, 151-153, 156, 157

D'Abernon, Viscount (British ambassador to Berlin), 72, 92

Daily Telegraph, 12, 182

Daladier, Édouard (French prime minister and foreign minister, Radical leader), 66, 67, 101, 177, 186, 187, 206

Dalton, Hugh (Labour Member of Parliament), 22, 23, 47, 55, 57, 98, 122, 164-166, 185, 211

Danzig, 21, 119, 124, 151, 152, 161

Dariac (deputy), 186-187

Dawn (film) controversy, 48-49

Dawson, Geoffrey (*Times* editor), 12, 62, 71, 171, 199

Desjardins, Charles (deputy), 19

Dickinson, G. (professor), 47

disarmament, 1, 4, 5, 7, 14, 16, 18, 23, 25, 29, 30, 32, 52, 59, 62, 63, 66, 67, 69, 72, 73, 90-92, 95-97, 100, 102, 103, 105-107, 109, 116, 119-123, 138-140, 152, 166, 167, 171, 179, 183-189, 191, 194, 195, 198, 199, 202-204, 215

Disarmament Conference (1932-4), 128-136; *see also* disarmament

Dominions (British empire), 11, 24, 36, 37, 106, 150, 158, 159, 166

Doumer, Paul (French president), 66-67

Drummond, Eric (secretary general of the League of Nations), 35, 36, 118, 119, 135, 157, 165

Dugdale, Edgar (translator), 199

Écho de Paris, 13, 52, 59, 60, 125

Economist, the, 9-10, 58-59, 110-111, 122-124, 166, 171- 172, 192, 195

Egypt, 11, 26, 105, 122

Elliot, Walter, 197

Fisher, Warren (Permament Secretary to Treasury), 30-31, 198

Fleuriau, Aimé de (French ambassador to London), 33, 49, 92, 134, 163, 185

Foch, Ferdinand, Marshal, 23-24, 149

Foreign Office, 22, 32, 36, 39, 48, 51-55, 57, 72, 82, 87, 90, 92, 98, 100-103, 122, 124, 135, 146, 149, 155, 159, 163, 164, 167, 185, 196, 200, 205

François-Poncet, André (French ambassador to Berlin), 81, 101-102, 134, 170

Franklin-Bouillon, Henry (deputy), 19, 60, 88-89, 151, 188-189, 205-206

Fromageot (jurist, French delegate, League of Nations), 36

Garvin, J.L. (journalist), 92, 182, 196

Gaus, Friedrich (jurist, German delegation, League of Nations), 36

Geneva Protocol, 24, 119, 151

Géraud, André (journalist "Pertinax"), 13, 191

Gilbert, Parker (Agent-General for Reparations), 54

Giraudoux, Jean (dramatist), 50

Gleichberechtigung, 111, 133

Gooch, G.P. (historian), 192

Gosset, P.W. (British military expert, Berlin embassy), 86-87

Graham, Ronald (British ambassador to Rome), 162

Grahame, George (British ambassador to Madrid), 36, 94

Grant Duff, Shiela (journalist), 72

Graves, Robert (writer), 110

Grey, Edward (former foreign secretary), 34, 195

Hague conference (1929), 45, 54-57, 91, 101, 108, 120-121, 151, 159

Hankey, Maurice (leading British civil servant), 45, 95, 118, 122, 134, 136, 152; on developments in Germany and Britain's military posture 102-109, 133, 137, 197-205; on disarmament and pacifism, 182-184

Hart, Basil H. Liddell (military theorist and writer), 182

Hartog, Phillip (professor), 199

Henderson, Arthur (British foreign secretary, Disarmament Conference president), 171; pro-League, pro-French policy clashes with MacDonald and Snowden, 56-57, 69-70, 75, 99, 121-122, 213; on disarmament, 121, 132; on Briand Plan, 158-166, 169

Herbette, Jean (French ambassador to Moscow), 20-22

Herbette, Maurice (French ambassador to Brussels), 55-56

Herriot, Édouard (French prime minister and foreign minister, Radical party leader), 81, 101, 102, 107, 109, 127, 128, 146, 186, 212-214; support for Briand, 66, 68-69; in Geneva (1932), 132-134; on Four-Power Pact (1933), 190

Hitler, Adolf, perceptions about, 2, 4, 9, 60, 91, 92, 99, 100, 102, 104, 111, 116, 136, 171, 177, 179, 180, 182, 184-186, 188, 191, 192, 195-201, 203, 205, 206

Horne, Robert (member of parliament), 75-76

Houghton, Alanson (U.S. diplomat), 68

Howard, Esmé (British ambassador to Washington), 33-36

Hungary, 21, 60, 98, 103, 116, 119, 153, 156, 170, 185, 191

Imperial Conference, 11, 104

India, 5, 11, 22, 26, 72, 105, 122, 137, 165

Indochina, 125, 138-139

Irwin, Lord, 213

Journal des débats, 13, 52, 154

Kaas, Wilhelm (German Center Party leader), 104

Kellogg-Briand Pact (1928), 3, 7, 17, 23, 32-37, 39, 85, 118, 121, 136, 152, 168, 172

Kennedy, Aubrey Leo (journalist), on conversations with British and French leaders, 23, 36, 49, 62-63, 70-71, 99-100, 115, 130-132, 134-136, 138-139, 155, 167-168, 170-171, 202-203, 213

Knatchbull-Hugessen, Hughe (British diplomat), 61, 100, 167

Koch-Weser, Erich (German Democratic Party leader), 58

Labour Party (Britain), 10-11, 54, 55, 57, 69, 119, 121, 150, 198, 201

Lagrange, Léo (deputy), 186-187

Lausanne Conference (1932), 45, 57, 75-76, 107-109, 133-134

Laval, Pierre (French prime minister and foreign minister), 67, 75, 127, 170

Layton, Walter (publisher, the *Economist*), 192

League of Nations, 4, 7, 10, 12, 14, 16-19, 23-26, 30-33, 35, 36, 47, 54, 58, 63, 67, 75, 83, 90, 103, 105, 107-110, 115-140, 145-148, 150-151, 153-155, 157, 163-167, 169-172, 179, 183-188, 190, 193, 194, 203, 204, 212, 215

League of Nations Union, 32, 75, 115, 120, 131, 138, 183, 184

Leeper, Reginald (Foreign Office official), 163

Léger, Alexis (secretary-general, French foreign ministry, poet), 70, 168-170, 186
Léon, Maurice (French financier), 94
Levinson, Salmon, 33
Liberal Party (Britain), 10-12, 54, 195
Lindsay, Ronald (Permanent Under-secretary, Foreign Office), 37, 38, 57, 122
"Liquidation" of the war (of 1914-18), 1, 45-64, 91, 133, 159, 160, 215
Little Entente 18, 21, 97, 154, 193
Litvinov, Maximilian (Soviet foreign minister), 126, 128
Lloyd George, David (prime minister, Liberal party leader), 10, 11, 14, 53, 150
Locarno agreements, 3, 10, 15, 19, 21, 24-26, 30, 36-39, 53, 60, 62, 73, 84, 85, 88, 97, 98, 101, 107, 116, 118, 119, 126, 129, 133, 147, 150-152, 168, 214
Londonderry, Lord (Air Minister), 130-132
Loucheur, Louis (French minister of finance, commerce, labor), 146, 147, 159
Lugano meetings (1928), 53-54
Lytton Commission, 136

MacDonald, James Ramsay (British prime minister), 27, 88, 93-95, 101, 106, 107, 109, 119, 122, 131; discord with foreign secretaries, 24, 55, 57, 75, 179; pro-German stance, 58, 133-136; criticism of France, 70, 72, 109, 133-136, 177, 194-196, 206, 211, 213; improved relations with U.S., 74, sense of crisis, 71-72, 75, 95, 121, 128; Four-Power Pact (1933), 5, 185-188, 194-196

Manchester Guardian, 12, 182, 196
Manchurian crisis, 106, 116, 129, 136-140
Mandel, Georges (deputy), 205-206
Marin, Louis (deputy), 19, 60, 187, 205, 206
Marshall-Cornwall, *see Cornwall*
Massigli, René (French diplomat), 52, 57, 125, 138
Matin, 13, 149, 158, 191
Mein Kampf, 198-199
Milne, George (Field Marshal, Chief of the Imperial General staff), 28-29, 108-109
Mitteleuropa, 65, 155, 158, 170
Montagu, Lily, 194
Montigny, Jean (deputy), 17-19, 125-126, 149
Monzie, Anatole de (deputy), 155
Müller, Hermann (German Socialist Party leader), 61
Murray, Gilbert (professor), 75, 121
Mussolini, Benito, 5, 18, 37, 60, 104, 116, 163, 167-168, 185-186, 191, 196

National Socialism (Germany), 1-2, 4-5, 22, 37-38, 59-60, 62, 66, 76, 89-92, 94, 99-102, 111, 129, 136, 139, 166, 170, 177, 181, 185-6, 191-193, 195-196, 200-201, 203, 205, 211, 214
Naval Conference (1927), 16, 27, 73
Naval Conference (1930), 61, 64, 74, 94-95
Nicolson, Harold (diplomat), 86
Noel-Baker, Philip (British delegate to the League of Nations), 63, 122, 129, 139, 164, 192
Norman, Montagu (Governor, Bank of England), 119

"Old Adam," 61, 81, 90, 91, 98, 104, 111
Optional Clause, 121, 125, 151
Ordinaire, Maurice (senator), 158

Ormesson, Wladimir (journalist), 15, 213-214
Ormsby-Gore, William (member of parliament), 196-197, 206
Oxford University, 25, 72, 181

Pan-European Union, 145-146, 156-157
Papen, Franz von (German chancellor), 101, 134
Paul-Boncour, Joseph (foreign minister), 101, 125, 127, 130-132, 199, 206; on Rhineland, 51-52; on German danger, 185-186; on Four-Power Pact, 190-191
Péri, Gabriel (deputy, Communist leader), 188
Pertinax, *see Géraud*
Phipps, Eric (diplomat), 52, 154-155, 200
Pietri, François (Minister of National Defense), 132
Pironneau, André (journalist), 59
Poincaré, Raymond (president (WWI), prime minister), 9, 11, 19-20, 55-56, 92-94, 119, 147, 149, 150, 158, 213
Poland, 18, 24, 39, 52-54, 57, 90, 103, 105, 107, 108, 116, 169, 204; corridor question, 21, 23, 55, 85, 95, 97-98, 110, 124, 149-152, 185
polls, public opinion, 47, 153
Populaire, 14, 60, 65, 66, 155, 170

Quai d'Orsay (French foreign ministry), 11, 13, 17, 22, 27, 32, 36, 39, 51, 67, 68, 87, 92, 93, 126, 127, 138, 139, 149, 154, 155, 157, 158, 165, 166, 170, 185, 186, 202, 214

Radical party (France), 11, 13, 17, 65-67, 69, 94, 115, 125, 149, 169, 177, 180, 186-188, 214
Radical-Socialist, *see* Radical
rearmament, 60, 103, 107, 135, 136, 138, 189, 197, 204
Rechberg, Arnold (German businessman, amateur diplomat), 149-150
Reichswehr, 60, 85, 87, 96, 135
revisionism, 2, 5, 17, 62, 81, 88, 102, 156, 161, 177, 214, 215
Reynaud, Paul (deputy), 69, 89, 94, 150-152
Rhineland, occupation and evacuation of, 1-3, 5, 15, 19, 23, 24, 31, 33, 36, 45, 46, 51-53, 56, 57, 59, 61, 62, 73, 82-85, 97, 107, 108, 159, 192, 201, 215
Robertson, Malcolm (British diplomat), 191-192
Roosevelt, Theodore, 115
Roosevelt, Franklin, 139
Rosenberg, Alfred (Nazi official), 192, 196
Rothermere, Lord (newspaper magnate), 12, 37, 192
Rowe-Dutton, Ernest (diplomat), 38
Ruhr occupation (1923), 85, 147
Rumbold, Horace (British ambassador to Berlin), 54, 81-83, 85, 87-90, 100, 124, 135, 161-162, 198-199

Saarland, 159
Sauerwein, Jules (journalist), 13, 149, 158
Schleicher, Kurt von (general, German chancellor), 96, 101, 110, 135
Schubert, Carl von (secretary general, German foreign ministry) 54, 57
Seipel, Monsignor (Austrian chancellor), 156
Selby, Walford (Foreign Office official), 36, 37, 53, 71, 82-83

Siegfried (play), 50

Silesia, 85, 161

Simon, John (foreign secretary), 179, 185, 191, 192, 194, 199, 201, 202, 206; style, 71-73, 130-132; clashes with MacDonald, 134-135; dissatisfaction with, 196-197, 213

Smoot-Hawley Tariff Act (1930), 179

Snowden, Philip (Chancellor of the Exchequer), 55-57, 70, 121, 122

Socialists (France), 22-23, 60-61, 76, 89, 147, 180

Soulier, Édouard (deputy), 83-84

Soviet Union, 3, 8, 20-22, 26, 37, 93, 115, 116, 126, 128, 135, 137, 149, 169, 178, 187-188, 201

Stahlhelm, 59, 96, 101, 102, 135, 150, 153

Stresemann, Gustav (German foreign minister), 21, 23, 25, 32, 37, 39, 53, 54, 58, 150; impact of demise, 81-85, 87, 88, 91, 98

Tabouis, Geneviève (journalist), 191

Tardieu, André (French prime minister and foreign secretary), 57, 62, 67, 75, 92, 94, 127, 171, 185, 187, 213; reform proposals, 68, 201; on disarmament, 130-132

tariffs, 17, 84, 139, 179

Temps, le, 13, 15, 38, 130, 138, 154, 158, 160, 191, 213

Ten Year Rule, 14, 29, 103, 106, 137, 179

Thomas, Albert (French socialist), 67

Times, the (London), 12, 16, 23, 48, 49, 62, 65, 70-71, 75, 99, 129, 130, 155, 167, 169, 170-171, 182, 195, 196-197, 199, 205, 213

Toynbee, Arnold (Professor, Royal Institute of International Affairs), 5

Treasury (Britain), 14, 29, 133, 179, 197

Tyrrell, William (British ambassador to Paris), 13, 14, 51-54, 67, 132, 155, 212; on French government and public opinion, 62, 68, 92, 93, 109; on need for Anglo-French cooperation, 99, 201-202; on Briand Plan, 158-162

Vansittart, Robert (Permanent Under-secretary, Foreign Office), 63-64, 83, 102-104, 106, 122, 134, 194; on economic causes of European crisis, 72; "Old Adam" paper, 90-91; on Ten Year Rule, 102-104

Waugh, Evelyn (novelist), 1

Weiss, Louise (journalist), 16

Weizmann, Chaim (Zionist leader), 199

Wellesley, Victor (Foreign Office official), 72

Wheeler-Bennett, John (writer), 169, 177, 192

Whitham, G. (writer), 86

Wilson, Woodrow, 115, 193, 215

Wolfe, Humbert (writer), 182

Woods, Edward (Bishop of Croydon) 182-184

Young Plan (1929), 45, 54-56, 61, 64, 100, 103

Zaleski, August (Polish foreign minister), 54, 57, 151, 169

Studies in Modern European History

The monographs in this series focus upon aspects of the political, social, economic, cultural and religious history of Europe from the Renaissance to the present. Emphasis is placed on the states of Western Europe, especially Great Britain, France, Italy and Germany. While some of the volumes treat internal developments, others deal with movements such as liberalism, socialism, and industrialization which transcend a particular country. The series editor is:

Frank J. Coppa, Director
Doctor of Arts Program
in Modern World History
St. John's University
Jamaica, New York 11439

Volume 1: *Between Pope and Duce: Catholic Students in Fascist Italy* by Richard J. Wolff, 1990, ISBN 0-8204-0478-0. 337 pages, $52.95.

Volume 3: *Prophet in Exile: Joseph Mazzini in England, 1837-1868* by William Roberts, 1990, ISBN 0-8204-1051-9, 226 pages, $37.50.

Volume 4:*Edmundo Rossini: From Revolutionary Syndicalism to Fascism* by John J. Tinghino, 1991, ISBN 0-8204-1297-X, 256 pages, $49.95.

Volume 5:*The Formation of the Italian Republic: Proceedings of the International Symposium on Postwar Italy* by Frank J. Coppa and Margherita Repetto-Alaia, 1993, ISBN 0-8204-1530-8, 368,pages, $42.95.

Volume 7: *The Partisans and The War in Italy* by Dante A. Puzzo, 1993, ISBN 0-8204-1951-6, 112 pages, $38.95.

Volume 8:*The Third Reich and Ukraine by Irene Ievins Rudnytzky*, 1993, ISBN 0-8204-1964-8, 688 pages, $63.95.

Volume 9:*Benedetto Croce between Naples and Europe* by Giuseppe Casale, 1994, ISBN 0-8204-2054-9, 240 pages, $49.95.

Volume 10: *Fascist Thought and Totalitarianism in Italy's Schools: Theory and Practice, 1922-43* by George L. Williams, 1994, 0-8204-2264-9,280 pages, $49.95

Volume 11: *The World of the Manager: Food Administration in Berlin during World War I* by George Yaney, 1994, 0-8204-2434-X, 424 pages, $71.95.

Volume 12: *Munich in the Cobwebs of Berlin, Washington, and Moscow. Foreign Political Tendencies in Bavaria 1917-1919*, by Siegfried H. Sutterlin.

Volume 13: *Democracies at the Turning Point: Britain, France and the End of the Postwar Order, 1928-1933* by Maarten L. Pereboom.

Volume 14: *Out of the Shadows: Women and Politics in the French Revolution, 1789-95* by Shirley Elson-Roessler.

Volume 16: *Italy Today: A Country in Transition* by Mario B. Mignone, 1995, 0-8204-2659-8, 252 pp., $29.95.

Volume 17: Rosa Luxemburg and the Nobel Dream by Donald Shepardson